Praise for
St. Andrews Sojourn

"[This] is a terrific book and a golfer's delight. George Peper is and always has been a wonderful writer."

—Donald J. Trump

"If you've ever played up the 18th fairway of the Old Course, alongside the stately stone dwellings that line it on the right, and wondered what it would be like to live there—for a month or a year or a lifetime—you will want to read this extraordinary book. And if the one place above all to be in the world of golf is St. Andrews, the second place is in your own easy chair relishing this account."

—James W. Finegan, author of *Blasted Heaths and Blessed Greens*

"Anyone who holds a fascination for the home of golf will find plenty of interest, as Peper offers an insider's look at all that St. Andrews has to offer."

—Ron Cobb, *St. Louis Post-Dispatch*

"Peper's an expert storyteller with a wry enough wit to keep readers entertained, even if golf's not their game."

—Karen Algeo Krizman, *Rocky Mountain News*

"*Under the Tuscan Sun* for golfers, with all the bittersweet pleasures that implies."

—*Booklist*

"An enjoyable look at a slice of a much different life, one that a person could easily get hooked on. . . . A fine wee book."

—Bryan French, *Fort Worth Star-Telegram*

"Golf fans will savor this . . . appreciation of their greatest shrine."

—*Publishers Weekly*

Also by George Peper

The Secret of Golf: A Century of Groundbreaking, Innovative, and Occasionally Outlandish Ways to Master the World's Most Vexing Game

Golf Courses of the PGA Tour

Playing Partners: A Father, a Son, and Their Shared Passion for Golf

The 500 World's Greatest Golf Holes (with the editors of *Golf Magazine*)

The Story of Golf

Golf Magazine's Complete Book of Golf Instruction (with the editors of *Golf Magazine*)

Golfwatching: A Viewer's Guide to the World of Golf

Shinnecock Hills Golf Club, 1891–1991

Golf Magazine's Encyclopedia of Golf: The Complete Reference

Grand Slam Golf: Courses of the Masters, the U.S. Open, the British Open, the PGA Championship

Golf in America: The First One Hundred Years

The PGA Championship, 1916–1984

Golf's Supershots: How the Pros Played Them—How You Can Play Them

Scrambling Golf: How to Get Out of Trouble and into the Cup

As Co-author:

Cinderella Story: My Life in Golf (with Bill Murray)

Greg Norman's Instant Lessons (with Greg Norman)

Shark Attack!: Greg Norman's Guide to Aggressive Golf (with Greg Norman)

ST. ANDREWS
SOJOURN

*Two Years at Home on the
Old Course*

George Peper

previously published as
*Two Years in St. Andrews: At Home on
the 18th Hole of the Old Course*

SIMON & SCHUSTER PAPERBACKS

New York • London • Toronto • Sydney

SIMON & SCHUSTER PAPERBACKS
Rockefeller Center
1230 Avenue of the Americas
New York, NY 10020

This title was previously published as *Two Years in St. Andrews: At Home on the 18th Hole of the Old Course*

First Simon & Schuster paperback edition 2007

SIMON & SCHUSTER PAPERBACKS and colophon are
registered trademarks of Simon & Schuster, Inc.

For information about special discounts for bulk purchases,
please contact Simon & Schuster Special Sales at
1-800-456-6798 or business@simonandschuster.com

Designed by Jaime Putorti

Manufactured in the United States of America

1   3   5   7   9   10   8   6   4   2

Library of Congress Control Number: 2006044309

ISBN-13: 978-0-7432-6282-8
ISBN-10:   0-7432-6282-4
ISBN-13: 978-0-7432-6283-5 (Pbk)
ISBN-10:   0-7432-6283-2 (Pbk)

Contents

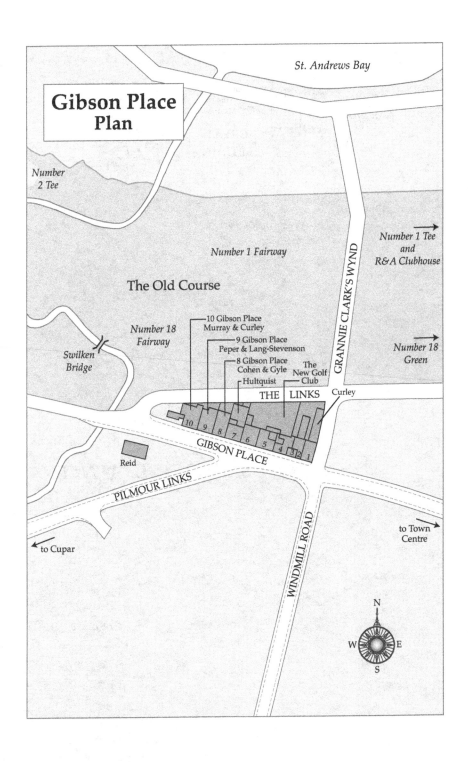

Gibson Place
Plan

St. Andrews Bay

Number 2 Tee

Number 1 Fairway

The Old Course

Number 1 Tee and R&A Clubhouse

GRANNIE CLARK'S WYND

Number 18 Fairway

10 Gibson Place
Murray & Curley

9 Gibson Place
Peper & Lang-Stevenson

Number 18 Green

Swilken Bridge

8 Gibson Place
Cohen & Gyle

The New Golf Club

Hultquist

THE LINKS

Curley

10 9 8 7 6 5 4 3 2 1

Reid

GIBSON PLACE

PILMOUR LINKS

WINDMILL ROAD

to Cupar

to Town Centre

N
W E
S

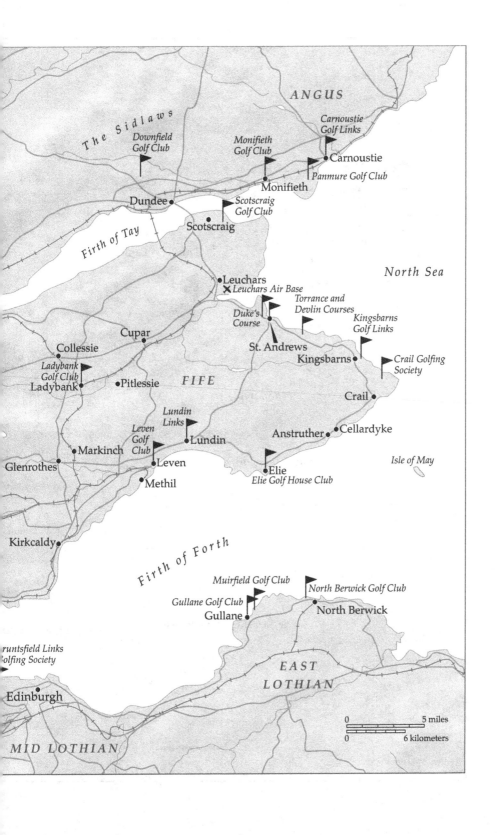

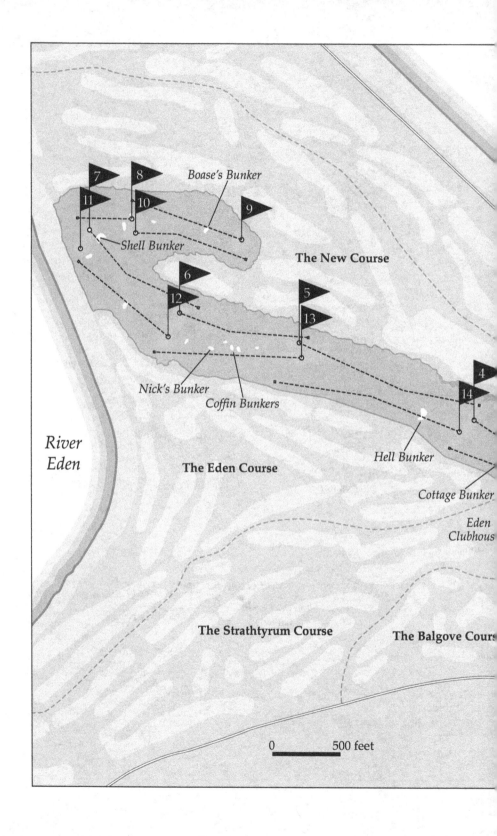

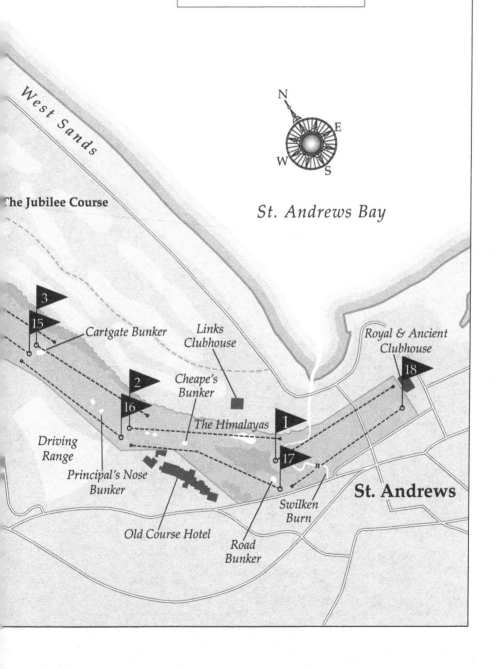

The Old Course
St. Andrews

West Sands

The Jubilee Course

St. Andrews Bay

N
E
W
S

3

15

Cartgate Bunker

Links Clubhouse

Royal & Ancient Clubhouse

18

2

Cheape's Bunker

16

The Himalayas

1

Driving Range

Principal's Nose Bunker

17

Old Course Hotel

Swilken Burn

St. Andrews

Road Bunker

ST. ANDREWS
SOJOURN

1

The Slice of My Life

t was a ghastly, careening push-slice—the mongrel of all golf shots—that changed the course of my life. Okay, maybe that's a bit breathless, but there's no question that the banana ball I perpetrated on July 16, 1983, was the finest shot I've ever missed.

The scene was the 18th tee of the most famous golf course in the world, the Old Course at St. Andrews, Scotland. As the editor-in-chief of *Golf Magazine,* I'd been invited, along with half a dozen or so colleagues from other American golf publications and newspapers, on a pre–British Open boondoggle, courtesy of a man named Frank Sheridan.

Sheridan had purchased the Old Course Hotel, the modern five-story monster that looms inharmoniously over the penultimate hole of the ancient links, the balconies of its sixty deluxe rooms jutting impudently outward from a chunky stucco frame. When the hotel first opened, back in 1968, Henry Longhurst aptly described it as "a dresser with its drawers pulled out," and despite its advantageous location, the place had never really caught on.

Sheridan, however, was determined to transform the hotel (which he'd rechristened the Old Course Golf & Country Club) into Scotland's premier hostelry, and to help make his point he'd drafted Jack Nicklaus and Seve Ballesteros to launch a weekend-long celebration with a head-to-head match on the Old Course, to be reported upon by us conscripted scribes.

But at the eleventh hour, there arose what the Scots refer to as a wee glitch. Commandeering a tee time on the Old Course is not a simple matter, even if your names are Nicklaus and Ballesteros. The St. Andrews Links Trust—which controls play on all six of the town's courses—had ruled that Sheridan's circus would not come to town— it would create too much disruption to the regular Saturday morning play. And so, rather hastily, the battle of the titans had been relegated to Ladybank, a comparatively unknown parkland course in a nearby town of the same name.

"It's just down the road—you'll see the sign," said the hotel porter on the appointed morning as I headed out the door to my rental car along with *Golf Digest*'s Ross Goodner, Ron Coffman of *Golf World,* and Furman Bisher, the venerable and feisty sports columnist for the *Atlanta Constitution.*

Down the road Ladybank was, but a bit farther down the road than we'd expected. We'd driven roughly ten miles, all four of us craning our necks at every little sign, placard, and poster, when Bisher boomed from the back seat, "Aw hell, why don't we just forget about it and go play some golf."

It was an offer none of us could refuse. And so, approximately 300 yards short of the intersection I now know to be signposted "Ladybank," I U-turned my Vauxhall Viva and headed back to St. Andrews.

Up to the first tee of the Old Course we marched and lo and behold there was an open slot. Today this would never happen, and even back in July of 1983 it was relatively astounding. What was even more remarkable, however, was that upon learning of our good fortune, all four underpaid and overprivileged members of the golf media immediately reached into our pockets and not only paid to play but sprung for caddies. (My colleagues, I assumed, had the same intention I had—to do some creative writing at expense account time.)

Four blissful hours later, we were tramping back into the lobby of the hotel, bags over our shoulders, when suddenly we found ourselves the focus of some highly unwanted attention. There, in the center of the lobby, standing in a semicircle and looking directly at us, were Nicklaus, Ballesteros, and Sheridan, in the middle of a press conference with our invited colleagues, including the BBC, with its klieg lights glaring and cameras rolling. Absolutely horror-struck, I moved into "perp walk" mode, shoulders hunched, head bowed, hand shading brow.

Old Furman had no such compunctions. Striding straight up to Nicklaus, he said, "Jack, we're awfully sorry we didn't come to watch you boys down at Ladybank, but you see, we *were* able to get a tee time on the Old Course!"

It was during that illicit round that I hit the fateful slice of my life. Understand now, the home hole at the Home of Golf lies seamlessly side by side with the opening hole, comprising a target the approximate breadth and contour of Nebraska. But as any devout golfer knows, the Old Course is not just a golf course, it's a shrine—golf's version of the Vatican—and number 18 is its culmination, its Sistine Chapel, the last place you want to demonstrate a proclivity to stray.

Moreover, running along the entire right edge of the hole is a sturdy, gleaming white fence, marking out of bounds, and just beyond that fence, across a narrow street, is a row of stately slate-roofed townhouses, their bulging bay-windowed facades adding considerably to the intimidation of the final tee shot. Yes, when a golfer puts his peg in the ground at number 18 on the Old, every fiber in his being tells him "Don't go right."

Which of course I did, with a swing so convulsive that, from the moment the ball left the clubface all four players and all four caddies knew it was gone, destined for not grass but glass—or steel or granite or human flesh or some calamitous combination of them all.

Curiously, however, it just disappeared, diving without bounce or clank into the nether regions of the gray stone neighborhood. I never found that ball. But while searching for it I did find something else—a For Sale sign. Incredibly, the bottom two floors of one of those town-houses—2,000 square feet of private residence—was on the market, and fate had drawn me (actually sliced me) to it.

On Monday morning, instead of heading down to Birkdale with my cohorts, I phoned the listing broker and asked the price. When I heard it, my heart skipped a beat—£45,000, or about $65,000 at the then prevailing exchange rate. The previous owner, an elderly woman, had died earlier that year and left everything in the hands of lawyers and accountants who had been instructed to accept the first offer to hit the asking price. In six weeks, no such offer had been received.

I took a quick walk through the place and that evening called home for permission. My wife, although a confirmed nongolfer, had been to St. Andrews and I knew she liked the town.

"The interior's not in great shape," I said, "but that's okay—the layout is ideal, the rooms are big, the ceilings are high, and there are four working fireplaces. Besides, we're never going to actually live here—it's an investment. We can rent it to students to help with the carrying costs, and in the summers it'll be free if we want to visit. I know it's a chunk out of our savings, honey, but wait until you see the view."

Happily, she didn't need much selling. And so, two months later in a solicitor's office in Dundee, George and Libby Peper became the proud owners of 9A Gibson Place, St. Andrews, Fife.

2

Transatlantic Landlord

t. Andrews, in addition to being golf's mecca, is home to the third oldest university in Great Britain, founded in 1412. Only Oxford and Cambridge are older or, for that matter, more prestigious. To the full-time residents, the University of St. Andrews is a sustained source of pride, commerce, and annoyance. Each autumn roughly 7,000 students converge from all corners of the world, instantly swelling the little burgh's population by fifty percent. Unfortunately, the university facilities can house only about half of these students, so in late August a tetchy sort of town-gown ritual begins to unfold as everyone tries to cram fifteen Titleists into a dozen-ball box.

It was perfect for us—we had no desire to visit our flat between September and May, and the rental income was exactly what we needed. We could put the squeeze on the lads and lassies without being squeezed by them.

Or so I thought. The day after we took possession of our place, I paid a get-acquainted visit to my neighbor upstairs. When I mentioned our intent to seek a student rental, his face went ashen. Sandy Brewster had just retired after a long and distinguished career in the international division of Gillette. Years earlier, he and his good wife, Kathleen, had bought the three-story flat directly above ours and converted it into a comfortable, tastefully decorated home. All he'd wanted from his golden years was to play a bit of golf, tend to his investments, and enjoy some peace and quiet.

"Do you realize what you're doing?" he said to me with the severity of a Calvinist deacon. "Do you realize what the students do? They play rock music at peak volume, they crash in and out at all hours of the night, they cook strange-smelling food, they leave rubbish on the stoop, they . . ."

I listened patiently to this litany, nodding sincerely while at the same time thinking "Tough darts, Sandy," until he got to his closer:

"And they will, I assure you, destroy the structure and contents of your home with the cruel comprehensiveness of a tornado."

"Well then," I gulped. "I guess we'll have to find some nice ones."

We did get lucky that first year—a young divinity professor and his wife whose idea of a wild time was a long walk on the beach followed by an evening of scripture reading. They took better care of the place than we would have. Over the ensuing two decades, however, things steadily deteriorated—a succession of lesser professors followed by graduate students, followed by undergraduate students, followed by undergraduate students with personality disorders, the last group so traumatizing the poor Brewsters that they fled their idyllic nest for a tiny cottage up the street.

I must admit I wasn't proud of having fostered the intimidation of an innocent septuagenarian couple, but I managed to assuage my guilt with the thought that, number one, the Brewsters had had a nice run—a good fifteen of their twenty years of residence had been passed in serenity; number two, they'd really become a bit too old to be lugging sacks of groceries up three flights of stairs; and number three, they'd made a handsome profit on the sale of their flat.

Our rental income had been relatively meager—about $500 a month to start, with only slight increases over the years. It hadn't covered the mortgage, taxes, and insurance, let alone the repairs.

And repairs there had been. Despite Sandy Brewster's warnings, the students were less than devastating as house wreckers. The real scourge was Mother Nature. In the first year of our ownership, a spring flood wreaked havoc with the sewer system, which backed up and belched its contents across our entire ground floor, leaving a stench that lasted for months. When we visited that summer, the odor in the kitchen was evocative of a Yankee Stadium men's room midway through a July doubleheader.

A couple of years later, while sitting innocently at my desk in Manhattan, I got a phone call that struck terror in my veins.

"Mr. Peper," said a clipped British voice, "it's Fiona here, at Murray & Donald Solicitors" (my real estate agent). "I'm afraid there's been a nasty business at your flat."

"Wh . . . what is it?" I asked, mentally speed-sorting through a catalogue of potential disasters. Conflagration? Mass suicide? Bagpipe recital?

"I'm afraid, sir, that you have dry rot."

I wasn't sure how to react. The term rang a bell, but only a faint one. Dry rot, as I recalled, was a medical condition along the lines of yellow fever or athlete's foot. I know now that it's something far more serious—a sort of cancer of the woodwork whose favorite prey is quaint-but-prohibitively-expensive-to-restore British buildings. There is in fact nothing dry about dry rot. Moisture is its cause, moisture that seeps through exposed brick and stone and settles into enclosed timbers. Like an army of termites, it eats away at everything in its path. Once the wetness evaporates, the wood rots. The only cure is to amputate, which we did at excruciatingly high cost, our insurance covering just a fraction of the work.

The only thing that saved us that year was the British Open. Too impoverished to enjoy the place that week ourselves, we rented it for a windfall of $5,000. Our tenant was International Management Group, the enormous sports management and marketing firm founded by the late Mark McCormack. When I made the deal with one of the IMG vice presidents, a chap named Bev Norwood, I had stars in my eyes. Greg Norman was then on the *Golf Magazine* staff of playing editors and I'd envisioned him and his young family ensconced at our place for the week. After all, it offered way more privacy and space than he'd get from a hotel and the location couldn't be beat.

I guess, if I'd taken a hard look, I'd have known better. In the few years we'd owned the place, we hadn't had the time or money to do much with it, just added a few pieces of furniture here and there. A couple of large televisions and a few, sturdy overstuffed chairs now vied with the pink-shaded lamps and chintz-covered sofas left by the deceased widow. The resulting decor was a tribute to schizophrenic tastelessness—Arsenic and Old Lace meets Animal House.

Moreover, there was only one bathroom, painted Easter egg purple (a decorator color for which the Scots seem to have a perverse predilection), and it had no shower, just a large tub, which, when filled with our rusty water, took on an unsettling peach hue, as if mildly radioactive. Worst of all, no matter in what corner of the residence you stood, aromatic traces of our sewer fiasco lingered.

So quite rightly, I suppose, IMG's location scouts decided old 9A Gibson Place was not suitable for the Great White Shark (or for that matter any of the briefcase-carrying sharks on the IMG payroll).

"So who's taking the flat?" I asked Norwood when I saw him at the U.S. Open.

"We're putting Mark's assistant in there, along with three girls from the London office," he said.

"Secretaries?" I said, a bit wounded.

"More like . . . hostesses," he said with a sly smile.

"You're kidding me," I said, suddenly seeing myself as a glorified whoremaster.

"Yes, I'm kidding you," he said. Bev Norwood, perhaps due to a lifetime of dealing with his peculiar first name, had a delightfully cynical view of the world.

A month later, I arrived in St. Andrews, checked into the bed-and-breakfast where I was staying for the week, and was headed toward the British Open media center when I bumped into Norwood again.

"So do the ladies have everything they need?" I asked.

"Almost," he said. "I'm just headed into town to buy them some red light bulbs."

Happily, our little house on the fairway survived that week, as well as the next decade and a half of student abuse, with remarkable strength and dignity. Throughout the 1980s and 1990s, in fact, 9A Gibson Place assumed a sort of back-burner role in our lives as Libby and I (mostly Libby) focused on raising our two sons and I kept my nose to the grindstone. I managed to visit St. Andrews about two summers in three, usually in connection with a British Open or Ryder Cup. Libby made it about two in five, and one year the boys came with us for a weeklong visit.

As time passed, we were able to make improvements—modern appliances, nicer furniture, new carpeting and drapes, and a variety of semi-tasteful golf-themed wall hangings. We even managed to squeeze in a second bathroom. Ultimately, the decor came to evoke neither old maids nor frat boys, just Pepers.

We created a place that for us was very livable—but only for a few days at a time. Indeed, if there was one thing on which Libby and I had come to agree, it was that our St. Andrews flat, although a fine investment, was like New York City—a nice place to visit but we wouldn't want to live there.

3

An End and a Beginning

The 2002 Ryder Cup was held at The Belfry near Manchester, England. Libby and I had earmarked the weekend prior for a St. Andrews visit. As was our custom, we left from Newark airport on the Friday-evening Continental Airlines flight that arrives at about 7:30 on Saturday morning. It's a six-hour flight, and typically I'm able to sleep for about four of those six hours, but this time my eyes never closed. I had some thinking to do.

For twenty-five years—nearly half my life—I'd had what I considered to be the greatest job in the world, running the editorial side of *Golf Magazine.* But the company had been purchased, new management had been installed, and the new president and I hadn't seen eye-to-eye. Over a period of two months or so each of us, for very different reasons, had begun to wonder publicly whether I should stay in my chair.

And so, during the long, dark silence of that flight I began considering my options. I still loved my job as much as I did the day I'd started—or almost—and especially enjoyed the easy camaraderie with

my colleagues on the editorial staff. On the other hand, I'd never considered myself much of a team player, and a part of me had always
wondered how I might fare as a one-man show, a freelancer working
from home. (Like all New York commuters, I was less than fond of
arising at 5:30, jumping in my car, and racing a few thousand fellow
maniacs into Manhattan.) I'd accumulated a good pension, more stock
options than I deserved, and a couple of real estate investments had
flourished in the boom times. My retirement seemed secure enough.

On the other hand, I knew next to nothing about money and in-
vesting. Besides, I was more than a decade short of retirement age, I
still had one son to put through college, a hefty home mortgage, and
myriad monthly bills. For reasons both psychological and financial, I
needed to work.

I'd shared my thoughts with Libby and she was as conflicted as I.
She wanted, and usually knew, what was best for me, and also knew I'd
become frustrated with the corporate conniving, but she was even
more anxious than I about the uncertainties of freelance life. Also,
being just as independent a person as I, she'd always treasured her solitude during the weekdays and wasn't particularly enthusiastic about
my becoming her constant companion—a classic case of "I married
you for better or worse but not for lunch."

That autumn weekend in St. Andrews was a particularly beautiful
one, with plenty of the golden kind of sunshine that only Scotland
seems able to produce. On Sunday evening, we were sitting at our bay
window, sipping a pre-dinner glass of wine and watching the shadows
stretch across the billowing 18th fairway when Libby popped the
question.

"You know," she said, "if you're thinking about leaving your job,
maybe we should sell the house in New York and move here. Tim
[our older son] is about to head out on his own, Scott will be going to
college next year, and it'll be just the two of us rattling around in that
big house. We could renovate this place, stay for a couple of years, and
then sell it at a profit and return to the States. What do you think?"

Never have I felt more in love with my adventurous, thoughtful, imaginative wife than at that moment. I was, in British parlance, gob-smacked, equally astonished and delighted. It was an idea that had never occurred to me, partly I suppose because I'd never dreamed Libby would go for it.

"Will you say that one more time?" I said.

She hesitated a moment. "You know you love it here, and granted it's not exactly my kind of place, especially since I *hate* golf, but I'll agree to live here if you'll agree to let me fix it up the way I want. It'll be expensive, but we can pay for it with the proceeds of the sale of our house in New York. Besides, whatever we put into this place you know we'll get it all back and more when we sell it."

"Well . . . yeah," I said. "And the British Open is coming here in 2005—that would give us plenty of time to fix it up and it would be the perfect moment to make a killing. Then we can come home and decide what we want to be when we grow up."

"Meanwhile we'll have an adventure," she said.

I don't think either of us slept much that night, me fantasizing about two years of life in a town with six golf courses and Libby mentally dismantling, reconfiguring, and redecorating every inch of the flat.

And so, on the Monday following the Ryder Cup, I walked into the boss's office and told him I'd decided to retire (technically, I asked him to fire me, which he kindly did, entitling me to an exit parachute that gave me plenty of time to start my new career).

Workwise, things fell into place with astonishing speed. Within a couple of months, I managed to land a column with *Links* magazine, a scriptwriting assignment from CBS, a consulting gig with Workman Publishing, and contracts to write four books. It all made me wish I'd taken the leap a couple of years earlier!

With our financial concerns thus at least temporarily at bay, I could join Libby in confronting the most daunting challenge of our lives—uprooting our house and home, deserting our sons, and absconding to Scotland.

We'd taken the plunge with our eyes open and knew it would be difficult both logistically and emotionally, but I don't think either of us appreciated all the moving parts. Suddenly our closest associates became lawyers, bankers, accountants, real estate agents, insurance brokers, cargo shippers, and storage facility managers. And that was just on the U.S. side of the pond—in the U.K. we began to face off with another set of lawyers, bankers, and accountants plus a brigade of architects, engineers, historic preservationists, contractors, carpenters, electricians, plumbers, upholsterers, and painters.

The most overwhelming assignment was the sorting out of our belongings. When a family of four lives in the same house for twenty years, they accumulate a mountain of possessions. Now, every item in every room had to be consigned to one of four fates: take it, toss it, store it, or donate it.

Many of the calls were easy to make. For instance, all rain gear and heavy sweaters were packed for Scotland. The antique dining room chandelier went into storage. The Franklin Mint collection of simulated silver coins commemorating fifty legendary artists and musicians of the twentieth century, bestowed on me grandiloquently by my great-aunt in 1981 with three of the anointed geniuses absent from their blue-velvet slots, got tossed.

The process became most vexing when I got to my den and confronted my trove of golf treasures. How did I amass all that stuff? A preliminary inventory revealed: nearly 1,500 books, magazines, journals, and tournament programs; just under a hundred videos; six complete sets of clubs plus seven backup drivers, seventeen wedges, and twenty-six putters; eight pairs of shoes, half of them encrusted with mold and curled up at the toes; nine golf bags, two of which had never been used because they were PGA Tour size and shouted my name in six-inch-high letters on the front pocket; approximately 200 paintings, prints, photos, and other assorted wall hangings; and a broad and horrifying array of golf-themed tchotchkes.

How did I acquire a first-edition copy of *Arnold Palmer and the Golfin' Dolphin*? What am I doing with a Power Pod driver and a Basakwerd putter? When did I come into possession of a bright red twenty-pound tee marker for Het Girdle, the par-3 5th hole at the Gleneagles Kings Course? What prompted me to purchase a full set of fourteen sterling silver olive picks in the shape of golf clubs?

And what was I going to do with all of it? The decisions were slow and painful, but ultimately I sorted it out as follows:

Packed for St. Andrews:

Clubs/Gear: My starting fourteen: TaylorMade 540 driver; Callaway Hawkeye 3-wood; Adams 5-wood; TaylorMade rac irons (3-PW); Cleveland 56-degree sand wedge; Ping beryllium copper L-Wedge; Odyssey Rossie II putter; my high school sweetheart, a Billy Casper Biltmore mallet head putter (in case the Rossie didn't hit hard enough for those double greens on the Old Course); the 1880 vintage long-nosed wood I'd bought at an auction during the 1982 British Open (it needed to return home).

Books: A complete set of Mark McCormack's *The World of Professional Golf Annuals,* 1968–2003; all thirteen books having to do with St. Andrews, the Old Course, and the Royal & Ancient Golf Club; everything written by Bernard Darwin, Bobby Jones, Herbert Warren Wind, P. G. Wodehouse, and me.

Art/etc.: Libby's magnificent oil painting of the 7th hole at Pebble Beach; twenty-eight years' worth of press credentials from golf events around the globe (the fruit of my misspent adulthood) soon to be encased in a self-congratulatory glass-topped display table.

Tossed Out:

Clubs: All wood woods; a set of Wilson Staff Dynapower irons and a set of MacGregor Tommy Armour CF 4000 irons, both from about 1971 (for a while these were regarded as collectibles and sold for thousands, but I'd neglected them in the basement, allowing them to become rusted and worthless); a complete set of barely used 1978-vintage Lynx Tigress woods and irons (my wedding gift to Libby, used only three times).

Books/Videos: All seven definitive biographies of Tiger Woods; all books whose titles included the word "Golfing"; all fiction and humor (there has never been a great golf novel, nor has there ever been a truly funny golf book—at least not on purpose); all instructional videos (beginning with the six-part series where the laughably awkward host was yours truly).

Art/etc.: All photos showing me with a full head of hair; all foursome-grinning-on-the-tee photos except those where I'm standing next to famous people.

Gave Away:

Clubs: One Putter Royale, a wooden-headed mallet with an insert crafted from the propeller blade of the *QE2*. (I probably should have put it on eBay, but one of my friends professed a penchant for athletic gear made from dismantled luxury liners.)

Books: A bulging collection of ill-conceived instruction manuals, including a couple I'd had a hand in writing. I mistakenly gave these to a golf charity aimed at helping kids with little chance of learning the game—now they had no chance.

Art/etc.: All but about a dozen items in my museum-quantity collection; one commendably weighty but rampantly unattractive "100th Anniversary of the U.S. Open" limited-edition bronze sculpture, purchased at a weak moment and a high price; one Michael's Invitational 1981 Children's Memorial Hospital simulated-leather golf-bag-motif trash receptacle.

Put in Storage:

Clubs: All twelve of my Acushnet Bullseye Standard original red-brass putters (I don't know why, I just couldn't part with them); my maroon-shafted Wilson R-90 and all other cool-looking old wedges (someday I know I'll be able to make one of them work).

Books: Everything on the history and architecture of the game, especially copy #125 of *Scotland's Gift: Golf* signed by the author, C. B. Macdonald (probably worth more than the rest of my library combined).

Art/etc.: All photos of me on the course with my sons; one stick-figure pen-and-ink self-portrait signed by the artist, Jack Nicklaus; one framed copy of *Time* magazine from September 1930 with Bobby Jones on the cover; one photograph of me in the locker room of the Players Championship with Rex Caldwell, Keith Fergus, Peter Jacobsen, Greg Norman, and Payne Stewart, where I'm the only one wearing clothes (don't ask); one framed montage of a photograph, scorecard, and the $8 won at Medinah Country Club in 1989, with a note from the poor chump I beat, two-time defending U.S. Open champion Curtis Strange; one long-drive contest trophy won at a Magazine Publishers Conference while I was working for *Golf Magazine,* utterly meaningless except for the inscription "Presented by Golf Digest."

It was Libby who masterminded the quick-and-the-dead calls on the rest of our worldly possessions—all the pots and pans, clothing and furniture, artwork and knickknacks. Libby, in fact, choreographed ninety-nine percent of our transatlantic transplant, just as, for twenty-five years, she'd shouldered most of the day-to-day responsibilities of our marriage—everything from changing the batteries in flashlights to changing our sons' diapers to changing the oil in our cars, all the while working as a freelance illustrator. I will never be able to thank her enough.

As the spring and summer sped by, there was much to do—bank accounts to close, newspaper subscriptions to cancel, phone and cable services to discontinue, three cars to sell (and one to buy in the U.K.). And since for various reasons we needed to maintain a U.S. address, an apartment had to be secured. When we decided New Jersey (not New York) was where we should be, a slew of additional assignments arose—new driver's licenses, new insurance companies, new income tax issues.

Most important were the concerns of a nonlogistical nature. Each of our sons was at a delicate stage. Tim had just graduated from NYU's Tisch School of the Arts, a drama major, and was about to embark on the precarious career of acting. Scott, four years younger, had been accepted to Princeton. Before Libby and I could make a move, we needed to be satisfied that both boys were happily settled. We were, in fact, four people in transition, each of us leaving family, friends, and home behind for an exciting but uncertain new life. By mid-September, however, we'd all made our leaps.

4

Dogged Pursuit

inety-three professionally packed boxes and one professionally crated baby grand piano were extracted
from our home, loaded onto a truck, and driven to the Port of New
York, where they were packed into a forty-foot container that was
lifted onto a 455-foot cargo ship that sailed 3,500 miles to Southamp-
ton, England, where, after passing through customs, everything was
loaded onto a lorry and driven 500 miles north to St. Andrews. The
whole process took nearly two months.

Libby and I, with just one suitcase apiece, made much better time,
but our journey was not without travail. Instead of flying into Edinburgh or Glasgow as was our preference, we were forced to fly via
London, rent a car, and drive 475 miles to St. Andrews. Our circuitous
route had been compelled by an item we'd brought with us, the one
item we couldn't load onto a ship—our single most precious possession—Millie.

She'd entered our lives on the Fourth of July, 2000. When Libby,
Scott, and I first saw her, cavorting with her brothers and sisters in the

front yard of a farmhouse in eastern Pennsylvania, we all fell in love. Just ten weeks old, a cotton ball with three black buttons for her nose and eyes, she somehow stood out from the half dozen other West Highland white terriers in the litter.

"Look at those big goofy ears," said Scott. "One sticks straight up, the other kind of flops over backwards."

"And her eyes," I said. "Don't they seem brighter than the eyes on the other dogs?"

"That's because she's paying more attention to us than the others are," said Libby. "She seems to be telling us to take her home."

We'd always been a dog-nutty family. Libby and I had barely moved into our first house when I presented her with Alice, a basset hound that stole our hearts despite being the dumbest mammal in North America. Alice was followed by Sandy, a golden retriever and best friend to our growing boys, and then by Cleo, a bright and feisty little schnoodle (mixed schnauzer and poodle).

Cleo was still with us but nearly ten years old and slowing down a bit when we brought home Millie. The notion was to rejuvenate Cleo with a playmate for her golden years. Unfortunately, Cleo at first viewed Millie more as competition than companion. After the ritual butt-sniff, she retreated under the kitchen table from whence she re-pelled Millie's advances with a series of snarling nips. Happily, Millie, in the manner of all Westies, felt no rancor and continued her courtship undeterred, eventually winning Cleo over just as she had the rest of the family, the two of them playing, eating, and napping together and par-ticularly enjoying their romps in the enclosed area of our backyard re-served for them and known affectionately as the defecatorium.

When she wasn't with Cleo, Millie tended to hang out with me, especially after I became a home-based freelancer. I think we bonded because we enjoyed the same things—taking early-morning walks, eating often and sloppily, scratching ourselves, staring mindlessly out the window, and above all, watching television.

When we made our decision to move to St. Andrews, we realized Cleo would not be able to go with us—she was simply too old and frail—but we were able to find her the perfect situation, living with a contemporary who had the same need for companionship that she did: Libby's mother in Kansas City. Millie was a different story—there was never a question that she would go with us. At least not until the day I was chatting with a friend.

"I guess you won't be taking your dogs with you," he said.

"Well, not Cleo, but we'll definitely take Millie," I said. "After all, being from the West Highlands of Scotland, she needs to return home."

"How are you going to handle the quarantine?" he said.

"What quarantine?" said I.

Back in 1901 a spate of deaths attributable to rabies had prompted sweet old Queen Victoria to impose a set of strict regulations on foreigners bringing their pets to Great Britain. Basically, the dog or cat had to sit in a detox cell for six months before it could rejoin its owners. Over time, however, the policy had become both cruel and idiotic. There had not been a case of rabies in the U.K. in decades—meanwhile, thousands of dogs and cats had died in their detention pens.

When we learned all this, we didn't know what to do. The notion of being separated from our dear little Millie for six months—and the vision of her in canine solitary—was more than Libby and I could bear. The nearest holding area was a drive of several hours from St. Andrews, meaning our choice would be to make regular visits and feel put upon or make no visits and feel guilty.

There had to be another way. Feed Millie a couple of Valium and smuggle her in the shoe pocket of my Club Glove? Bribe a trawler captain to drop her on the beach at Folkestowne? Pretend I'm blind and seek exemption under the seeing-eye-dog clause? Suit up in black tights and ski cap and stage a midnight raid on the pet prison?

As much as we disliked it, there were only two options—obey the law and be separated from Millie for the entire fall and winter, or scrap the whole idea of moving to St. Andrews.

Then an amazing thing happened. The quarantine was lifted. After a hundred years, the British government decided to loosen up a bit. As suddenly as we'd been throttled, we were released. There were still hurdles to be jumped—essentially Millie had to satisfy the six-month rule before rather than after her arrival. That meant a gauntlet of rabies vaccinations, blood tests, and tick and tapeworm treatments, as well as the subcutaneous insertion of a microchip that would allow her to be identified instantly by officials at any port of call in the world (presumably so they could eliminate her as a terrorist suspect).

Libby and I paid half a dozen visits and several hundred dollars to the local vet, accumulated a two-inch-thick file of customs documents, and on the day of our trip spent nearly three hours in the cavernous pet check-in area of Newark airport, getting Millie bonded and boarded. I'm not sure where on the plane they put her, but I can only assume she had a fully reclining seat, champagne service, and a choice of movies, because while Libby and I traveled gratis on frequent flyer miles, Millie's one-way ticket cost $589.

At Heathrow, we were dispatched to a grim little office to wait for our girl to clear customs and immigration. A Frenchman sitting next to us had been there nearly five hours, waiting for his cat. Over the previous forty-eight hours he'd traveled from Paris to Houston to pick up Fifi, then—following U.K. requirements—accompanied her to Heathrow (then the only airport in Europe that allowed pet arrivals). While we were with him, a uniformed official emerged from the customs area to inform Pierre that he was missing the original copy of one of the twenty-seven required immigration forms. He produced a photocopy but that would not do, and since it was Saturday morning and no one could help him until Monday, he and his cat would have to remain in London for the weekend, with Fifi's quarantined cat house pegged at $250 a day.

So I guess we were lucky when after just under three hours Millie leapt into our arms. She was a happy dog, and about to become immeasurably happier. For while Libby and I faced a host of challenges and uncertainties in our expatriate life, for Millie it would all be upside—a town full of playful, aromatic hounds, a home full of cozy chairs and twenty-four-hour cable, and a vast new backyard defecatorium called the Old Course at St. Andrews.

5

Arrival

There's a memorable scene in *The Wizard of Oz* when Dorothy and her cohorts come skipping around a bend in the Yellow Brick Road and suddenly stop in their tracks. There before them, on the far side of an enormous field of poppies, is the shimmering skyline of the Emerald City, the magical place where dreams come true.

In much the same way, Libby and I rounded a corner on the A91 just east of Guardbridge and there, rising against the autumn twilight, were the distant spires and gables of St. Andrews. I'd made this trip dozens of times—the appearance of that skyline was no surprise—but a bolt of excitement shot through me nonetheless. This time I'd come not to visit but to live—and to live out a dream.

It was just shy of six P.M. We'd been barreling north in our rented Ford Focus for eight hours, following the six-hour flight and a three-hour wait at International Pet Control. Now, at last, the finish line was in sight. Normally, I would have gunned it through the last two miles of winding, stone-wall-lined road, past the horse stables and the pig farm, past three of the six links courses, past the athletic fields, and through the town's ancient southwest gate. Instead I slowed the car down, to savor the moment we'd awaited for over a year—our arrival. There was, after all, no reason to rush. No one was waiting for us, we had no deadlines to meet, and there was no better time to stop and smell the flowers.

That fanciful notion lasted about ten seconds. Then I slammed my Type-A foot to the metal, and we roared into the Auld Grey Toon.

The three stone townhouses at the south end of Gibson Place are among the first major buildings you see as you enter St. Andrews. Our house was built in 1866 for a chap named David Cunningham at a cost of £800. I have a copy of the original deed, which looks like a first draft of the Declaration of Independence—twelve pages of single-spaced calligraphy that concludes with a list of two or three dozen signatures.

There were some vicious zoning laws back then. Among the conditions imposed upon Mr. Cunningham by the town planners was that he not use his premises "for any Brewery, Spinning Mill or Factory, Distillery, Workshop or yard for Masons, Wrights, Smiths, Coopers, Weavers, or Candlemakers or for Slaughter Houses or for carrying on any nauseous operations, noxious or noisy manufacturers, or anything that can be deemed a nuisance or occasion annoyance or disturbance to the neighborhood." Remarkably, student rentals had made the cut.

Mr. Cunningham built a grand five-story home for himself and his family, but sometime during the early twentieth century the place was bisected at the chest to form two flats—9A downstairs and 9B above. Our place, I suspect, was originally the servants' quarters—a first floor (sitting about two feet below ground level) comprised of a kitchen, pantry, sitting room, and bedroom, and a second floor with a living room, another bedroom, and a bathroom.

Not much had been done to the place in half a century or so, and I would have been happy to keep it that way. In my view all it needed was a coat of paint, a few light bulbs, and cable TV. But I'd made a deal with Libby, so a somewhat grander vision had been put in motion: a complete remodeling of the kitchen with all new cabinets and appliances—including a restaurant-quality icemaker and a dumbwaiter—along with an opening-up of the floor plan so that the kitchen, pantry, and sitting room merged into one large family room, American-style, complete with a granite-topped island for food preparation, recessed lighting throughout, and two walls' worth of custom-built bookcases and cabinets. The blueprints also called for refurbishment of all four fireplaces, redesign of both bathrooms, built-in closets in the downstairs bedroom, and the creation of a raised bay window area upstairs to provide a more commanding view of the golf course and the sea beyond. The Sultan of Brunei would've approved.

It had been nearly four months since our last visit, when we'd had a final conference with the architect, approved the plans, and pulled the trigger. Progress reports had followed—letters, e-mails, and phone calls—but they were suspiciously nonrevelatory. "We've had the odd wee glitch but we're making progress" was about as much as anyone would say.

Most dismaying was the absence of any visual updates. I'd dearly hoped to see the occasional photo attached to an e-mail, but it seemed the only St. Andreans familiar with digital photography were the caddies who snapped the obligatory "here-I-am-at-the-Home-of-Golf" photos with cameras thrust at them by American and Japanese golfers.

I was, however, able to do some Orwellian surveillance thanks to www.standrews.com. Among the gizmos of this full-service site is a Webcam stationed on the roof of the Old Course Hotel that may be aimed and zoomed in for ninety seconds of real-time viewing of anything within its scope. When I beamed it in on a view of the Swilken Bridge, roughly one hundred yards down the 18th fairway, the backdrop included a remarkably clear view of our back door.

It was thus that, throughout the six weeks prior to our arrival, I made it part of my morning routine to log on and zoom in for an invasion of my own privacy. Most of the time I didn't see much, but one morning, just a few days before we were due to head over, I hit pay dirt. The activity was frenetic, a constant stream of burly blokes shouldering in and out of our doorway with an assortment of tools, supplies, and items too small for the Webcam to discern. The show was a riveting mixture of *This Old House* and *24*—except that each episode lasted not one hour but ninety seconds. Undaunted, I repeatedly rezoomed on the proletarian parade until darkness fell on St. Andrews and the last guy finally lumbered to his van. That day, I decided, one of two remarkable things had happened—either the lads had pulled off a whirlwind completion of the kitchen or they'd robbed us of everything in the flat.

So we were anxious in every sense of the word to see what had transpired in our nascent nest. When we finally pulled up to the curb that evening, we didn't bother to gather our luggage, just beelined it for the front door.

Which barely opened, so crammed was the front hall with lumber, pipes, boxes, and grit-covered debris. We had entered not a home but a bomb site. Sheetrock and planks lay everywhere, along with scraps of metal, lengths of wiring, and shards of tile, all of it under a thick layer of gray-white soot. The bedroom and living room looked as if they'd been hit by a tsunami, with furniture and debris stacked to the ceiling. Only the upstairs bathroom was untouched, as in no one had lifted a finger to work on it. Dust bunnies—big ones—had taken over the stairway and were beginning to breed.

Downstairs, where we'd expected to see gleaming appliances and new cabinetry, there was nothing, and I mean nothing—just a grim, gray, hollowed-out hovel, a tomb. The interior walls had been banged away, and the old kitchen cabinets had been removed, but that only made it worse—exposed timbers, bare walls, and a cold concrete floor with the only light coming from a hanging bulb-in-a-cage.

Libby's tears and my stupefaction lasted only a moment before being replaced by the sickening reality: Our home was uninhabitable!

6

Two Andrews

A renovation that had been slated for completion in September, then pushed back to Thanksgiving, now seemed targeted for Easter. Of 2008. Our situation was beyond despair, beyond anger. A week into our sojourn, all we could do was laugh, count our blessings, and give thanks to the man upstairs.

Namely, Andrew Lang-Stevenson. In 2001, the Brewsters' flat, directly above ours, had come on the market. For a brief, unguarded moment we'd thought of buying it, with the pipe dream of converting the top three floors into St. Andrews's premier bed-and-breakfast, operated from below by George and Libby. Then I'd run the numbers while picturing the lifestyle we'd be shackled to—a couple of trolls in the cellar, rising at six each morning to shovel out bacon and eggs, then wash bedspreads and swab bathrooms soiled by strangers. Thereupon, sanity had returned.

The flat was bought instead by a delightful Englishman who was to become both our good neighbor and good friend. Andrew Lang-

Stevenson was a golf-loving alumnus of the University of St. Andrews who never quite got the place out of his system. Thirty-five years after his graduation, married with three teenaged children and a thriving practice in orthopedic surgery, he'd convinced his good wife, Sue, that a holiday home in the town of his alma mater was an altogether smashing idea.

Almost from the moment I met him, I realized Andrew and I were kindred spirits. We were about the same age, in a similar semi-retirement mode, were the same height and weight, both bespectacled, and both all but bereft of cranial covering (though he at least had a mustache, something I'd never been able to muster). More important, we were both hopelessly addicted to golf and married to decidedly golf-averse women who suffered our obsession with sufficient understanding and good humor that they'd agreed to invest in domiciles hard by the Old Course.

At the same time, however, we were very different souls, each of us somewhat typical of his national origin. In contrast to my Yankee competitiveness was Andrew's gentler mien, to my self-absorption, his thoughtful generosity, to my time-consciousness and linear focus, his tendency to get lost in the moment.

We loved playing matches against each other, but neither of us paid much attention to who was winning—I became manically focused on shooting the lowest number I could, while Andrew floated serenely along, singing to himself, sniffing the sea breeze, and musing about whether his weight shift was too pronounced. He was a better man than I, a man who made me wish briefly that I'd been born British (as if that might have made a difference).

It was no surprise, therefore, that on the day before we were due to head back to the States after our summer reconnaissance visit, Andrew said, "If your flat's not ready when you return in September, you'll just stay upstairs."

When I demurred, he was adamant. "Don't be silly," he said, "we won't be coming back north until late November and meanwhile there will be no one to keep an eye on the place, so you'll be doing us a favor. You'll stay as long as you need." With that he'd handed me a set of his keys.

Thus it was that our residence in Scotland began not in 9A Gibson Place but in the far more commodious 9B, five hundred square feet larger and twenty feet more elevated, with a view of the links and beach that put ours to shame. Standing in Andrew's bay window and enjoying that view for the first time, I thought I would never be able to lower myself.

One of the first people I saw from that window (speaking of Andrews, saintly and otherwise) was Andrew Albert Christian Edward Mountbatten-Windsor—the Duke of York. At precisely eight o'clock on the morning of September 18, 2003, His Royal Highness, fourth in line to the British throne, smoked a drive 275 yards down the first fairway of the Old Course as a small tee-side cannon unleashed a deafening blast. The occasion was the ritual "playing-in" of the captain of the Royal & Ancient Golf Club, HRH becoming the sixth member of the royal family—and the first in sixty-six years—to assume the position.

That single stroke is the only one the captain plays, but it's enough to win him the Queen Adelaide Medal, which, following tradition, he wears at all official club functions. I wondered whether he'd been nervous standing up to that shot. He was a golfer about the same caliber as I, roughly a 7-handicap, and I was far from immune to the terror-induced top, snap-hook, push-slice, and whiff. Moreover, he had known about his captaincy for several months and thus had had ample time to engender a full measure of paralytic fear. The history of the Royal & Ancient is full of tales of captains who've foozled their playing-ins, notably Andrew's ancestor HRH the Prince of Wales, who in 1922 hit his tee shot onto the front of the 18th green, less than fifty paces away. The newspapers of the day, somewhat more respectful than the current London tabloids, described the drive as "a bit to the left."

On the other hand, Andrew was no stranger to public demonstrations of grace and power. I decided, on balance, that he'd been nervous but not nearly as nervous as I would have been.

7

Round One

No matter who you are, to stand for the first time on the 1st tee of the Old Course at St. Andrews is to experience the greatest natural laxative in golf. So intimidating is this opening shot that Dwight Eisenhower, a five-star general who once held the fate of the free world in his hands, couldn't handle the pressure. He slinked to the second hole.

There you are, barely a dozen steps from the front porch of the Royal & Ancient Golf Club, the full weight of its four-storied grayness upon you. Thirty-two clubhouse windows face that tee, and you can feel eyes piercing from every one of them, especially from the Big Room—front and center on the ground floor—where the blue-blazered members sip their gin and tonics and peer imperiously through graduated bifocals.

You feel their eyes, lasered into your temples. You feel the eyes of every golfer in your group, every golfer waiting to play, every lurking caddie, raking greenkeeper, and passing motorist, every shopkeeper, dog walker, street cleaner, beachcomber, and windsurfer, every gull, snipe, and pigeon, every fisherman on every trawler in the North Sea. Most of all you feel the eyes of Old Tom Morris and Harry Vardon, of Henry Cotton and Bobby Jones—of every great player, live or dead, who has ever walked these fabled links. And you don't want to disappoint them.

Which, of course, I did. My first round on the Old Course—at least my first as a resident—came two weeks after our arrival. It was a relatively quiet weekday afternoon, and I was able to walk up to the 1st tee and join a group of three Glaswegians named Jamie, Jock, and Ian.

They didn't know me and there was little likelihood I would ever see them again. That was a good thing. They were all worse players than I (or at least confessed to higher handicaps). That was also good. They had each paid £110 (nearly $200) to play the Old Course, while as a local I'd paid next to nothing—that induced a feeling of inner warmth that only a cheap bastard like me can appreciate. Finally and perhaps best of all, Jamie, Jock, and Ian had never played the Old Course while I had played it a dozen times.

Surely, therefore, they would be petrified by that opening tee shot, which was exactly what I needed, because I myself had been petrified for weeks. With the moment of truth now at hand, I desperately needed all three of these blokes—or at least two of them—to hit shots of such unimaginable ineptitude that I, hitting after them, would be empowered with the *Schadenfreude* necessary for solid contact.

Sadly, all three used tidy Scottish swings to spank their pellets down the middle. Then it was my turn. The palsied trembling of my hands was so severe that I could barely get the ball on the tee. I'd come up with a dozen different swing keys—"Slow back, slow through," "Stay behind it," "Head down, wait for the hit"—but such worthy thoughts seldom take hold if, at the moment you take the club back, your mind is spinning like a gyroscope.

To be honest, I made a decent pass at the ball. But to counter my fear of the worst of all results—a whiff—I'd teed the ball so high that I hit it off not the face of the club but the crown. The result was a shot that went almost straight up in the air—a trajectory of roughly 87 degrees vertical. And there was a headwind. I didn't know whether to run for cover or call for a fair catch. My tee shot returned to earth roughly thirty paces forward of the point from which it had been launched.

"Bad luck," said Jock with typical British bonhomie.

I played my second shot as quickly as possible, reached the green in 3, and 3-putted for my double-bogey. Normally for me, a double at the 1st hole is sufficiently dispiriting to destroy the remainder of the round. This time, for whatever reason, it didn't. Once down the 2nd fairway, beyond the evil theater of number 1, I calmed myself and found a rhythm, enjoying the wind on my cheeks, the soft, springy turf beneath my feet, and the exhilarating notion that this wondrous place was now my home course. I managed to play the last 17 holes in 3 over par, for a round of 77, a round that gave me enormous encouragement and hope.

You see, I'd come to St. Andrews with three tacit goals, two of them shared with Libby, one entirely my own. Our first goal was purely venal—to transform our hovel into a palace and sell it at an obscene profit. In the twenty years since we'd bought our flat, housing prices had skyrocketed in Great Britain, just as they had in America. The part of the U.K. that had seen the fastest growth was Scotland, the hottest city in Scotland had been St. Andrews, and the most desirable street in St. Andrews was the one on which we now lived. Our aim was to get everything gussied up by July of 2005, slap up a For Sale sign for the Open Championship, and reap a seven-figure bonanza, to be used for a retirement home in the States.

Our second goal was to make our two years as happy as possible. For me, the idea of living in St. Andrews was a dream, and I knew I'd warm to the golf delights, but I had concerns about my non-golfer wife. We were, after all, a couple of New Yorkers arriving in a small Scottish town where we knew almost no one. Would we meet people? Would we like the people we met—and would they like us?

Would our friends from America visit us? Would we be able to adapt to the slower pace, the shorter winter days, the rampant wind and rain? Could we ever adjust to the fact that we'd abandoned our two sons, left them three thousand miles behind? Would we ever feel at home in the Home of Golf? We hoped to be able to answer all of those questions with a yes.

The final goal—my goal—was a more solemn mission: to shoot par—maybe even under par—on the Old Course. One of the first things I'd unpacked upon arrival in St. Andrews was a framed scorecard from the round I'd played on October 23, 1985. The occasion was the biennial "Writer Cup" matches contested between teams of ink-stained wretches from the U.S. and Europe. Like the Ryder Cup, it was a three-day affair with an opening day of four-ball matches followed by foursomes (alternate shot) on day two and twelve singles matches on the final day. That year the sites were Carnoustie, the New Course at St. Andrews, and the Old Course.

Thanks to two superb partners—Bruce Berlet of the *Hartford Courant* at Carnoustie and Ron Thow of CBS-TV on the New Course, I'd had an impeccable start, winning three out of a possible three points—front 9, back 9, 18—on each of the first two days, to become the leading point-earner in a little competition-within-the-competition for Man of the Match honors. At the opening cocktail party, the event's organizers had announced that a 14-karat-gold Girard-Perregaux wristwatch, valued at close to $2,000, would be presented to the highest point earner on each team. This of course was in blatant violation of golf's rules of amateur status, which at the time prohibited nonprofessionals from accepting any award worth more than $250. However, shameless graft-grabbing slugs that golf writers are, no one had breathed a syllable of protest. Indeed, there seemed to be a tacit agreement that no report of the matches would mention the illicit timepiece. Honor among thieves.

Since no other American had compiled six points, I was a lock for the watch if I could score another three-point sweep in my singles match on the Old Course. My opponent was Renton Laidlaw, then the golf correspondent for the *London Evening Standard* and commentator for the BBC and now the stalwart anchor of European Tour events on the Golf Channel. If you've watched him broadcast—burly and baldheaded, with a lilting Scots accent—you undoubtedly see Renton as a wise, warm, avuncular sort of fellow, and he is just that. However, on the 1st tee of the Old Course in October of 1985 he was a scrappy 14-handicap, the team title was at stake, and he wanted to win just as badly as I did.

Speaking of tight, on that 1st tee, my esophagus was so constricted with fear that I couldn't have ingested a raisin without consulting Dr. Heimlich. To make the usual intimidation more brutal, a microphone had become involved. Let me tell you, when you hear a stentorian British voice utter "Now playing for the United States" followed by your own name, every normally compliant muscle and tendon goes on sabbatical.

I'd chosen a 2-iron, to keep the ball in play, and I did that, cold-topping it 150 yards down the middle as Renton nailed a beauty nearly 100 yards past me. Being the sort of person who embraces bad omens, I figured the day was over, that I'd finally found my choking-dog game, would shoot 110, lose to Renton what would surely be the pivotal point in the match, and return home in shame.

Instead, for no apparent reason, things once again turned around. With a series of scrambling pars punctuated by birdies at the 5th and 9th, I somehow made the turn in 34—2 under par. After bogeying 11 and 13, I chipped in at the 15th and parred 16. That put me on the tee of the 17th hole, impossibly, at 1 under par.

By this time, poor Renton had been dispatched, despite playing beautifully, at least a stroke or two better than his handicap. I'd also won the ignominious wristwatch and the U.S. had sewn up the match. All that was left was a personal quest. I had a chance to do something I'd never done, on any course: shoot under par for 18 holes.

In the twenty years I'd played the game I'd stood on the 17th tees of golf courses underdressed, underappreciated, under umbrellas, under false pretenses, and under misconceptions—but never under par. I was in completely foreign territory—and facing the most difficult hole on the course, maybe on the planet: a 461-yard par-4 that had made fools of countless players better than I.

So I topped it again—this time only 50 yards or so, barely to the corner of the stone wall that lines the right side of the hole. From there, however, I was able to gunch two irons forward to the front of the green and sink a 2-footer for the best bogey of my life. Thus, I came to the 354-yard final hole needing a 4 for even-par-72, a 3 for the Holy Grail of 71.

When my fatted 9-iron approach left me in the Valley of Sin, 60 feet from the pin, all hope of a birdie was gone. I did, however, slap the putt to within 4 feet of the hole. Then, in a masterful imitation of Doug Sanders on the final hole of the 1970 British Open, I lurch-stabbed the ball so comprehensively that it never touched the cup. It had been one of the two or three greatest rounds of my life, but in the final twenty minutes I'd thrown up on myself.

Ever since that day, I'd felt I had a score to settle with the Old Course, and now I'd come back to settle it. My handicap was still 7, but now I would have the time to study the old lady, discover her charms, decipher her challenges, and perhaps unlock her secrets. I knew I could coax a 72 out of her, maybe even better, and I couldn't wait to start trying.

8

Molishing

Nearly a month passed before our flat began to look as though it might become habitable for someone other than a Gypsy.

"We've just about completed the demolishing," said George Davidson, the balding, wild-eyed, goateed architect who'd honchoed the project from day one.

He and Libby and I were holding our weekly Monday-morning meeting, standing in the middle of our bomb-crater kitchen, where three beefy fellows had just hoisted a twenty-foot-long I beam into a slot in the exposed ceiling. We had not expected this heavy-metal arrival, let alone the pair of floor-to-ceiling support beams now standing defiantly in the center of our planned food preparation area. The lovely granite-topped island we'd long envisaged would now be a lovely granite-topped island with two massive steel palm trees.

"Great," I said, surveying the devastation. "When do we start molishing?"

It was mid-November, we were laughably behind schedule and

hilariously over budget—Libby's budget—which itself had begun at a figure one zero wider than mine.

Our conclave that morning was significant because of the appearance of a fourth attendee, our contractor. Not surprisingly, he had been making himself scarce.

Not that we would have noticed. A chap of medium height, average build, and middle age with a countenance bereft of expression, he was from the Retief Goosen School of Personal Magnetism. When he walked into the room, it was as if someone had just left.

On this day, as on the two other occasions I'd seen him, he barely spoke, just nodded earnestly at everything George Davidson, Libby, and I said while jotting the occasional note into a small spiral-bound pad. These notes, I surmised, were for the general amusement of his office pool, to help fine-tune the over-under bet on the completion date of our job.

The only good news was that, since the day we'd installed ourselves in Andrew Lang-Stevenson's upstairs flat—getting literally on top of things—the pace of work had become decidedly more feverish. One morning I came down the stairs to find no fewer than eight tradesmen at work in various corners of the rubble. Two plumbers were widening a copper gas pipe to accommodate the turbo-charged, seventeen-speed, GPS-equipped stove Libby had ordered. One electrician was installing rheostats to operate the sconces and chandelier in the living room, a second had his nose against the bedroom circuit breaker, while a third flipped manically through the installation instructions for the cable TV. All noise was drowned out by an electrical saw wielded by a joiner (British for carpenter) crafting a cabinet for my golf clubs while two visiting gentlemen from Stannah Lifts took measurements for the hoist (British for dumbwaiter). Hoist, in truth, is far more descriptive a term for a small elevator used to transport food and crockery. Dumbwaiter is what I had become.

With the speed and precision of a gunslinger, one of the Stannah boys whipped out his tape measure, fired its aluminum tongue three feet up the side of a wall, and snapped it back. As someone whose mechanical dexterity does not extend much beyond gripping a pencil, such maneuvers leave me gaping in awe. I have nothing but reverence for those who can saw neatly and effortlessly through sheets of plywood or hammer a nail without hammering a fingernail. Most baffling is anything electrical. In the little over a month since we'd arrived, I'd managed to short out Libby's hair dryer, melt an espresso maker, and upset the circuitry of our absurdly expensive Bose Wave radio, necessitating absurdly expensive repairs. Three times. My new best friend was the local appliance repair guy.

It is thus that I also feel a peculiar vulnerability when in the presence of skilled laborers, a paranoid certainty that they're muttering things about me behind my back. Things like "I'll bet you three grommets and my hard hat this guy's favorite color is pink."

Never was that feeling more palpable than during our renovation. The workers—two of whom had arms tattooed with slavering reptiles—knew I was less than pleased with the progress they'd made, and I knew they were less than pleased with the frequency of my visitations from above. My fears culminated on the day I discovered three lines of chat-room graffiti scrawled in blue chalk on one of the Sheetrocked bathroom walls.

"I hate this job . . ."

"I know how you feel . . ."

"Me, too . . ."

Those words struck fear in my heart. Clearly, at least three manly men were chomping to coldcock me with their Allen wrenches. And so I began to steer clear of the flat during working hours, except at lunchtime when most hands were occupied with coffee, sandwiches, and tabloids rather than implements of blunt-force trauma.

But there were a few less fearsome fellows as well. Michael Matthews, the painting contractor, was an efficient, sunny chap who unhesitatingly agreed when I asked him to commit an act of public vandalism. Six cast-iron Victorian street lamps line the road that runs parallel to the 18th hole of the Old Course, each of them issuing the distinctive Day-Glo-salmon-colored light that every Western European municipality seems to favor. The second of those six lamps stood smack in front of our home—its soccer-ball-sized light bulb barely six feet from our second-story bay windows.

At first I rather liked it. The light was so piercing and powerful, no interior lamps were needed, which meant a savings on the electric bill. It was also highly effective as a reading lamp—even the smallest type was clear and bright—notwithstanding the fact that all paper took on the distinctive hue of the *Financial Times*. As time passed, however, we couldn't deny the truth—sitting in our living room during the evening hours was like sitting on the inside of a jack o'lantern. So I approached Matthews.

"Look," I said, "I realize this isn't exactly kosher or cricket or whatever you guys call it, but I'd like you to slap a coat of paint on the bulb of the street lamp. Not the whole thing, just the southern hemisphere, the half that sends its napalm glow through our windows."

"No worries," he said cheerily, "we'll give it a coat of primer and then a coat of Ebony Satin—you'll have it made in the shade, so to speak."

Another solid citizen was Andy the Joiner, a wiry little man of perhaps sixty years with a thick shock of Einstein-wild white hair and two expressive 180-degree eyebrows to match. Andy had a penchant for tartan-plaid flannel shirts, just as many American workmen do, but being from the source, he had an impressive collection. In six weeks, I never saw the same one twice and wouldn't be surprised if he had a plaid for every clan in Scotland.

Andy was a craftsman from the old school—patient, honest, wise, and able to translate our visions into exquisite cabinetry. When, more than a year after he'd finished his work for us, Libby and I received the news that he'd died suddenly of a heart attack, we were shocked and greatly saddened. We'd lost a friend.

One of Andy's assistants, a strapping young fellow named Alistair, was adopted by Libby as her personal joiner, installing coat hooks and doorknobs, crafting extra shelves for closets, and generally granting her woodworking wishes. As one of the first Scots with whom she spoke on a regular basis, he also taught her a thing or two. One evening, on his way out the door to his truck, he pirouetted and said, "That's me then."

"Uh . . . yep, that is definitely you," she replied.

They held each other's quizzical gaze for a moment before Ali caught on.

"Oh, I just mean I'm done for the day—that's me."

It was the first time either she or I had heard the expression that we would come to hear—and use—on a daily basis. Libby liked it so much she began signing off her e-mails "That's me then."

Truth be told, our experience with the St. Andrews tradesmen belied what I'd been warned to expect. They were uniformly polite, diligent, well spoken, and above all, exceedingly able—even the electrician, the only person I'd ever met whose very name was an accident report—David Fell.

Most of all, I was impressed with their punctuality—especially one of Michael Matthews's assistants, a paint and wallpaper magician I came to know as Seven O'Clock Jock. Jock was a fellow of about my age and build, but conversing with him was something of a challenge. To begin with, he had Marty Feldman eyes—the left one looked straight ahead but the right wandered a bit. I never knew where to position myself, and holding his gaze was out of the question. On top of that there was his accent, the strongest Scottish brogue I'd ever heard. Every sentence sounded roughly the same: "A hoot ma heet but a canna doon a meedie," to which I decided I had two viable responses, the sage, smiling nod of agreement or the somewhat more risky "No way!"

But despite our difficulty communicating, Jock and I had something in common—we were confirmed morning guys. The day he appeared on the job, he asked whether we'd mind if he arrived for work a bit early.

"How early?" asked Libby the night person.

"Seven's me time," he said. "Seven o'clock, aye."

And so for the better part of five weeks, I tiptoed out of the master bedroom of Andrew's flat at 6:30, took my shower, walked Millie, put on the coffee, and clomped downstairs to unlock for Seven O'Clock Jock.

The longer the job took, the more ideas came to Libby—ideas for new nooks, storage places, and decorative touches—and the more expensive things got.

"Anything's possible," George the architect would say in his nerdishly playful way. "At the end of the day, it's all about the extra pennies."

Extra pennies there were, and said pennies were losing value fast. For most of the twenty years we'd owned the flat, the dollar-to-pound exchange rate had remained relatively stable—essentially the pound had stayed between $1.40 and $1.60. It had been $1.55 when the job began, but in the space of a few months it had risen to $1.75, and since our arrival it had seemed to go up a penny a week. Ultimately it would hit close to $2.00.

The cost of our renovation had doubled and we were getting literally pounded.

9

The Saint Hood

strangely, for an apartment of barely two thousand square feet, our home was accessible from two different streets, with the result that Libby and I were never able to agree on which of our doors was the front. Logic was on her side, the Gibson Place side. That, after all, was our official postal address. It was also the larger and more formidable of the two entries—four broad stone steps from the sidewalk to a pair of ten-feet-tall pocket doors that slid apart to reveal four more stone steps to a pair of side-by-side glass-paneled wooden doors with polished brass mail slots at their feet—the Pepers' 9A residence to the right, the Lang-Stevensons' 9B to the left.

The first time I used that entrance, I was annoyed to see that 9B had a doorbell and we didn't. There was no buzzer, no door knocker, no chime, air horn, or pots and pans to bang with a spoon. How, I wondered, did one announce one's arrival? Then, on the stone wall to the right of the door, I spied a curious brass protuberance, roughly the size of a tennis ball. By all appearances, it was a doorknob, but a doorknob to nowhere. I turned it and nothing happened. Then I pulled it and nothing happened. Then I pulled it really hard and ignited the carillon from hell, a cacophony of ding-donging cowbells that must have throttled half the citizens of northeast Fife.

The opposite side of the building—the golf course side—was, to my mind, the front. This was where the big bay window faced, where all furniture pointed, where all eyes turned. It was the only door I ever used. The entry, however, was dodgy. First, there was no sidewalk, no separation at all from the street. When you stood at our little wrought-iron gate, your heels were on a double-yellow line that marked the south boundary of the road known as The Links and you were well advised to pull in your butt lest you be sideswiped by a passing motorist.

The gate punctuated an undistinguished stone wall—two feet tall, a foot or so thick—that was our only protection, the only structure that kept wayward vehicles from plunging into our kitchen. The door was more in the nature of a slot. (My guess is that it had begun its life as a window, then the owners decided they needed either a service entrance or an easier way to slip out to the golf course.) The passageway was barely eighteen inches wide and the door opened outward less than 90 degrees, permitting entry only by house pets, children, and adults without serious weight problems.

Among our first visitors was a notably endomorphic carpet salesman from Dundee. Roughly five foot eight but nicely over 300 pounds, he could have been a poster boy for stomach stapling. He'd come to show Libby samples for the master bedroom, had parked his car on the golf course side, and as a point of pride insisted on exiting that way, acutely underestimating the assignment he faced.

As luck would have it, I was returning from a round of golf just as this fellow began his egress. His arms outstretched and his back pinned against the door casing as he squeezed himself sideward, he looked liked someone trapped on the ledge of a tall building. At the most extreme moment, his elephantine girth filled the entire entry cavity and the door strained at its hinges. Our flat seemed in the final throes of childbirth.

Just as I reached the gate, he exploded through. I was so astonished, I couldn't think of anything to say or do, so I just put my head down and kept walking to the end of the block, around the corner, and in the door Libby called the front.

A most welcome aspect of having doors on two streets was the intense feeling of neighborhood. Having lived in the New York suburbs for the previous twenty years, with our house perched on the side of a steep hill that sloped to the Hudson River, we'd had few neighbors, and those we had were so far removed that we'd never gotten to know them. It had been less than ideal for our boys, who'd never known the joys of a neighborhood gang, but it had suited Libby and me just fine, both of us being relatively reclusive types. Besides, there's that old saw, "You choose your friends, you're stuck with your relatives and neighbors." Now we were a flop wedge from a dozen people—and we got to know them very quickly.

In the house just next to ours—one door closer to the 18th green—were Sydney and Deirdre Cohen. A tall, perpetually tanned South African approaching his eightieth birthday, Sydney had had a highly successful career as a research professor before retiring to St. Andrews in the 1980s. He was a quiet fellow with a kind smile, and still played golf occasionally, carrying his bag on his shoulder despite a pair of ailing knees. I liked him from the start. Deirdre, several years his junior, was a charming and elegant Englishwoman with a playful sense of humor that endeared her to Libby.

Sydney's area of expertise had been microbiology, and although he never mentioned it, I knew he'd done something pretty big, because a piece of misdelivered mail had been addressed to Professor Sydney S. Cohen, CBE.

A quintessentially British institution is the Honours System, a complex hierarchy of awards that have been presented for six centuries or so to recognize personal bravery, achievement, or service to the country. Best known of these are the Orders of Chivalry, of which there are ten, including the curious Most Noble Order of the Garter (founded in 1348, presumably by someone in the marketing of under-garments) and Most Honourable Order of the Bath (which I would assume to be ladies first).

The majority of modern honors comes under the breathless heading Most Excellent Order of the British Empire. They are awarded in five classes—Knight or Dame Grand Cross (GBE), Knight or Dame Commander (KBE), Commander (CBE), Officer (OBE), and Member (MBE).

The first two groups are limited to 945 people (100 GBEs and 845 KBEs). These are the folks who get to call themselves Sir or Lady. One of them has to die before a new one gets dubbed. The third group—Sydney's group—is limited to 8,960. (How these odd quotas are arrived at is a complete mystery to me. I suspect there's someone tucked away in Windsor Castle or Parliament or somewhere—someone with a title such as High Chancellor of the Most Excellent Personages—who runs the numbers.) The bottom two groups are unlimited and include manifestly lesser souls, the likes of David Beckham and Alan Greenspan (yes, foreigners are allowed). The awards are bestowed personally by the Queen or the Prince of Wales, and are presented semiannually, on the Queen's birthday in June and at the end of the year.

I knew Sydney was far too modest a man to want to discuss his CBE, so I Googled him. Back in the 1960s, at the National Institute for Medical Research in London, he'd made breakthroughs in the study of human proteins that had led to the development of a vaccine for malaria.

Sydney and Deirdre occupied the first three floors of 8 Gibson, also known as Jamieson House. (Our place was called Arran House—in the U.K. homes are like pets and babies; the moment you get one you give it a name.) On the fourth floor was the longest-standing resident of the neighborhood, Maureen Gyle, a single woman and avid golfer. For months I'd labored under the misconception that she had worked for the British government as a code breaker in MI5, but when at a party I asked her about it she said, "Oh no, I was never anything so glamorous. I just worked for the University of St. Andrews. But you know who did do the work you're referring to—Robina Stewart, the lady who owned your flat before you." Wow, I thought, we're living in Miss Moneypenny's place.

For several years, the third floor of Jamieson was owned by a good friend and longtime *Golf Magazine* colleague of mine, Ron Riemer. Back in the late 1980s Ron and his wife, Kathy, had joined Libby and me on one of our summer visits to the flat. It was Kathy's first visit to Scotland, and to Ron's delight she loved it as much as he did. A long-time employee of IBM, Kathy had some stock options she wasn't sure what to do with, and the answer came one morning during their visit when I noticed an ad in the *St. Andrews Citizen*.

"You won't believe this," I said to Ron, "but one of the flats next door, at 8 Gibson Place, just came on the market." Two days later the Riemers had a contract on it, and for the next ten years they and we were absentee neighbors. In 2002, with Sydney and Deirdre in a vertically expansive mood, Ron and Kathy sold to them, took a tidy profit, and poured it into a retirement dream home in Arizona, the same sort of plan Libby and I now had in mind.

Shortly after the Riemers left the neighborhood, two other American couples arrived. The most recognizable home on the street—the Swilken, a sort of mini-Moorish castle painted bright white in stark contrast to every other building on the street—was bought by Tim and Cindy Hultquist while Jack and Mary Ann Curley took ownership of two properties, the bottom two floors of 10 Gibson Place (The End House) and a three-story residence at the other end of the block, which they immediately gutted and rebuilt.

Tim and Jack were friends and colleagues, both big hitters with the investment firm of Morgan Stanley. They'd bought their places as vacation homes to be enjoyed a few weeks a year. Each of them had a primary residence in an upmarket New York suburb (the Hultquists in Greenwich, Connecticut, the Curleys in Saddle River, New Jersey) and belonged to a venerable golf club (Winged Foot and Ridgewood, respectively). We got to know the Hultquists more quickly and closely than the Curleys, who visited less frequently, but we liked both couples and looked forward to their visits. Besides, with help from a local decorating firm—Farmore Interiors (which true to its name charged far more than any other)—they'd created a trio of magnificent homes that had greatly spruced up the neighborhood.

In the wake of those renovations, a story in a London tabloid had raked some muck about the onslaught of Yankee carpetbaggers on the Auld Grey Toon. Our block was singled out as Millionaire's Row, a line that caught the fancy of more than one resident.

When I first heard it applied to me, I wasn't sure how I felt—flattered, offended, or simply miscategorized. I took pains to assure my accuser that we Pepers were no parvenus, that we'd been paying St. Andrews taxes for twenty years and had been on the block longer than just about anyone. We were locals, dammit.

"Hmmph," he sniffed, looking at me as if I were a carpet stain, "you're no locals. Do you realize how long you have to live in St. Andrews before you're a local?"

"Uh . . . no."

"Well, you don't have enough years left to find out. There are families who've been in this town for three or four generations and *they're* not locals."

"How far back must one's lineage go?" I asked. "To Old Tom Morris?"

"More like his grandfather."

Okay, we were carpetbaggers—but our bag was the smallest on the block.

Happily, the preponderant attitude toward us ostentatious, opportunistic, rapacious Americans was a bit friendlier, and the warmest welcome came from our neighbors across the street, Eric and Margaret Reid. Two more long-standing, upstanding, or likable St. Andreans you will not find. Eric, a retired architect, had been a member of the Royal & Ancient Golf Club for forty-nine years (his annual dues payment, therefore was £5). Before him, his father had been an R&A member. Margaret, likewise, had grown up in the town. The Reids raised their three children in St. Andrews and, shortly after we arrived, they'd celebrated their fiftieth anniversary.

They were a very cute couple—Margaret, a wee lass of perhaps five-foot-three with a modified Cleopatra hairdo that was pure white, and Eric, just a few inches taller, also white-haired with a permanently impish look in his eyes. Despite approaching their eightieth birthdays, both were remarkably fit (as were most of the folks we were to meet; there is surely some sort of hardiness chromosome bred into the Scots DNA). Margaret thought nothing of beginning the day with a two- or three-mile stroll down the links or along the beach, while Eric toted his clubs jauntily around the Old Course and maintained a handicap of 16.

Libby got on instantly with Margaret, despite the difference in their ages, as I did with Eric, whose mind was as nimble as his gait. Each time I was in his company, he came up with at least one or two repartees that left me wondering, How the hell did he think of that so fast?

Their home, perched behind the 17th green of the Old Course, was designed by Eric and built in the 1970s for Margaret's parents. (The famed Swilken Burn—creek—that guards the first green also runs through the Reids' side garden.) Being roughly a century younger than anything else in the neighborhood—a stucco-sided raised ranch with most of the living space on one broad, shallow level, set ten feet above ground level, with a carport below—it stood out a bit. But the size of the place was perfect for the two of them, and the front facade—essentially one long wall of floor-to-ceiling windows, extending from the kitchen across the dining and living rooms all the way to the master bedroom—took full advantage of their spectacular view.

The Reids drew several yards of opaque beige curtains across their windows at night, but opened them bright and early each morning. They thus spent their days in a sort of elevated fish tank, an eternal episode of Big Brother, but they liked it that way. They were, after all, always neatly dressed and coiffed, seemed able to confine potentially embarrassing moments to the evening hours, didn't mind the stares of strangers, and quite enjoyed exchanging cheery waves with passing friends.

I must admit, in the first few days after we met them, I didn't know quite how to handle the look-up-and-wave thing. The inveterate voyeur in me compelled a quick peek. On the other hand, I didn't want to get caught snooping. On the third hand, I didn't want them to think I had no interest in them.

For a day or two I experimented with furtive glances from under the brim of my cap. I knew where to zero in—either the bedroom, where Eric sat at his computer, or the living room, where one or both of them routinely padded around or sat with a book. More often than not, they were there and ready for me. Our eyes met and the happy hands went up. I realized that to pass the Reids' house and not check in was tantamount to ignoring your mother when she steps onto your elevator.

The stealthy peeks quickly became full frontal scans of the fish tank. Whether walking Millie, playing down the 1st hole of the Old Course, or playing up 18, I looked up toward the Reids' in search of white-haired activity, the way a pilgrim to St. Peter's Square scans for a sign of the Pope. If I didn't see something immediately, I continued to ogle the breadth of their home until, invariably, the sheer force of my gawk pried one of them into view. Some days, the Reids and I exchanged six or seven vigorous waves.

Most often the appearance came from Margaret, who took a keen interest in everything that went on in St. Andrews. Her home gave her an ideal reconnaissance post.

"You missed your putt," she told me one morning.

"What?"

"Yesterday," she said. "You missed your birdie putt at number 1. I think you pulled it."

Since I had teed off at 7:30 A.M., I assumed she'd randomly spied my palsied stab while doing the breakfast dishes. The truth was, she'd known exactly when I was scheduled to play and had been watching for me. The tee times for the Old Course are posted each afternoon at several points in the town and are also made public on the Internet. Margaret always seemed to know who was playing with whom, who'd be heading to the various clubs for post-round lunches, who'd been foolish enough to battle bad weather, to rise at dawn or race against sunset.

"How was the fish?" she asked me another day.

"Huh?"

"The haddock. It looked very nice when I saw Libby buy it from the fishmonger yesterday. He comes down the street in his van every Tuesday, you know. I believe she bought some dressed crab as well."

"Really," I said.

"Yes, you'll be having that tonight, I expect. You don't want to let crab go for too long. Which reminds me, would you like to use our extra wheely bin?"

"Extra what?"

"Extra wheely bin, for your rubbish. You left your bin bag uncovered on the walkway the other morning and I'm afraid the crows got at it before the rubbish collector could. We have an extra bin in our garden and you should use it whenever you need."

I thought Margaret was unusual in the degree of interest she took in everyone and everything going on, but I was soon to realize that St. Andrews is a very small town and that every move by every citizen was monitored closely by a large percentage of the populace.

The truth is, we were very grateful for the concern Eric and Margaret had taken in us. In a sense, they adopted Libby and me, were the first and foremost to make us feel at home, and it was through them that we began to meet not only our other neighbors but many new friends. One fall evening the Reids held a cocktail party on the deck that adjoined the west end of their home. All the neighbors were there, even the visiting Hultquists and Curleys. It was a lovely evening and we were all in a fine mood, sipping Chardonnay and reveling in the view over the golf course and sea.

"I love this view," said Margaret, "but what I really love these days is seeing the lights in all those windows across the street. It's so wonderful to have those homes occupied by all you people. We're so lucky."

"Yes," said Eric with a rascally smile. "The other day one of my golf pals was boasting about his trip to the U.S., and all the people he'd met there. I told him, 'Oh, I have lots of American friends—they're my neighbors.'"

10

Perfect Golf

was stark naked, standing in the Lang-Stevensons' master bathroom on a Wednesday morning in late October, when I discovered the real joy of living in St. Andrews.

Just before stepping into the shower I glanced out the window to behold an arrestingly beautiful dawn. The sun had come up a brilliant deep pink against a sky that was nothing but blue. Thin white waves rolled lazily onto the West Sands barely two hundred yards away and the gently fluttering flag at the 1st green told me the breeze was soft, perhaps fifteen miles an hour from the southwest. It was the ideal morning—the ideal moment—for a game of golf.

Trouble was, I had no game scheduled, no time booked, no one to play with. In the month or so since we'd been in town I'd met only a few people and hadn't had the gumption to phone and ask any of them to play. I did, however, have a key to the realm—a St. Andrews Links Pass, which allowed me free run of the town's six courses. And I knew they opened at 8:00 A.M. So on a naked-giddy whim, I shut off the shower, dug yesterday's clothes from the hamper, speed-brushed my teeth, raced downstairs, inhaled two chocolate chip cookies and half a glass of milk, slipped on my golf shoes, threw my bag over my shoulder, and hotfooted it to the 1st tee.

Not of the Old Course but the New. Our place was blessedly situated smack between them. From our back door, the route to the 1st tee of the Old began with a hurdle of the three-foot-high white out-of-bounds fence (a maneuver that, incidentally, can carry a high degree of difficulty, depending on one's leg length and overall physical condition, not to mention the girth and weight distribution of one's golf bag), followed by a northeasterly walk of about two hundred yards, across the 18th and 1st fairways. To get to the New, it was the same hurdle, then a northwesterly walk of about three hundred yards to the Links Clubhouse from which both the New (opened in 1895) and Jubilee (1897) Courses emanate. (The three other courses—the Eden, Strathtyrum, and Balgove—start from a point roughly a thousand yards west of our flat.)

I hoofed it as fast I could, hoping to be the first guy in line. More than anything, I wanted to play alone. A century or so ago, British prime minister A. J. Balfour said, "A tolerable day, a tolerable green, a tolerable opponent supply, or ought to supply, all that any reasonably constituted human being should require in the way of entertainment." Wise words indeed, but to my mind, two out of three of those conditions were plenty.

The ultimate "tolerable opponent" is myself. I can think of no one I like better. Don't get me wrong—I consider myself neither a snob nor a recluse—I don't long for the absence of my fellow men. The truth is, I enjoy a few hours of bonding with golf buddies—whether of my own skill, better, or worse. But I have little interest in pickup games with strangers. I'm far too self-obsessed, too focused on my own game, my own swing, my own score, to muster the time and energy for small talk and forced niceties.

Unforced nastiness is closer to my style. I enjoy few things so much as the good-natured needling and banter of a match among friends. Indeed, even when I'm not playing well, I can manage to keep my spirits high through what Bernard Darwin so aptly described as "a decent, reasonable rejoicing in the misfortunes of others."

Had I been around seven hundred years or so ago, when all those alleged progenitors of golf—kolf, kolven, jeu de mail, pall mall, etc.— were afoot, I'm convinced I would have lobbied passionately for the worldwide adoption of a game called chole.

Originated in northern France, chole was a team activity played cross-country with an air of arrogant spitefulness that perhaps only the French could embrace. The two teams established a target, say a church door in the neighboring town, and then proceeded to bid for the chance to play toward it. "We can get there in 48 choles," the first team would say, after which the other team would huddle for a bit and reply, "We can do it in 45." The bidding would continue until one team said to the other, "Okay it's yours at 38 choles—*bonne chance, mes amis.*" The bid-winning team then played three shots (one chole) toward their target, after which the opposing team was allowed one shot (a déchole), the object of which was to deposit the ball into the worst imaginable trouble. From there, the offense got another three advancing shots, followed by another thwart by the defense, and so on until the church door was either reached in the predicted number of strokes or not.

Sadly, chole never caught on. Maybe they lost all the balls. Maybe no one survived the mid-match brawls. Whatever the reason, it's a great personal disappointment—chole, I think, would have suited me far better than golf.

So it was probably in the public interest that I play alone. Besides, there are some clear advantages to going out as a single. Your yipped 3-footers aren't embarrassing, your cuss words go unheard, your fist pumps and throaty "yeah!"s don't annoy anyone, your missed shots cause you less aggravation, and you always finish in first place.

It was thus with no small measure of delight that I arrived at the New Course starter's window that morning to find not another soul in sight, just the starter himself, who gave me a cheery hello, echoed my rapture at the glorious morning, ran my Links Pass through the computer, and dispatched me with a sprightly "Off you go, sir, the course is all yours."

He also handed me a scorecard, but not a pencil. Indeed, never until recently on the Old did any of the St. Andrews courses offer a pencil. If you begged, you could occasionally pry one loose, but only after you'd been made to feel as if you'd requested an audience with the Queen.

I realize that keeping a hole-by-hole score is an American thing, and that most British golf is match play where you don't need to write numbers in boxes. I also realize that many golfers carry writing implements in their bags. But is that any reason to be so cheap about pencils? After all, on any given day, a large percentage of the play at St. Andrews comes from visitors who want to record their scores for posterity.

I suppose, being a nonprofit enterprise, the St. Andrews Links Trust wants to show some restraint in spending on golfer amenities. That makes sense. After all, they churn out only two hundred thousand rounds or so each year, and hey, if they were to go doling out pencils to everyone, can you imagine the cost—at, say, two cents apiece, it could run as high as $4,000! You just don't throw that kind of money around, not when your annual income is a measly $15 million!

But I digress. On the idyllic morning in question, nothing—not even pencil parsimony—could detract from my joy. There I was on the 1st tee of one of the most delectable links courses in the world, just me and Mother Nature, with nary a soul in front of us. I would be able to play the game at my speed (which often has been likened to polo), drop extra balls after missed shots, improve my lies, cuss and fart freely, and generally assume the character of a lowlife. When that happened, I invariably played brilliantly.

It was little surprise therefore that my opening tee shot was, in Scottish parlance, a beezer. With help from a following breeze and a huge first bounce on the firm turf, it scampered all the way to the green, 320 yards away. The 3-putt that followed did nothing to dampen my enthusiasm.

Rain had fallen steadily the day before, but there were no puddles on the fairways, no mud—just a touch of early wetness—and the sand-based turf was at once hard and soft as only linksland can be, yielding sweetly to the thump of a well-struck iron. Likewise, there was just enough wind to make me feel cleverer at combating it than I actually was.

And so I walked in blissful solitude, enjoying the fresh salt air, thinking self-laudatory thoughts, dreaming self-indulgent dreams, and playing the game without letting it play me. As I moved from shot to shot, the only sounds I heard were the clinking of the irons in my bag and the occasional squawk of a gull. Not even the greenkeepers were out. The only sign of life came at the 6th tee, where a red hare leapt from the gorse bushes and raced across the fairway.

The 9th tee of the New Course runs just above the east bank of the Eden Estuary heading out to the sea. Before playing my tee shot to this, the toughest par-3 in St. Andrews—a semiblind shot of over 200 yards with the water on the left side, gorse and dense rough on the right—I gazed across the estuary. The tide was out, and perhaps 200 yards from the shore, a dozen or so seals frolicked on the slippery river bottom.

A bogey 4 at that hole took me to the turn in 40. On the New Course number 10 turns back toward the clubhouse. Into the wind now, I expected (even wanted) things to get tougher, but instead I surprised myself with a 4-iron to 6 feet and a successful birdie putt—exactly the kind of putt I would have jerked out of the hole had I been playing in the company of any human. Two more birdies at the short par-4 11th and the par-5 12th had me back to 1 over par and basking in a delusion of aptitude. Then the wind freshened for the last third of the course. With five bogeys over the last six holes I reached the low end of my comfort zone with a score of 77.

It was nonetheless very satisfying, as was the elapsed time—1 hour and 47 minutes. I'd played two approach shots to several holes, dropped balls around the greens to practice chips here and there, and dragged back a few missed putts for second tries. On the tee of the par-3 13th, I'd hit four 8-irons before getting one of them to stop on the slippery green. And still, I'd finished in well under two hours!

By ten o'clock I was back home, standing in the warmth of my postponed shower, planning the rest of my day, and wondering if life could possibly get any sweeter.

11

In at Last

t was not until mid-November, a full two months after our arrival, that we finally vacated our temporary quarters in 9B and moved our clothing and gear downstairs. The place still was not finished, but at least—at last—all the utilities were working, the kitchen was semi-operational, and the daily onslaught of tradesmen had ebbed to an occasional visit. We'd entered a new and brighter phase: the decorating phase.

In my view, it was a moment that called for shrewd strategy. First, inasmuch as we were going to live in this place for only two years, we didn't want to lose our heads over the choice of draperies, wallpapers, floor coverings, etc. Second, we needed to think carefully about who the likely buyers would be and target them with our decor.

Somewhat nervously I shared my thoughts with Libby.

"I can't decide," I said. "Should we be going after Americans? I've always thought they were the prime market, but the way the dollar's plummeting, I'm beginning to reconsider. What do you think, should we aim the furnishings at Brits or maybe Europeans or even Asians?"

"None of them," she said flatly.

"None of them. Well, then, who?"

"Me."

"Oh . . ."

"I don't care whether we're going to live here two years, two months, or two lifetimes," she said. "It's our home and while I'm here I want to enjoy it. That means we decorate it my way. I told you that a year ago."

I knew that. And Libby knew I knew that. She also knew that my only strategy was to save money—that I'd been attempting, rather pitifully, to manipulate her, because I feared her way would be prohibitively expensive. What ensued was the first in a series of spirited exchanges on the fate of our home, our union, and our long-term financial security, an exchange from which I emerged with two new strategies: 1) do not offer opinions on home decor unless asked and 2) do not moan about the cost. Just shut up and pay up.

The truth was, when it came to interior decorating, I didn't deserve a vote. In the world of dust ruffles, duvet covers, and pillow shams, my ignorance is exceeded only by my lack of interest. Besides, I owed Libby big-time—she'd uprooted herself and come three thousand miles to a notoriously bleak corner of the world so I could enjoy a couple of years of golf heaven. The least I could do was cede control of the home couture.

Anyway, I needn't have worried about the bottom line. Through a combination of artistic talent, shopping savvy, and elbow grease, Libby managed to save as much money as she spent. Having majored in fine art at Skidmore and trained as a commercial illustrator, she'd developed a strong sense of color, texture, and proportion. Beyond that, she'd always enjoyed the whole process of nesting. Our home in the States had been a 1920s vintage Arts and Crafts design, acquired in fair-to-poor condition. Over the course of a decade or so, Libby had transformed a dozen moping rooms into stylish and comfortable living spaces.

In more recent years she'd kept a file of decorating ideas clipped from *Architectural Digest* and *House & Garden*—photos of tartan-plaid valances, leather-bound sisal stair runners, and Delft-tiled fireplaces. This was her chance to turn some of her visions into reality.

A whole new decorating world opened up for her, however, when she learned how to Google on the Internet. Suddenly every major store, every big-time catalogue, every purveyor of every purchasable item in the universe was at her fervent fingertips. Like most women—most humans—Libby loves finding items at reduced price. Unlike most women, however, she has no particular zest for shopping—the traffic, the parking, the crowds, the inevitably fruitless pawing through merchandise.

Thus it was that she became a Googling fool. During the six months prior to our move to the U.K., nothing struck greater panic in my veins than to pass by Libby's computer and see in the Google Search box a phrase such as "19th century Persian rug" or "genuine ostrich leather Chesterfield sofa" or "gold handspun silk draperies." Blessedly, each search phrase also included the word "discount."

Once in Scotland, her favorite site became LauraAshley.co.uk. For a time it seemed as if our home had become the company's newest retail outlet, so frequent were the deliveries, so numerous the purchases (all, of course, at madcap markdowns). When one morning I noticed an article in the London *Times* business section on the decline of the Laura Ashley brand, I was incredulous. Surely our orders alone should have been enough to bolster the company.

But it all worked out, thanks not only to Libby's nose for e-sales but her willingness to do much of the painting, hammering, cutting, pasting, and stitching herself. Working hand in glove with Murray & Murray the kitchen people, Tyler's the tile makers, Watson the stonemason, Matthews the painter, Morpheus the bed builders, Overmantels the mirrormongers, Open & Shut the blinds makers, Gillies the carpeters, Walker's the upholsterers, Stewart's the fireplace installers, and Templestone's the mantel craftsmen, Libby served as chief designer, forewoman, and Jill-of-all-trades, assuring that all assignments were completed as expeditiously and economically as possible. This pleased me more than I could say.

To my brief distress, however, one item seemed not to be destined for our new home—the icemaker. Back in the States, there was no kitchen accessory for which I'd developed greater affection than my Scotsman DC33, a two- to three-foot under-the-counter marvel that clunked out an endless supply of crystal-clear, softly rounded one-inch cubes. So utterly spoiled was I by this machine that I was prone to fits of petulance whenever subjected to a Diet Pepsi or Mount Gay rum and tonic or Macallan single malt poured over cubes of lesser merit.

Thus, one of the first items on our list for the St. Andrews kitchen had been a proper icemaker. In Scotland, however, ice is seen largely as something that gathers in street puddles on winter nights. When at a pub you order a gin and tonic, the bartender grabs a small glass, fills it a third of the way with gin, adds the contents of a mini-can of Schweppes, and then, using a teaspoon, ladles a miserly sliver or two of ice from the plastic Johnnie Walker bucket that has been sitting on the bar, unreplenished for six hours or so.

If you go to a party at someone's home and ask for a whisky, your host invariably returns with a sad little snifter containing an inch or so of scotch and asks, "Would you like a splash of water?" When you reply, "No thank you, but could I have some ice?" he looks at you as if you've asked him to add ketchup, then turns sullenly and disappears for fifteen minutes or so. (What he does during that time is a matter of conjecture. In winter I suspect he scales a ladder up the side of his house and hacks icicles from the gutter; in the three other seasons, he presumably scurries to the pub for a raid on the Johnnie Walker bucket.) Your drink is returned with an icy stare.

I knew the British were cool toward ice, but nothing could have prepared me for the paralyzing moment when Libby said, "I've been surfing the Net for three days—there are no home icemakers in the U.K." Astonishingly, in all of Scotland there was not a Scotsman, model DC33 or otherwise, to be found. Indeed, in the entire Kingdom of Fife only one icemaker had been installed in the previous six months, when the St. Andrews Bay Hotel had taken delivery of an industrial-strength behemoth capable of flash-freezing Loch Lomond.

The implications of all this were more than I could bear. After two decades of plopping picture-perfect little cubes into my glass, I was simply not prepared to arm-wrestle with ice trays or lug plastic-bagged cubes from the supermarket. There had to be another way. Eventually Libby found one, although it was not an entirely happy solution. We were forced to acquire a model made by Sub-Zero, the vaunted American import aptly named for its concomitant ability to cool your comestibles and obliterate your net worth.

While Libby was doing all this domiciling, I was not completely idle. I had three assignments: set up the phones, set up the computers, and set up the televisions. The first two, considering my ineptitude with all things electrical, went smoothly, thanks to British Telecom. After a few dozen back-and-forths, we even got the laptops hooked up wirelessly so we could walk around the flat untethered yet online.

Setting up the TVs turned out to be an undertaking similar in complexity to the Allied invasion of Normandy. In the U.S., getting a television is pretty much a two-step process—you buy it and you plug it in. If you want cable, you make a phone call to your local provider and within anywhere from a few hours to a few days you're hooked up and happy.

Not so in the U.K. First every television owner is required by law to have a TV license. When I first heard this I was stupefied. What on earth could a TV license be? Was it like a driver's license—a certification that you were fully trained in how to operate it? Was it like a dog license, an identification tag in case the TV wanders off or bites someone? Or was it more like a license to own a firearm, ensuring that the TV is used by responsible adults and only for recreation and, in extreme cases, self-defense?

No, it turns out, a TV license helps ensure that the state-owned British Broadcasting Corporation, the BBC, maintains high standards of programming without need of commercials. Once I understood this, I had no real problem with it. After all, I'd always enjoyed the Beeb's wire-to-wire telecast of the British Open, not to mention the weekly coverage of the British Dart Throwing Tour.

The annual fee was a hefty £126. I could have chosen not to pay it, but I would then have risked being prosecuted for harboring a rogue television. The British government actually employs teams of inspectors who patrol the country in unmarked vans inside which are devices that can detect the presence of a television signal. If you're caught, you must make a court appearance and pay a £1,000 fine—and they catch over a thousand violators every day. So I paid.

Far more daunting was the business of hooking up to Sky, the cable purveyor that extends one's viewing options from the five standard terrestrial channels, BBC1, BBC2, ITV1, Channel Four, and 5, where the offerings consist largely of news, old movies, nutty British sitcoms, snooker tournaments, and reruns of *Everybody Loves Raymond* plus the odd special on *Croatia Today* or *Up Close with the Spotted Salamander.* Sky provides an array of nearly 400 global channels, everything from *Men & Motors* to *Garden Spot,* the Golf Channel to the God channel, Fox News to Al-Jazeera, plus myriad pay-per-view options—a dozen or so Sky Movies channels and at least another dozen channels offering explicit sex of all varieties. Needless to say, I was eager to get things up and running.

"I have some news about your building," our architect George Davidson told us one Monday morning, a slight tremor in his voice. "It's listed."

"You mean like the Tower of Pisa?" I said, the tremor now in me.

"No, not listing, listed," he said. "More like the Tower of London. According to 'Planning Act 1990—Listed Buildings and Conservation Areas,' 9 Gibson Place is a Grade C listed building."

"What does that mean?"

"Good news and bad news," he said, with a geeky I-know-something-you-don't twinkle in his eye. "It means you live in a structure of historical and/or architectural significance, a protected building. The good news is you don't have to pay VAT on any of the

structural improvements we've made—all those beams and supports—and that will save you a few hundred quid in taxes."

"Fine, what's the bad?"

"The bad is that, if you want to alter the building's character in any
significant way you will have to apply to Fife Council for Listed Building Consent."

"What does that mean?"

"It means that attaching a Sky dish to your slate roof will take a bit
of doing."

I must say, it felt special to be listed, despite the fact that our desig-
nation had little to do with the architectural magnificence of our home
and everything to do with the fact that our facade showed up in every
painting and photograph of the 18th hole of the Old Course. However, the honor wore off when I did a bit of research and learned that
the listed list wasn't exactly elite. There were no fewer than 370,000
listed buildings in the U.K., nearly 50,000 in Scotland, nearly 5,000 in
Fife, and a whopping 376 in St. Andrews alone! Suddenly it seemed
more prestigious to be unlisted.

And Fife Council. What was that? *Where* was that? Was it like the
Tribal Council on *Survivor*? Was I about to begin matching wits with
mean-spirited, self-involved jackasses, generally humiliating myself
for the sake of a one-in-sixteen chance of winning?

When I arrived at the council's headquarters in nearby Cupar, I
was told my application for a TV dish would have to be submitted not
in duplicate, not in triplicate, but in octuplicate, to satisfy Fifedom's
byzantine network of magistrates and factota. The process, I was further informed, would take a minimum of eight weeks and would
likely include a site visit by an inspector, who would make a final judg-
ment as to whether the presence of a twelve-inch dish, tucked in the
shadowy base of a soaring gable, would materially rupture the St. Andrews skyline.

The groveling took exactly eight weeks, but the answer from Fife
Council was yes. (If it had been no, I'm not sure what I would have
done—probably voted myself off the island.) And so, suitably licensed

and permitted, I phoned Sky cable, only to learn that they couldn't in-stall my dish. The roof was too high, and because of health and safety issues, Sky engineers were not authorized to do the work—I would have to hire an independent installer. Thus began a desperate kingdomwide search for a cable-ready SWAT team willing to climb a hundred feet or so and slither across the rain-slicked slates of our 140-year-old roof.

At length I was directed to Fife Aerials—the Flying Wallendas of residential wiring—who completed the job three weeks later than I wanted at a sky-high fee of £200 ($360).

But that was only the outside half of the hookup. Since I'd ordered not only Sky but Sky+ (the British equivalent of TiVo), and since I wanted it to work on three different televisions, one of which would serve as a mother ship for the other two, the job was sufficiently com-plex to flummox the local electrician. Another two weeks went by be-fore a Sky technician arrived to sort out the various cables, tethers, switches, and remotes.

The whole process, which had begun in September, finally came to an end in early December. But it was the last major cog. Oh, there were still one or two light fixtures to install, the kitchen ceiling needed a final coat of paint, and Libby continued to Net-surf for area rugs and occasional tables, but essentially our renovation was complete.

It had strained both our marriage and our piggy bank, but at the same time we'd created a lovely nest, a place that in Libby's words was "room for room, the nicest home we've ever owned." The end had justified the lack of means.

One evening at around six, having returned from a windy winter round on the Old Course, I was sitting on the comfy new Laura Ash-ley couch in the cozy new kitchen/family room as Libby prepared din-ner in the versatile new oven she'd come to love. A glowing fire warmed the room, Sky News was on the telly, Millie was on my lap, and a perfectly iced Macallan was in my hand. At that moment, I didn't care who bought our flat—or when—because I felt completely and ut-terly at home.

12

Gordon

When we returned stateside for the Christmas holidays, many of our friends had the same question for us: "How are you handling the Scottish winter?"

"It's really pretty mild," I said, doing my best not to sound defensive. "The temperature rarely dips below 40. Plus we get almost no snow. Something to do with the microclimate or the Gulf Stream or El Niño or something." (Unless pressed, I never mentioned the wind— the relentless, biting, bone-chilling wind—or the rain or the sleet or the hail or the sixteen hours a day of darkness.)

Our November and December had in truth been relatively balmy—including a couple of days when golf was played in shirt-sleeves. By mid-January, however, full Scottish grimness had set in. One particularly cruel morning, a gale raged in from the North Sea, the wind chill dived below zero, and snow began dusting the fairways of the Old Course. Inside, Libby and I were layered in two sweaters apiece while Millie huddled next to the largest radiator in the kitchen. I'd just put the kettle on for coffee when there was a knock at the door.

It was Margaret Reid, popping by as she often did, to see how we were getting on. "Well," she said, brushing snowflakes from her parka, "I wonder what hole Gordon is on."

St. Andrews, I'd come to realize, was full of colorful characters but none more compelling than the fellow who lived next door to us, Gordon Murray. Ironically, he'd been the last neighbor we'd gotten to know—in all the summers we'd visited, we'd never bumped into him. And yet I felt as if I knew him well. During the months leading up to our move, I'd received phone calls and e-mails from several friends and acquaintances, all saying the same thing: "When you get over there, say hi to my buddy Gordon Murray."

Somehow, this chap knew many of the same Americans I knew. Golf people, all of them—golf writers, golf architects, golf pros, rules officials, equipment manufacturers, tour operators, resort owners. There wasn't a corner of the American game where Gordon Murray hadn't made his presence felt. Forget six degrees of separation—this guy needed no more than two or three. Yet somehow I'd missed him.

Then one day, a week or two after our arrival, I was hauling some groceries out of the car when from behind me came a voice.

"Excuse me, are you George Peper?"

There, standing at the door of his own car—a navy blue S Class Mercedes—was a figure best described as Nicklausian: just under six feet but sturdily over 200 pounds. His broad, ruddy face was topped by a full head of graying blond hair that on this day held a back-tilted pair of Oakley sunglasses.

"At last we meet," he said, flashing an orthodontically engineered smile that lit up the gray afternoon. "I'm Gordon Murray. Welcome to the neighborhood."

We stood there on the street and talked for nearly an hour, a getting-acquainted conversation that felt more like catching up with an old friend. Although we'd come from widely different back-grounds, golf and St. Andrews had brought us together, and that was more than enough.

Gordon was a local boy, born in a St. Andrews hospital and raised in Cellardyke, a tiny coastal town ten miles to the south. The odd name Cellardyke had come from "sil'er (silver) dykes," which referred to the gleam of herring scales in the fishing nets hung over the harbor walls (or dykes) to dry in the sun. During the nineteenth century it had been a busy fishing village with over two hundred boats, but in 1898 a massive storm had wiped out the harbor and the fleet had moved half a mile down the coast to the larger and better protected port of Anstruther, leaving Cellardyke to an inexorable decline.

Gordon's kin were all fisherfolk, originally in Anstruther and then in Aberdeen where his parents moved when he was young. He, too, had been expected to go into the fish business but resisted, joining the Aberdeen police force instead.

"I wasn't much of a cop," he told me. "I arrested only one guy in two and a half years, a drunk driver, and in his case I had no choice. When I opened his car door, he fell out onto the pavement. I was way too lenient on the drinkers—probably because I had so much empathy with them."

Inevitably, the pull of the sea and the push of the family were too much and Gordon became a fisherman, first as a *Perfect Storm* type, shipping out for weeks at a time in quest of cod, halibut, sole, or whatever found the nets, and later as an inside man in the processing end of the business, using his considerable people skills to rise through the ranks. When he eventually became a partner, he expanded the business, adding a separate frozen-food division, then sold it all and retired at age fifty.

At about the same time, he became the beneficiary of some extraordinary good fortune. His elderly maiden aunt had died, and in her will she'd left Gordon her home in St. Andrews—the top two floors of the End House (10 Gibson Place), which overlooks the 17th hole of the Old Course with extended views to the west across all six of the town's links.

For Gordon, an avid golfer all his adult life, there was never a question—he would pick up stakes and move to the Auld Grey Toon. For his nongolfer wife, Shelagh, however, the decision was less simple. They'd spent twenty-five years making a good life for themselves in Aberdeen (nearly eighty miles up the northeast coast). They'd raised two fine sons there and made numerous friends. Shelagh, a former model for Pringle knitwear, had even started a women's clothing store in the city. To leave Aberdeen would be wrenchingly difficult for her.

So they compromised. They kept their home in Aberdeen but also settled in St. Andrews, where Shelagh, like Libby, used a flair for decorating to create a beautiful and comfortable third-floor nest for the two of them as well as a separate apartment below which during roughly half the weeks of the year served as a bed-and-breakfast for FOGs—friends of Gordon—from around the golf world. The saintly Shelagh suffered this parade of affable but monomaniacal males with remarkable patience and good humor. I soon came to see that, as in my case, the very best thing about Gordon was his wife.

Once fully installed in town, Gordon wasted no time throwing himself into golf, quickly establishing a record of perfect attendance, or close to it, on the St. Andrews courses. The day I met him, he'd just emerged from the pro shop that is the trunk of his car. It was 11:00 A.M. and he'd completed a round on the Old Course with another one scheduled at nearby Crail that afternoon.

When not playing golf, Gordon spent much of his time setting up future games, either with his fellow members of the St. Andrews Club and New Club or with inbound FOGs. As the omniscient Margaret Reid said, "Gordon is always on one of two things—the golf course or his mobile phone."

And when not playing or arranging golf, he caddied. Not for the money—Gordon Murray didn't have to work another day for the rest of his life (although Old Course caddies do very nicely, thank you— £35 plus a tip that can range from £10 upward—that's a minimum of $80 for a single bag, and usually a light traveler's bag at that). No, Gordon caddied for the exercise, to alleviate the boredom that had beset him after retiring too young, and above all, for the contacts.

Americans were his favorites, especially well-connected members of prestigious clubs. It was no coincidence that he'd played Pine Valley, Cypress Point, Shinnecock, East Lake, and virtually every other elite course in the States. Most of his invitations were gained while lugging someone's bag around the Old Course.

He always worked his wiles the same way, greeted his man with a hearty, disarming "Hello, Bob, I'm Gordon Murray," and chatted him up a bit to settle the 1st-tee jitters, always asking the fellow where he was from. The reply—no matter what state in the union—ignited a discussion of nearby courses Gordon had played. By the time they reached the 1st green, Gordon and his loop were no longer caddie and player, they were fast friends, and if the fellow hadn't yet returned the question and asked Gordon where he lived, Gordon tapped him on the shoulder, pointed to the white bay window with the commanding view, and said, "That's my place, up there."

Sometimes it could be a bit hard to take. One of Gordon's favorite stories is about a doubter.

"A pal of mine from the States—a bloke from Philadelphia I'd caddied for several times—got a call from a buddy of his who'd just been to St. Andrews for the first time. The guy starts talking about his trip and says, 'You won't believe the character I got as a caddie on the Old Course. He claimed he'd played every Open Championship course and about half the U.S. Open sites, had been to the Masters, was a backer for Paul Lawrie when he won at Carnoustie, and went to school with the head coach of Manchester United. He also said he'd caddied for the Queen of Malaysia and the Japanese ambassador to the Court of St. James's and was friends with everyone from Wayne Huizenga to Rod Stewart. Then, as we're heading up the 18th hole, he points to this big house at the end of the block and claims he owns it. Have you ever heard such a load of crap?' 'Yes, I have,' says the friend, 'from Gordon Murray, and it's all true.' "

Despite 200 or so rounds of golf per year, Gordon had never gotten his handicap lower than 10, and when I met him he was hovering around 14. Given his muscular build, and the fact that he'd been a fine rugby and soccer player in his youth, he had only moderate power off the tee, partly due to an unorthodox downswing in which he allowed his right foot to lift off the ground and step forward so that in his follow-through he faced the target with his hands in front of his face, resembling something between a gladiator in mid-battle and a basketball player on the free-throw line. Many of his tee shots duck-hooked until I presented him with a TaylorMade R7 driver with the adjustable headweights. Then he developed a rich variety of misses.

But Gordon's most frequent haunt was the Old Course, and on the Old Course, length—and even accuracy—is of relatively little importance, if you know how to tack around the worst bunkers and gorse. Much more important is an ability to scramble from 50 yards in, and in that area Gordon was among the best. Long before the 2004 British Open, when Todd Hamilton showed the world how to wield a rescue club from short range, Gordon was bump-and-running his ball across the humps and hillocks of St. Andrews with an uncanny feel for distance. On top of that, he was a fine putter, especially under pressure. On days when his spin-through lurch was in sync and his drives were flying straight, you didn't want to oppose him in a match.

Nor did you want to take him on in any sort of dispute. It didn't take long for me to discover that Gordon had some rather strong views, particularly with regard to the conduct and operation of the St. Andrews golf courses.

Mind you, on the parallel fairways of the Old Course certain rules of the road apply, among them the notion that when two groups of players playing on opposite 9s converge, the group playing the inward 9 has the right of way. (The only exception is at the 1st and 18th holes, where the group teeing off at number 1 takes precedence.) Usually, there is not much of an issue, except at the par-3 11th hole, which, in a quintessential Old Course quirk, actually plays *directly across* the fairway of the par-4 7th.

Well, one day Gordon's group, on the 11th tee, was held up for several moments as a group of older gentlemen toddled obliviously down the 7th as if they were the only four-ball on the course. Gordon stood there watching them for a while, then could contain himself no longer.

"Don't you know the rules?" he shouted. "You're supposed to wait for us to play our tee shots!"

"You have no right to speak to us like that," came the reply. "I happen to be a member of the R&A!"

"Well," said Gordon, "then you should bloody well know better. Now get out of the way!"

Slow play irritated Gordon almost as much as it did me. (He and I, in a two-ball with no one in front of us, could have comfortably finished 18 holes in about two hours and fifteen minutes. I suspect we verged on being discourteously fast, although in Scotland I doubt there is such a thing.) Often are the days I saw him exhort the group ahead of us to pick up the pace. "They think that because they're playing at a pace of under four hours they're doing well," he said, "but they're a hole and a half behind the group in front of them!" I couldn't have agreed more—but I always allowed him to be the one to speak.

But the most irritated I'd ever seen Gordon related to an incident that had nothing to do with pace of play. It was one of those mornings when a long line of hopefuls had formed beside the Old Course starter's box, all of them visitors who had failed to gain tee times on the daily ballot. Their only chance was to hope for cancellations and no-shows, or hope that a two-ball or three-ball game would welcome them to fill out the group. (This is the normal practice—all St. Andreans appreciate the treasure they have in the Old Course and they are more than happy to allow visiting golfers to join their groups, knowing that, in many cases, it is the one opportunity those visitors will ever have to play the course.)

Gordon and I had gotten a time that morning but one member of our group had had to drop out, so we'd taken on the fellow at the head of the queue, a charming young RAF pilot who had traveled many miles, arrived at dawn, and stood in line for over an hour to get his shot at the old lady. He was clearly delighted to step onto the tee and proved to be not only a companionable bloke but a solid 10-handicap, and we'd had a spirited, enjoyable match.

As we walked down the 11th fairway that day, Gordon noticed that the group that had teed off half an hour behind us and were now playing the 8th hole was a two-ball, a couple of University of St. Andrews students.

"Look at those two," he said. "That's bloody shameful. All those guys in line to play and those two sods go out as a two-ball. Someone should teach them a lesson in courtesy." He didn't confront them, but I could see he wanted to. It was a classic Murray moment—anger tinged with self-righteousness but fueled by a fundamental sense of what is fair.

Gordon's designer shades and Pebble Beach logo cashmeres didn't wear well among some of the working-class guys with whom he consorted, nor did the stories he loved to relate of his far-flung travels and high-profile pals. He was also a thorn in the side of the Links Trust, constantly questioning its authority and practices. But I figured if these were his worst sins, they were weaknesses that could be forgiven. Gordon was simply the local fisherman whose ship had come in, the caddie who could pull his bib from the trunk of his Mercedes. In that sense, he wasn't unlike many citizens of St. Andrews, a town that had become a retirement haven as well as a golf mecca, where a growing number of nouveaux riches had flocked to live out their lives. The lure of the links, the vitality of the university, and the freshness of the sea air had brought them—just as they had brought Gordon and brought me.

The difference with Gordon Murray was that he was not the retiring type. He was the guy who got up at 6:00 A.M. and closed out the pub at midnight, the guy who knew the name, address, phone number, and handicap of every innkeeper, shopkeeper, and greenkeeper in town. He was the neighborhood concierge, the guy who offered not only to put out your trash and take in your mail while you're away but pick you up at the airport when you returned. With a phone call or two he could secure you an able electrician, a fresh-caught salmon, or an upgrade on your next flight. Gordon's acts of kindness, he knew, would not go unreturned, but they were nonetheless acts of kindness.

When, in one of my first columns for *Links* magazine, I made reference to Gordon and his good deeds, it prompted a letter to the editor that was passed on to me.

"I have a story to share with you about your neighbor Gordon Murray," it began. "Nine months ago I made a trip to Scotland and my golf clubs missed the connecting flight from London. The morning after our arrival, I'm standing on the sidewalk by Rusacks Hotel. I'm supposed to leave for Kingsbarns in fifteen minutes and the clubs still have not arrived. Up walks this stranger.

" 'Why the long face, my man?' he says. 'It's a beautiful Scottish morning.'

" 'Yes it is,' I say, 'except for the fact that I'm supposed to play golf in half an hour and my clubs haven't arrived.'

"Immediately, the guy offers me the use of his clubs for the day. He's never seen me before, knows nothing about me, but knows what it's like to not have your sticks on a day like this. We head down to his car, he grabs his bag out of the trunk, hands it to me, and I take off for Kingsbarns where I end up shooting 79, my best round of the trip. We had a memorable visit to Scotland, but one of the fondest memories was of Gordon and his generosity."

To many people both in and outside of St. Andrews, I would become known as Gordon Murray's neighbor, and to my mind that wasn't a bad thing to be.

13

Show Me Your Papers

One morning while on a stroll with Millie I came upon a fellow dog walker, an elderly Scottish chap who'd spent most of his working life in America. As our hounds sniffed each other's hindquarters we chatted a bit.

"What do you miss about the States?" he asked.

"Mostly our two sons," I said. "We talk to them on the phone about every other day and exchange e-mails, but until we moved here we'd never been separated from them by more than a few miles, so that's been a bit tough."

"Nothing else?"

"Yeah—rare, juicy cheeseburgers. No one over here seems to have broken the code on how to make an American burger."

"Yes, I guess I'd agree," he said, though it was clear he didn't quite share my rapture.

We chatted a bit longer, then allowed our dogs to pull us our separate ways.

"Oh, yeah," I shouted over my shoulder, "there's one other thing I miss—the *New York Times*."

I'd been reading "the newspaper of record" since I was eighteen. More to the point, I'd developed a thirty-five-year addiction to the *Times* crossword puzzle, especially the big one in the Sunday magazine section. I always allotted myself one hour to complete it. Some blessed Sundays I could whip through it in under half an hour—I always saw that as a positive omen for the week ahead. Other weeks, when as my hour expired and I'd filled in fewer than half the squares, I had no choice but to accept the brutal truth—the puzzle was somehow flawed.

Sadly, the only *Times* to be had in Great Britain was Rupert Murdoch's London *Times*. Oh, I could have logged onto www .nytimes.com, and occasionally I did, but as fervently as I love the Internet, I had trouble making the leap from a paper paper to a digital paper. Besides, the clever marketing folks at the *New York Times,* no doubt sensing my desperation, had excluded the puzzle from the site's free content, offering it instead as a pay-to-play option at $35 a year. That bit of niggardliness threw me into a proud-silly period of crossword self-deprivation.

Then one Saturday morning I remembered that the weekend edition of the *Herald Tribune,* published out of Paris, carried the *Times* cross-word. Immediately, I marched the two blocks to my local newsagent. (A British newsagent is a cross between our American newsstand and general store, offering a limited but eclectic range of goods, everything from disposable diapers to Walkers shortbread to porn magazines.)

"Do you carry the *Herald Tribune*?" I panted.

"Aye, we do sir," said the wizened little fellow behind the counter. "Would you like today's paper or yesterday's?"

"Er, today's," I said, mildly mystified at the question.

"Are you sure you'd like today's paper and not yesterday's?" he said.

"Yes, definitely today's," I said stiffly, nearly adding "you stupid old git."

"Aye," he said, "then I'm afraid you'll have to come back tomorrow."

I tried the three other newsagents in St. Andrews—unbelievably, on that Saturday morning the only *Tribune* in town was Friday's. And the publishers wonder why readership is decreasing.

There are over 1,300 regional and local papers across England and Scotland, most of them weeklies. In St. Andrews, the daily array included the London papers plus the *Glasgow Herald,* the *Edinburgh Scotsman,* the *Dundee Courier,* the *Scottish Express,* the *Northeast Fife Courier,* and, on Fridays, the *St. Andrews Citizen,* covering everything from town council meetings to homing pigeon tournaments.

I suspect the Brits would find our *New York Times* an extremely dull read. None of the London papers, I discovered, was as straightforwardly reportorial. Probably because they have to compete so fiercely for readers, both the broadsheets and the tabloids freely mix hyperbole and opinion with their reportage. Objectivity does not seem to be the core value it is for American journalists.

Nor, sadly, is accuracy, as I can attest from painful experience. Fifteen or so years ago, just before the British Open, a report came out of Britain that Princess Diana had played a round of golf at Royal Troon and scored a hole-in-one on the famed Postage Stamp hole. I didn't question it for a moment and immediately instructed one of my editors at *Golf Magazine* to include an item on the royal ace in the next issue. Two weeks later, well after that issue had gone to bed, the story was exposed as a hoax. Diana didn't even play golf.

In any case, with such a panoply of options, I wasn't sure which paper to make my own. The Homer Simpson in me leaned toward the tabloids, but as much as I enjoyed *The Sun*'s Page 3 girls and the *Daily Mirror*'s lurid take on life, they dumbed things down a bit too much. If I'd allowed my world to be shaped solely by the tabloids I'd be aware of only four countries—Great Britain, Ireland, the U.S., and Iraq.

I tried the London *Times* briefly after they took the daring step of changing their format from broadsheet to tabloid, but by then I'd come to enjoy the verve and nerve of British journalism, and the *Times* was just a bit too dry. Eventually, I settled on the *Daily Telegraph,* supplemented on Fridays by the *St. Andrews Citizen* and on weekends by *Scotland on Sunday.*

My chosen newspapers became an integral part of my morning routine, which began at about seven with the first of several daily "walkies" with Millie. Initially, we set ourselves an eastern loop, up Links Road, past Rusacks Hotel to Golf Place, where we hung a right past Auchterlonies golf shop, then a left around the Dunvegan Hotel and up to the newsagent. It was a perfect length of walk, about a quarter mile each way.

After Millie's exercise came mine. A year before coming to the U.K., I'd had both hips replaced (arthritis limps in my family) and the post-op rehab had put me into the habit of daily exercise. Nothing too vigorous, mind you—a half hour or so on a treadmill followed by some light work on the weight machines—but enough for me to lose a quick ten pounds and banish the backaches I'd had for a decade. It was a good habit that I didn't want to break, so in St. Andrews one of the first things I did was look for a gym.

There were three choices. The university athletic facilities were open to all and at a very reasonable fee, but they were a bit too serious for me. On the day I took a tour, the weight room was packed with Schwarzeneggerian specimens a third my age performing feats that vaguely frightened me. Neither my body nor my ego was ready for that den of testosterone.

That left me a choice of the two upscale spas at the St. Andrews Bay Hotel and the Old Course Hotel. The former was by far the more elaborate facility, with an Olympic-size pool, numerous weight training machines, and a titillating coed steam room. Word was that Prince William, a member of the university water polo team, was an active member with a preference for early-morning workouts. For a brief moment I envisioned me and Wills, spotting each other on the bench press, doing some synchronized swimming, maybe snapping towels at each other in the sauna. Just the two of us starting the day.

But the St. Andrews Bay Hotel, three miles out of town, was too far for me. The spa at the Old Course Hotel, on the other hand, was just 300 yards from my door, with a splendid set of facilities. Plus, for an extra £100 a year, any spa member could become a member of the Duke's Course, Peter Thomson's fine parkland layout set on a hill overlooking the town. So Libby and I both joined the spa and golf club. The Prince's loss was the Duke's gain.

On most days I completely undid the good of my workout by driving into town for a stop at Fisher & Donaldson, St. Andrews's justly famous bakery, where I treated myself to a mouthwatering confection called a yum-yum. If a Krispy Kreme glazed donut were to mate with a French croissant, the yum-yum is the child they'd produce—pure deep-fried carbohydrate and sugar—the rough caloric equivalent of forty minutes on a treadmill. (So enraptured was I with the yum-yum that I approached the co-owner of Fisher & Donaldson, Sandy Milne, and asked for the recipe. Alas, one of the prerequisites was a 100-gallon deep-fat fryer, an apparatus our kitchen could not quite accommodate.)

Once home, I completed my morning ritual by reading the newspaper while consuming my yum-yum with a large cup of coffee and watching the *NBC Nightly News,* dutifully recorded by Sky+ at 4:00 A.M. At around 8:30, I'd look at Millie and say "Upstairs?" That was our signal that this would be a day of writing, and it was time to get to work.

14

Window Office

Given the symmetrical nature of our flat—two floors, with a bedroom, bathroom, and living area on each—it was inevitable that Libby and I would sort ourselves onto different levels for most of the day, she in the kitchen/family room downstairs, where, in one corner, she'd set up an easel to pursue her oil painting, and I in the upstairs lounge, where, in the bay window area, I'd staked out my office.

Office such as it was. It consisted of a wing chair, a small padded bench I used as a footrest, and a laptop that sat literally atop my lap. Next to the chair was a round end table just large enough to hold a lamp, a tin full of pens and pencils, a paperback dictionary, and a phone.

As our first winter in the flat inched toward spring, there was plenty on my plate. Due almost immediately was an update of a book I'd written nearly two decades earlier—*Golf Courses of the PGA Tour*. It had proved a steady seller, had seen a second edition in 1995, and thanks to the eternal churn in PGA Tour sites and courses, it was once again up for a rewrite.

Next on the docket, six months down the road, was *The Secret of Golf,* an anthology of instruction methods. Happily, it required relatively little writing from me—just a series of introductions to the teachers and their theories, the bulk of the book being excerpts from the masters' own texts. Finally, there loomed the text you're reading now.

So I was fully booked. In addition there was the column for *Links* magazine, consulting for Workman Publishing, and an assortment of smaller assignments. I didn't fear getting it all done, but I did fear that, while getting it all done, I wouldn't have much time to play golf. And constantly, wrenchingly, golf called to me.

The best thing about my office was the view. The bay window itself was comprised of four eight-foot-tall panes, each of them fitted with bulletproof glass to repel the relentless barrage of wayward drives from the 18th tee.

The left-hand window faced to the northwest, where, if you pressed your right cheek tight against the glass, you could see the 17th green, including the feared Road Hole Bunker, where countless players great and small have come to grief. Just to the right of the bunker was the 18th tee, and to the right of that the 1st green and the 2nd tee.

In the foreground, fifty yards off our port bow, rose the arched gray stonework of the Swilken Bridge (or Golfer's Bridge as is its rightful name), its age a matter of vigorous debate among the locals with the estimates ranging from less than three hundred years to over a thousand. All that is certain is that it has been crossed by nearly every great player in history (with the exception of Ben Hogan) and photographed by nearly every visitor of the past fifty years.

The middle two panels of our bay faced straight across the 1st and 18th fairways to the West Sands, a broad crescent of beach best known for its role as the opening scene of the movie *Chariots of Fire.* Shortly before we arrived, the West Sands had been named Scotland's finest bathing beach. Given the rocky ruggedness of the Scottish coast, such an honor may seem akin to being named Florida's finest ski slope, but the West Sands is actually an impressive stretch, extending nearly two miles to a point where the St. Andrews Bay converges with the Eden Estuary to become the North Sea. It attracts visitors 365 days a year, but it's especially busy on warm summer weekends when hundreds of locals suddenly mistake themselves for Tahitians, flocking to the shore where they expose as much of their Bremner Wafer–white skin as legally permissible, like a vast convention of plucked fowl.

A ridge of grassy dunes separates the beach from the fairways of the New and Jubilee Courses, which unfurl from the back steps of the Links Clubhouse, a large modern-Gothic structure built in 1995. In the distance, just visible across the estuary, is Leuchars, a town more easily heard than seen. During World War II, RAF Leuchars was one of Britain's major air defense bases and it remains active today as home to two dozen Tornado F3 supersonic fighter jets and the people who fly and service them. Few rounds at St. Andrews are completed without at least one ear-splitting takeoff or landing, and each September, to commemorate the Battle of Britain, aircraft from around the world come to Leuchars to stage Scotland's biggest air show, an extravaganza that causes fifty thousand people to gape mindlessly skyward for several hours.

In the distance, ten miles beyond Leuchars, rose the Sidlaws, a range of hills cradling Dundee, Scotland's fourth largest city, and farther east were the farmsteads and towns along the Firth of Tay— Broughty Ferry, Monifieth, Barry, and directly across from St. Andrews, Carnoustie (twelve miles as the crow flies but forty minutes by car).

My favorite view, however, was through our right-hand window pane, at the 1st tee and 18th green of the Old Course, with the clubhouse of the Royal & Ancient Golf Club between them and the gray-blueness of the North Sea beyond. In the world of golf, there may be more beautiful views, but there is none more inspiring.

And so it was that, on the five days of the week that I didn't play golf, I sat in the wing chair that pointed straight at that pane. For eight or so hours a day, when my eyes weren't fixed on the screen of my laptop they were drawn inexorably to the comings and goings outside—golfers of every shape, size, and skill. But beyond them unfurled a parade of joggers, dog walkers, beachgoers, and kite flyers, of backpackers and ball kickers, windsurfers and parasailors, fence painters and window washers, fishermen and horsemen, codgers in tweed, toddlers in seersucker, and hand-holding couples of every age.

It was hard not to daydream, hard not to think about those people—who they were, what had brought them to St. Andrews, and where they'd be headed when they left. Sometimes I dared ask the same questions of myself: why exactly had Libby and I come here and where would we be headed when our sojourn was over? It was a bit like a round of golf—we'd teed off with high hopes, had hit a couple of bumps along the way, now seemed to be hitting a rhythm, a stride—but where were we going? In what directions would the bounding fairways toss us, and how might the fickle winds force us to adjust our strategy, alter our course? I had many more questions than answers.

15

The Club

Early one morning I wandered over to the Old Course starter's hut, hoping there might be a three-ball in need of a fourth. Luck favored me and I was able to join a trio of young American guys on their first trip to St. Andrews. They were from the New York area, it turned out we had a couple of friends in common, and the four hours I spent swatting and chatting with them were about as good as golf blind dates get.

Feeling expansive as we walked up the stone steps behind the 18th green, I said, "Would you guys like to come into the R&A for a drink?"

"The R&A? Wow, yeah," said one of them, "but are we dressed okay?"

"Sure, no problem, just follow me," I said over my shoulder, stiff-arming the brass push plate on the clubhouse door.

It didn't budge. I pushed it again and still it didn't move.

"Must be stuck—I'll have to let the club manager know about that," I said, leading my guests to a second door on the other side of the portico. "Just leave your clubs here in the vestibule."

We installed ourselves in the Trophy Room, a casual bar just off the main lobby, where I showed the lads some of the club's artifacts and began to hold forth on the history of golf. I'd reached the eighteenth century and was about to launch into a riveting dissertation on the global influence of the gutta-percha ball when I realized that no one had come in to take our drink orders. We were the only ones in the room—the only ones in the club as far as I could tell—yet we'd been utterly ignored.

"Bob!" I bellowed imperiously at the club porter standing at his desk in the lobby, barely twenty feet away, "can you get someone to come in here and take our drink orders, please?"

"Yes, of course, sir," he said, "but you do know you can do it easily yourself."

"I don't think so," I said testily. "We've been sitting here rather visibly for fifteen minutes and not a soul has appeared. I don't seem to have much clout."

"Did you ring the buzzer, sir?" he said.

"Huh?"

"The buzzer. On the wall next to you, sir. It tells the kitchen staff you're here. Just press it, and Pam will be with you in a trice."

"Oh . . . uh . . . yes, of course. I must have forgotten," I said, looking to my left at a little black wall switch, boldly imprinted with the word "BAR." There were, in fact, several such switches, conveniently located at various points around the room—and around every other room on the ground floor of the club.

I'd been a member of the Royal & Ancient Golf Club for sixteen years, but before moving to St. Andrews I'd entered the clubhouse only a handful of times and since arriving I'd visited only a handful more. The truth was, the place sort of scared me. Maybe it was the club logo, an image of St. Andrew holding the cross on which he was to be crucified. Presumably the founding members had a few cheerier options—why did they have to go with the image of a tormented saint?

In any case, I knew only one or two local members, and I hadn't had the courage to walk into the clubhouse alone. The three young

Yanks, by accompanying me that day, had done as much for me as I'd done for them.

The Royal & Ancient, or R&A as it is known to golf cognoscenti, is more than a club, it's a monument, an institution dating back to 1754 when twenty-two noblemen and gentlemen, "being admired of the ancient and healthful exercise of the golf, and at the same time having the interest and prosperity of the ancient city of St. Andrews at heart, being the alma mater of the golf, did contribute a silver club having a St. Andrew engraved on the head thereof to be played for on the links of St. Andrews upon the fourteenth day of May said year, and yearly in time coming."

Note the dual motive: 1) to have some organized fun and 2) to promote St. Andrews. At that time, the town was in a sad state, having plummeted over the course of two centuries from the height of prestige and prosperity. To appreciate the level of despair, consider this: The town had fewer than 2,500 residents, but there were over forty pubs.

It had all started a millennium or so earlier, with a bunch of bones. St. Andrew, it seems, was one of the movers and shakers of early Christianity. Along with his older brother Simon Peter (St. Peter), he was an apostle of Jesus Christ and was thought to be responsible for spreading Christianity throughout Asia Minor and Greece.

Tradition holds that St. Andrew was crucified by the Romans in southern Greece (the diagonal orientation of his cross is said to be the basis for the design of the Scottish flag). His bones were entombed and around three hundred years later were moved by Emperor Constantine to the capital city of Constantinople (now Istanbul). Legend suggests that somewhere in the sixth century a monk named St. Rule was warned in a dream that St. Andrew's remains were about to be moved, and was directed by an angel to take as many of the bones as he could to "the ends of the earth" for safekeeping.

St. Rule was able to make off with a tooth, an arm bone, a kneecap, and some fingers, and these he dutifully transported to the extremity of the then known world—a Pictish settlement on a spit of land jutting into the North Sea—a town that would come to be known as St. Andrews. The relics were enshrined in a specially constructed chapel, which was replaced in 1318 by a magnificent cathedral. The largest building for hundreds of miles, it took 159 years to build and positioned St. Andrews as the ecclesiastical center of Scotland. (After all, no other city within perhaps a thousand miles could boast the relics of a genuine apostle.) As a result, the town rocketed to the top of every medieval Catholic's must-see list. Each year tens of thousands of pilgrims traveled hundreds of miles, crossed mountains and rivers, braved wars, bandits, and brutal weather, just to reach St. Andrews—just as golfers do today.

Religion in those days being closely tied to learning, the cathedral was followed in short order by the University of St. Andrews (1412). The first in Scotland, it attracted and produced a parade of eminent scholars, scientists, and poets. By the sixteenth century, St. Andrews was arguably the hottest town in the kingdom. Then calamity struck in the form of the Protestant Reformation. Decrying the "idolatry of Catholicism," John Knox and company seized control of the town, murdered various and sundry prelates, pulverized every religious icon in sight, and reduced the great cathedral to a pile of stones, all in the name of reform. To appreciate what this did to the commerce of St. Andrews in 1550, imagine what would happen today if a battalion of backhoe operators were to plow through the Old Course and convert it into a potato farm.

With no bones to genuflect at, the pilgrims canceled their treks and the town lost its stream of tourism. A proud harbor that once held three hundred ships dwindled to a few small boats, and the university lost both students and funding, nearly pulling up stakes and relocating to Perth.

Into this breach, and not a moment too soon, stepped the twenty-two noblemen and gentlemen. They called themselves the Society of St. Andrews Golfers, but in effect they were the first St. Andrews Chamber of Commerce. Almost from the day they formed their club, the fortunes of the town began to turn.

Theirs was not the first golf club in Scotland. The Royal Burgess Golf Society (out of Edinburgh) had started in 1735 and the Honourable Company of Edinburgh Golfers had formed in 1744, complete with thirteen rules of play. But the St. Andreans had their act together and they were quick to make their presence felt. In 1764, when they decided that some of the holes on their 22-hole course were too short (perhaps the first concession to advanced equipment technology), they reconfigured to 18 holes. That 18 became the standard for the rest of the world.

Over the next few decades, the society would attract the best and brightest golfers and gentlemen, frame a new set of rules, and generally position itself as the last word on all questions related to the game. In 1834, England's King William IV became the patron of the society and declared it the Royal & Ancient Golf Club—an imposing name for a club if ever there was one—and twenty years later they had an imposing clubhouse to go with it. The enduring preeminence of St. Andrews was all but assured.

Today the R&A runs eleven championships and international matches, including the British Open (or Open Championship as it's known in the U.K. and will hereafter be referred to in this book). It is also the final authority on all matters relating to the Rules of Golf, amateur status, and equipment standards, except in the U.S. and Mexico, where the USGA prevails.

Of course, throughout this period of expanded influence there was always a more private side of the R&A, a club that had grown from those twenty-two noblemen and gentlemen of Fife to nearly 2,400 men from around the world (roughly 350 of them Americans), a club that was about to celebrate its 250th anniversary.

And that was all just a bit intimidating. The first time I walked up to the clubhouse as a "local" I was less than comforted by the brass plaque beside the front door. "Members of the Royal & Ancient Golf Club Only" it read, a phrase both forbidding and ungrammatical. Had I been standing over the engraver I would have insisted on a two-line sign: "Royal & Ancient Golf Club" on line one and "Members Only" on line two. It may seem a bit nitpicky, but "Members of the Royal & Ancient Golf Club Only" has an imperious "Thou shalt have no other clubs before me" implication, suggesting that an R&A member must renounce all other memberships before entering the door.

My first few visits had left me more than a bit cowed, questioning whether I would ever feel comfortable in a blazer and club tie, sitting in a leather chair in the Big Room, glass of port in hand and London *Times* in lap, whether I could ever be happy hobnobbing in a place where a third of the members looked like Noël Coward and the other two thirds like Winston Churchill. I was forever walking on eggshells, wondering whether I'd used the fish knife to cut my braised lamb, poured the table water into my claret glass, said something too loud, too tacky, too American. There were so many behavioral subtleties I needed to master, and I wasn't sure I wanted to.

If my three American friends had noticed my ineptitude they were far too polite to say anything, and they thanked me profusely as we headed out the door. Then panic struck—all four sets of golf clubs had vanished from the vestibule. (There had long been a problem in Scotland with the theft of clubs—especially the fancy new American models, which at British prices are extremely expensive.) I was mortified and angry.

"Uh, Bob . . ." I said. "I have some bad news. Our golf clubs are not here."

"Yes, sir," he said. "They're all downstairs in the Bag Room. You see, they shouldn't be left in the vestibule—not safe, you know, sir."

"Yes, yes, of course," I said lamely. "I'd forgotten that's where we put the clubs." Then hoping to salvage some face, I said, "By the way, I wanted to be sure you knew about the door on the golf course side of the entry. I tried it two or three times and it wouldn't budge."

"Right you are, sir," he said. "It's shut tight. Has been since 1983."

16

Tescoid Anthropology

he daily life and times of the Scots rarely make for international headline news. Imagine our pride and excitement, therefore, the day CBS-TV and the Associated Press seized on a story out of Glasgow. The subject was something that had theretofore been dismissed as an urban legend, a preposterous tale promulgated for decades. Suddenly, to worldwide astonishment, the legend had been proved true!

The Loch Ness Monster? No, the deep-fried Mars bar.

It seems that, beyond the Scottish borders, no one had believed it possible for an entire nation to embrace and ingest a 65-gram chocolate-coated, caramel-and-nougat-filled missile, dipped in egg batter and fried to resemble a Mrs. Paul's fish stick. But they'd underestimated those plucky Scots.

The news was delivered by Dr. David Morrison, a consultant to the British National Health Service. "We can now confirm that there is no doubt," he said. "The deep-fried Mars bar is not just a myth." His announcement came after a telephone survey of nearly five hundred fish-and-chip shops across Scotland had found that nearly one in four (22 percent) offered the down-market delicacy, some of them selling more than two hundred DFMBs per day. Indeed the whole inspired concept of adding a thick jacket of saturated fat to a 400-calorie candy bar had been born in Stonehaven, Aberdeenshire, the result of a bet struck between a chip shop owner and his corpulent pal.

In the minds of many, the demythologizing of the DFMB explained why parts of Scotland had the highest incidence of heart disease, cancer, and strokes, and why Scots had the biggest waistlines, worst teeth, and lowest life expectancy in the developed world. (In Glasgow, the nation's unhealthiest city, men were not expected to make it to the age of seventy.) For me, it merely confirmed the evidence I'd gathered while walking the aisles of the local Tesco store.

I'd come to believe, in fact, that if you want to get to the heart of the Scottish national character, the place to begin was the local supermarket. My research had begun on one of those husbandly saunters, where the male blank-mindedly pushes a cart up and down the aisles while his wife fills it equally with essentials and superfluities.

The Tesco chain has nearly two thousand stores throughout the U.K., roughly equivalent in penetration to Wal-Mart in the States but even more dominant. Most of the outlets are food stores but in recent years the company has branched out into clothing, electronics, financial services, and telecommunications. Across all categories, over one in every eight pounds sterling of retail sales in Britain is spent at Tesco.

The St. Andrews store, relatively modest in size, at first seemed a clone of the smaller supermarkets in America—the same row of checkout counters at the front of the store, the same aisles of neatly stacked items, the same competing aromas—baked goods, fresh fish, delicatessen. But I would soon realize there were some major differences between this store and the ones I'd known all my life.

The Indian section, for instance. To my knowledge, no food store in the U.S. dedicates fifteen hundred square feet of shelf space to the likes of chicken tikka and lamb Bangalore. Granted, there's that whole Colonial Empire thing to consider, but nothing could have prepared me for the dizzying array of curries, kabobs, and kormas. To the British, Indian cuisine seems to be what Mexican cuisine has become in the U.S.: a semi-exotic fast food that is relatively inexpensive, highly filling, and gastrointestinally challenging.

Another theory is that the Brits embraced Indian food because they themselves have no idea how to cook. I don't buy that. As my mother used to say, "If you can read, you can cook," and goodness knows, the Brits are inveterate readers. No, if what hits the table in England and Scotland isn't quite as tasty as in France and Italy, I'd suggest it's due not to the ineptitude of the chefs but the inferiority of the ingredients.

Beginning with produce. I don't know whether it's insufficient sun, overabundant rain, or uncooperative soil, but fruits and vegetables in the U.K. are remarkably unremarkable. Most disappointing to me was my favorite, the tomato, which in Scotland resembles an orange Ping-Pong ball. Where the Scots seem to hit their stride is with beans—not fresh beans but canned beans of every variety. In one astonishing aisle I discovered black beans, green beans, red beans, butter beans, broad beans, chili beans, and cannellini beans, not to mention another canned item called mushy, which the label yummily described as marrowfat and processed peas. Laudably, given this breadth of offerings, the Scots with whom I communed displayed no overt propensity toward flatulence.

As you might expect of an island nation, the fish throughout the U.K. is excellent, and I must admit there is nothing quite as nice as fresh-caught wild Scottish salmon, whether smoked, poached, or grilled. The shellfish, however, seemed a millennium or so less evolved than the specimens I was used to. An American lobster could eat a British lobster for breakfast, and British shrimp truly are shrimps.

The worst surprise, however, was the meat. The Scots are fiercely proud of their Aberdeen Angus, and I'm sure they are noble beasts, but somewhere between hoof and boeuf something happens—or more accurately, something doesn't. The Brits don't hang their meat for very long, and hanging is what makes beef tender and flavorful. In the U.S. many butchers and steakhouses will hang meat for a month or more before serving it. But that is costly—in time, storage space, refrigeration, and labor—and the Scots, famously frugal, have opted to pass. I suspect that somewhere along the line, in a sort of tacit national plebiscite, they agreed that it's more sensible to pay £5 for a tough steak than £10 for a tender one.

And so at most restaurants, when one orders the vaunted roast beef and Yorkshire pudding, what arrives is something similar in taste and texture to a shirt cardboard—a thin slice of grayness, bereft of juiciness and flavor and presumably carved from a creature just minutes beyond rigor mortis. Remember the mystery meat they slapped on your plate in the cafeteria line at school?

The only place in Scotland where we'd found bona fide New York–quality beef was the Champany Inn, an elegant little chophouse in the town of Linlithgow, nine miles above the Forth Road Bridge. I'd first read about it in the 1980s, in a *New York Times* article by R. W. Apple entitled "The Best Steaks in Britain," and we'd been loyal patrons for years thereafter. But sadly, the Champany's prices had skyrocketed beyond even New York levels—£35 ($60) for an eight-ounce rib-eye, Lilliputian vegetables extra—so Libby and I had learned to stifle our steak cravings until our trips to the States.

The Scots must surely know that their beef is somewhat lacking. How else to explain their propensity to boil, pulverize, submerge, and encrust it in a variety of quaint-sounding frozen pies—cottage pie, shepherd's pie, steak pie, scotch pie. Then there is steak and kidney pie, a veritably transporting experience—when you cut into it, you feel as if you've been planted facedown in a urinal. My personal favorites, however, are the comfort foods with discomforting names: toad in the hole, bubble and squeak, bangers and mash, bridies, stovies, and faggots. I love them all, except maybe the faggots, which are meatballs made out of pig's liver.

Of course, the meat dish most closely associated with Scotland is haggis. Let's be clear about what it is—a sheep's stomach filled with the minced heart, liver, and lungs of the sheep (appropriately called offal), mixed with oatmeal, onions, and spices. The supposition is that haggis was originated by a shepherd in the highlands, a hardworking bloke with limited grazing lands and perhaps only one or two spring lambs with which to get through the winter. A hefty haggis or two stretched the meat another week or so.

Times have changed, of course, and even in Scotland there are more appetizing items at the butcher's counter—cow's tongues and oxtails, for instance—but haggis remains not only a tourist attraction but, astoundingly, a mainstay in the menu of many Scottish families. I had some trouble comprehending that until I realized that more than two hundred years ago haggis became the beneficiary of the ultimate press agent, the poet whose writings and philosophy shaped so much of the nation's culture, Robert Burns. In 1786 the beloved Rabbie wrote a poem called "Address to a Haggis," hailing it as "great chieftain o' the puddin' race," and thereby secured its place alongside kilts, bagpipes, whisky, tartan, and Sean Connery as an endearing, enduring symbol of Scotland.

Each year, on the occasion of the bard's birthday (January 25), Burns Suppers are held throughout Scotland (and, increasingly, other parts of the world). These evenings begin when a bagpiper enters the hall in full squeal. Behind him walks the chairman of the dinner, bearing a silver platter that holds the haggis. Once everyone is seated, the "Address to a Haggis" is delivered, in whatever unintelligible Scots dialect was spoken back then. At the appropriate point in the recitation, the orator pierces the haggis with a knife, and thereafter everyone dines. The remainder of the evening is devoted to more poems, speeches, songs, and toasts, and it all ends with everyone standing up (if they're still able), holding hands, and singing another of Burns's greatest hits, "Auld Lang Syne."

What Robert Burns did for haggis is inestimable. Indeed, I've always believed a similar sort of boost could have—should have—elevated the American hamburger. Granted, the burger is already an icon, as sure a symbol of our national cuisine and culture as exists, but consider what might have been. After all, cooked and seasoned properly, the hamburger is every bit as savory as a steak *and you can eat it with your hands*—you don't have to hack it away from bone and fat with a knife and fork or chew through sinew and gristle. Hamburger is the caviar of meat. Believe me, if Longfellow or Whitman had jumped on the hamburger bandwagon a century and a half ago, you would never have heard of T-bones, filets, or porterhouses, and you could tack a zero onto the price of your Big Mac.

In any case, the Scots aren't much for meat, but they do know their candy. The whole Mars bar thing was merely a maniacal extension of what seems to be a national sugar fixation. What other country could come up with "tablet," a fudgelike confection made of nothing but sugar, milk, and butter and served in tiny squares because any portion larger than a domino would send most humans into diabetic shock.

An entire aisle at Tesco is reserved for candies and cakes of every description, from the Mars and Snickers bars (which seem to emerge mid-round from every Scot's golf bag) to an unending assortment of dots, thins, fingers, rounds, shortbreads, tim tams, and tooties. There are also a dozen different varieties of something called a digestive, a semisweet biscuit made from wholemeal flour. It sounds vaguely healthful, but the truth is it's as decadent as an Oreo, just less tasty.

The largest section of the store is reserved for what they call sweets (what we call desserts), most of them of the rich and gooey variety, with sticky toffee pudding and the lewdly suggestive spotted dick at the top of the list. No wonder that, for generations, a popular twenty-first-birthday present from upper-middle-income Scots parents to their children was a complete set of dentures.

Suffice it to say, Scottish food stores do not allocate the same space to diet foods and appetite suppressants that American stores do, nor is there the large pharmaceutical section we have. Instead, an enormous area—verging on a quarter of the store—is devoted to liquor. Maybe it's because of the rainy climate, maybe it's the millennium or so of disrespect from their English neighbors, or maybe it's just the fact that they've been making their own excellent hooch for centuries. Whatever the reason, Scots love their booze.

Prior to leaving the U.S. I was a moderate drinker—one scotch on the rocks, then a glass or two of wine with dinner. In less than six months as a St. Andrean I'd learned how to throw down four drinks before golf and another four after. At one overly lengthy Burns supper, astonishingly, I polished off a liter of Famous Grouse. It was simply a matter of keeping up.

Ironically in this whisky capital of the world, relatively few people drink single malt scotch. The R&A members—many of them Englishmen—tend to go for gin and tonics. The first time I asked for a Macallan twelve-year-old, the club steward gave me an odd look. Not only does Macallan not come in a twelve-year-old vintage in the U.K. (it's ten-year instead), but the club doesn't stock anything except its own two blends (R&A #1 and R&A #2, each affixed with a plain white label that makes it look as if it was brewed in a backwoods Kentucky still) plus literally a single malt, also the R&A's own brand.

Otherwise, the adult beverage of choice is beer. Tennants, Carlsberg, and Stella Artois lead the way, along with two cream ales—Belhaven Best and 80 Shilling. The Tesco stacks reflect these preferences but feature a wide assortment of other spirits as well, including most of the brands we're familiar with in the States plus an impressive selection of wines. Happily, wine is the one item that tends to be less expensive in Scotland than at home. Even the most modest French and Italian wines cannot be found in the U.S. for less than $10 or $15 a bottle, but there are dozens of wines for half that price in the stores in Scotland.

In addition, there are a few strange foreign potables, both alcoholic and non. Irn Bru and Lucozade were two soft drinks I'd never encountered on American soil, and when I tried them, I felt retroactively blessed. Reflective of the British craving for all things saccharine, they tasted as if they'd been concocted from one part water and four parts Aunt Jemima maple syrup.

More interesting—and far more posh—is Pimms No. 1, a 150-year-old brew first developed to aid in digestion and now a favorite among the English toffs. It's gin-based, roughly the color of cherry cough syrup until mixed per recommendation with what the Brits call lemonade (and we know as Sprite), at which time it turns a rusty orange and becomes a refreshing summer cooler.

For winter, there's something called Crabbie's Green Ginger Wine, which, when mixed with a dram of whisky, a smattering of cloves, and a teaspoon of sugar and stirred with a few ounces of hot water, becomes a Whisky Mac, an elixir to warm the bones and dull the memory after a cold, cruel day on the links.

The Irish have a reputation for drinking just as much as the Scots, but they're also apt to be by turns maudlin weepers, joyous crooners, rambunctious carousers, and belligerent brutes. The Scots are none of those. They just sip their drinks, chat and chortle, occasionally shake their heads, and order another drink. There's a patience and gentleness to the Scots—a sort of resigned forbearance with life's lunacy—and that, too, is evident at the local Tesco, where people never block the aisles with their carts, always say "sorry" as they squeeze past, and happily wait their turn in the checkout queue. Voices are never raised, clerks are never argued with, and everyone dutifully bags his or her own groceries. It's the way our American markets should be—except for the meat and tomatoes.

17

Wooing the Old Lady

Our first six months in the Auld Grey Toon, while bereft of major calamities, had brought a few moments of utter bewilderment. In the window of one of the barbershops a large sign said: "A Free Whisky with Every Haircut." Nice touch, I thought, and had settled into the chair, wee dram in hand, when the barber, a teenaged lass whose deep purple mascara accessorized nicely with her pink hair, appraised me briefly but disconcertingly and asked: "Would you like me to do a number two on you?" Only after I bolted down the whisky and began to projectile-perspire did she offer clarification—Scottish barbers coif by numbers.

We would encounter other imponderables—from gazumping to Guy Fawkes Day to the looming crisis from methane-laden cow farts. Some things in Scotland simply were beyond explanation. In one area, however, I was beginning to gain some understanding. Round by round, I was unraveling the mysteries of the Old Course, starting to feel that the old lady and I had a bit of chemistry.

I tended to hit the ball low, particularly off the tee, and that was helpful in the wind that is nearly constant on the east coast of Scotland. Thanks to modern equipment, I'd lost relatively little distance over the years (or so I'd convinced myself), so from the back tees of 6,609 yards, few of the deep, steep-faced fairway bunkers came into play. On top of that, my predominant shot pattern with the driver was right to left, and that worked just fine on the Old Course, where, except at the 9th and 10th holes, you can go left all day and get away with it, rarely finding anything worse than some light rough. In the words of the veteran caddies, "Left is right, right is shite."

Then there were my 18 best friends, the enormous Old Course greens—14 of which are doubles, with one surface serving two holes. They average 24,000 square feet in area, roughly four times the size of a standard green. The largest is the 5th/13th at 37,900 square feet—incredibly, the first 10 greens at Pebble Beach could fit on that surface.

These huge targets suited my riotously erratic iron game. At any other course on the globe, I averaged about 6 greens in regulation per round while finding every sort of greenside trouble. On the Old, I routinely hit twice that many, and once in a while hit all 18.

Of course, when you miss a green on the Old Course—and often, even when you hit it—you can be left with a rather lengthy assignment in pasture pool. Happily, I enjoy attempting all those pitches, punches, chips, and putts across the humongous humps and hummocks, enjoy what golf architect Alister Mackenzie called the "pleasurable excitement" of links golf. Although I'd quickly lost the American-style short game I'd arrived with (and lived in utter fear of having to play a Mickelson-style cut shot), the truth was that when within 50 yards of the hole, I rarely needed to loft the ball more than a foot or so off the ground. Meanwhile, I'd become reasonably adept in one area—the ability to 2-putt from 90 feet (a skill that is absolutely useless on the other 25,000 or so courses around the world).

But shotmaking was only a small part of my education on the Old Course. Shot *planning*—learning where to golf my ball around the ancient links—had become a consuming joy. I've always believed that, on the very best golf courses, you don't play them, you allow them to play you—to coax, coddle, tempt, tease, and teach you. The best courses can make you a better player, if you let them.

The Old Course has evolved over six centuries with relatively little thought and manipulation by man, at least compared to the intensive plotting and planning that go into today's layouts. And yet it may be the ultimate thinking man's golf course. Every shot makes you stop in your tracks and consider what confronts you.

Bobby Jones, perhaps the most cerebral of the game's great players, had a negative first experience with the course, tearing up his scorecard on the 11th hole of the third round of the 1921 Open Championship. Still a teenager at the time, he'd become frustrated by his inability to cope with the links and wind. But as he matured, and returned repeatedly to the course, his attitude changed.

"The more I studied the Old Course, the more I loved it," he said, "and the more I loved it, the more I studied it so that I came to feel that is for me the most favorable meeting ground for an important contest." When in retirement he built his own course, the Augusta National, which annually hosts the Masters, Jones, along with Alister Mackenzie, tried to incorporate the strategic genius of the Old Course. When the Augusta National course was completed he said, "There is not a hole out there that can't be birdied, if you simply think, and not a hole that won't be bogeyed if you stop thinking."

All that thinking had become the fun for me. One of the first things I realized was that in order to properly subdue the old lady I would need a slightly different set of weapons. My TaylorMade 5-wood, which in the U.S. had helped me play the high-flying, soft-landing shots that American courses call for, now was all but superfluous, and I replaced it in my bag with a long unused Ping 2-iron.

My 32-inch Odyssey Rossie II putter, with an insert that allowed for soft impact on the speedy greens of the U.S. Northeast, was not only unhelpful, it was hurting my game. Only once in every five or six years, when the Open Championship comes to town, do the Old Course greens get remotely fast. The rest of the time they range somewhere between 8 and 10 on the Stimpmeter. When you're hitting a steamship-length putt on a green of that speed, what you need is not a soft hit but a sledgehammer, so I called up one of my oldest reserves, the 1968-vintage Wilson Billy Casper mallet head that had carried me to a position on the Pearl River High School golf team.

Finally, I changed golf balls. This move, however, was one of economics rather than strategy. Bear in mind, from 1974 to 2002 I'd worked in the golf business, most of that time as a magazine editor. Over that span, I'd been fortunate to receive lots of free equipment for testing and review. I hadn't bought a golf ball since Nixon was president. Now, suddenly, I not only was off the dole but compelled to pay U.K. prices. In St. Andrews, the cost of a dozen Titleist Pro V1s was £36—about $65. That was utterly unacceptable to my long-standing sense of self-entitlement.

Happily, there was a solution. On average, at least one golf ball per week found its way into our back stoop area, thanks to the general nervousness and ineptitude of people driving from the 1st and 18th tees. Just as happily, since many of those people were playing the Old Course as a once-in-a-lifetime experience, they'd armed themselves with the best golf balls. Thus, while the thwack, doink, or ping of a ball against our residence left Libby annoyed and sent Millie into a barking rage, it always put a smile on my face.

Of course, it also presented me with a moral dilemma—whether or not to return the ball to the person who had launched it. A nice guy would dig it out of his petunias and toss it onto the fairway. An unmitigated jackass would scoop it up and deposit it immediately into the pocket of his golf bag.

I, being neither of those chaps, adopted a middle ground. When I realized we'd had incoming, I held my ground. If the assailant had the chutzpah to appear at our gate, snoop around the stoop, and find his ball, I figured he deserved to get it back. If no one showed up, then after the group had proceeded a safe distance, I went out to investigate. At that point, any pellets within the confines of our premises were mine to keep. I'm not particularly proud of this modus operandi, but hey, it kept me in ammunition. I figured, as long as I was able to lose golf balls at a slightly slower rate than my garden yielded them, I was golden.

Ball conservation was, of course, another reason to develop a game plan for the Old Course. In the broadest terms, it was a matter of learning to avoid the worst trouble—if I could do that, I knew I could score because, in contrast to just about every other course in the international top 100, the Old Course has several birdie holes. Thus, in my goal of shooting par or better, the key seemed to be to avoid making double-bogeys and worse.

A succession of painful iron shots into the Swilken Burn had taught me always to overclub at number 1—if the wind and yardage said I needed an 8-iron I began taking a 7-iron. A ball in the fronting creek meant the best score I was likely to make was a 5, while from the light rough at the back of the green, the *worst* I was likely to make was a 5.

For weeks I'd thought a tailwind made the front 9 vulnerable, but I'd come to realize that it also complicated the "keep it left off the tee strategy" at the 2nd, 3rd, and 4th holes, where the three Cs—the Cheape's, Cartgate, and Cottage Bunkers, respectively—awaited my running draw. When my game was in good form, I tried to play these three holes with a gentle fade.

By contrast, at the par-4 7th hole I decided on an aggressive game plan. Downwind, the enormous Shell Bunker was within reach of my driver, but I accepted that, knowing the ball would never get near the high front wall and that a softly thudding sand shot was as good a way as any to attack the green that falls vertiginously from front to back and left to right.

I'd developed a bad attitude toward the Loop, the four holes from 8 through 11 that moved in a circle, 8 and 9 heading briefly back into town, 10 and 11 looping back out toward the Eden Estuary, the farthest point from the 1st tee.

What misguided shepherd had come up with that idea? I mean, this could have been a perfectly good 14-hole golf course—7 holes straight out, 7 returning straight back—and every course following it would have been 14 holes as well. A round of golf would have taken closer to three hours than four (or five), 28-hole double rounds would have been a breeze. What's more, in the case of the Old Course the halfway point would become the crest of a ridge overlooking the Eden Estuary, a spot that golf writer Jim Finegan has called "in the world of golf, the one place to be above all others." But no, some dizzy shepherd had decided to make a circle before heading home—a loop that began with a nondescript par-3 and two all-but-featureless, drivable par-4s.

Of course, had there been no loop, we would miss out on the single most exciting moment on the course (except perhaps for the drive at 17), the tee shot at the par-3 11th, a distance of 172 yards, where depending on the wind conditions I'd hit everything from a soft 9-iron to a full driver. It was a tough hole for me to come to terms with. Every cell in my adolescent brain told me to go for the pin, usually positioned behind the cavernous Strath Bunker, which eats into the right front of the green. For anyone whose ball finishes against the front wall of that bunker, saving par is less an achievement than an accident. The wiser shot is to the left, although on that side the 10-foot-deep Hill Bunker (where Bobby Jones came a cropper in 1921) lies in wait. Distance control is also vital—too short, even by an inch, and the ball rolls 30 feet back down the fairway, leaving a highly challenging pitch or putt; too long and it may topple down a steep bank, or even worse, sail over everything into the Eden Estuary. I never did figure a strategy for number 11, except to somehow get the ball on the green in fewer than three strokes.

Thirty years ago, Jack Nicklaus called number 12 his favorite hole on the Old Course. Given the distance players now hit the ball, I suspect he'd revise that view. The hole is only 316 yards, and from the tee it looks unassuming enough, but what the player does not see is half a dozen deep bunkers scattered at various distances across the middle of the fairway. In Nicklaus's heyday this meant the tee shot—with a fairway wood or long iron—had to be carefully directed to a safe sector of the minefield. Today, even from an extended tee, most of the longer hitters just take aim at the green and let it rip. From the regular tees, I did the same. Downwind, that put the green in reach, and into all but the worst headwinds, a driver enabled me to clear everything but a final bunker just short of the green. One day I was rewarded with a drive that ran up the slope to the back of the two-tiered green, stopping less than 4 feet short of the hole. My eagle putt never reached the cup.

At the longest hole on the course, number 14, a stone wall running down the right side induced an out-of-bounds phobia in me, so on most days I tacked hard to the left, down the paralleling 5th hole, which also allowed an easier entry to the green. There were many secrets to learn about the approach to this hole, but my sense was that they would be slow in making themselves known to me. Until then, every time I was able to escape with a 5, I was quite happy.

With the wall back in view and mind at the 16th, I again adopted the coward's line, actually hitting into the left rough rather than flirt with either OB or the Principal's Nose and Deacon Sime Bunkers in the left center of the fairway. I also liked the left-side approach to the humpy green, though an informal survey of playing partners suggested I was in the minority on that one.

Number 17 is one of the most difficult holes in the world, a 461-yard par-4 that doglegs sharply around the east face of the Old Course Hotel en route to a narrow green perched between the famed Road Bunker and the road itself. It began its life as a par-5 and still plays that way. I'd decided my strategy was to be aggressive from the tee, cautious into the green. The drive had to be played over a series of dark green cottages—reproductions of the sheds that had been part of the railroad that once ran into town. On the side of one of the sheds the enterprising hotelier had painted the words "The Old Course Hotel" in white two-foot-high lettering.

Initially, I'd chosen a line over the "The" only to find that when I hit the ball squarely in that direction I ended up in the left rough—some of the thickest on the course. Hitting over "Old" put me farther down the rightward dogleg but still in the rough. Ultimately, I settled on the space between "Course" and "Hotel," "Course" into a breeze, "Hotel" or even a bit right of it when downwind.

For the second shot, I decided never to go for the flag, unless it happened to be on the small front apron of the green (which it almost never was). Instead I took one to two clubs less than the distance called for, and tried to punch a low running shot that, if I hit it perfectly or got a lucky bounce, might slide up the slope to the top tier of the green, but in most cases would leave me a putt up that slope. "Never hit a ball into the road" became my mantra on 17 just as "stay out of the burn" was the mandate on number 1. Occasionally, the flag would be positioned at the extreme left of the green, near the 18th tee. On such days, at the peril of those playing in front of us, I aimed straight for that tee in an attempt to take the bunker, road, and front slope of the green out of play. Sometimes it even worked—usually I chickened out somewhere in the middle of the downswing, pushed the shot into the bunker, and made 6. There are myriad ways to make a 6 at 17.

The final hole, a bunkerless 354 yards, didn't require much in the way of strategy, except to keep the tee shot well left—partly so I wouldn't hit either my car or my house. Yet strangely, I went several months before birdieing this relatively simple par-4. I think it was a matter of nerves. You see, the 18th green at the Old Course is something of a monument, and at any given moment there are a dozen or so tourists, townspeople, and assorted loiterers leaning against the fence to the right and back of the hole. If you hit a good shot, they applaud you, if you hit a bad one, the silence—or occasional snicker—can be mortifying. Just as it had taken me months to settle myself on the 1st tee shot I'd had trouble summoning a smooth stroke on the 18th green.

One Saturday in late March was particularly frustrating. Gordon Murray and I had faced off against a couple of guys who were about the same age and handicap as I. We'd all played well that day but Gordon and I had ham-and-egged a bit better, and when my putt found the hole for birdie at 16, the match was over.

It was then that I realized I was 1 over par with two to go—with a par at 17 and a birdie at 18 I'd have the 72 I'd been questing after. Normally, such a realization is enough to cause me to top my next shot, but I managed a good drive at the Road Hole and then a career 6-iron settled 20 feet from the hole, setting up an easy par. At 18, my approach with an 8-iron was even better, stopping 3 feet from glory.

It was a lovely Saturday morning, and the gallery was larger than usual, perhaps twenty people peering at us from all angles. As my partners played their approach putts and holed out, I let my mind drift to a thousand unproductive places, occasionally making eye contact with one of the spectators. By the time I stood over my birdie putt it was no longer a question of whether I was going to miss it, merely how.

The putt could not have been longer than the width of a door jamb—and my attempt sent the ball precisely half the width of a door jamb. It was at that moment that I heard the worst sound in golf, when the twenty onlookers simultaneously gasped in horror.

Still, the 73 tied my record of nineteen years earlier and left me with the confidence that someday in the not too distant future I would be making my score of par or better—albeit with a tap-in from 2 inches.

18

A Special Experience

Two hundred yards or so behind the 18th green of the Old Course, on a broad street called the Scores, sits a sturdy stone townhouse with a shiny silver plaque at its entrance. Inscribed on the plaque are the words "The Old Course Experience."

Could this possibly be what it suggests, I wondered on the day I first strolled past it. Behind this unassuming gray facade, could this really be a Disney-type exhibit, complete with surround sound and virtual reality, the purpose of which is to show exactly what it feels like to be 150 acres of windblown, divot-riddled dirt?

Brimming with ignorance, I pressed the doorbell. Surely it would trip off something special—perhaps a choir of falsetto-voiced, computer-animated greenkeepers trolling a chorus of "It's a Sod, Sod World."

What a letdown. The place turned out to be nothing more than a golf tour operator. ("The Old Course Experience" refers to what they guarantee anyone who books a trip with them—a tee time on the ancient links.) There were no strobe lights, no streaming videos, no pixilated pyrotechnics, just a little eight-page brochure.

Ah, but one of those pages caught my eye, the one that trumpeted "The St. Andrews Father-Son Tournament." As it happened, my younger son and favorite golf partner, Scott, was about to head over on a spring break and the dates of his visit coincided exactly with the week of the tournament. The timing was perfect.

And so was the site. It was in St. Andrews, after all, that father-son golf made its big-time debut with Old and Young Tom Morris. Tom Morris, Sr., born in 1821, was an accomplished player, clubmaker, and course designer. In 1851, he became the greenkeeper at the Prestwick Golf Club and the same year, his son, Tom Morris, Jr., was born. In the inaugural Open Championship at Prestwick in 1860 Old Tom finished second to Willie Park, then went on to win the title the next two years and four times in all. He returned to St. Andrews in 1865 as the greenkeeper of the Old Course. By that time, Young Tom had begun to show the qualities that would make him the game's first certified prodigy. In 1868, at the age of seventeen, he won the first of three consecutive Open Championships; like his father, he would win four overall. But his story is ultimately a tragic one. In 1875 his wife of one year became ill during childbirth, and both she and the baby died. Young Tom never recovered from his grief and a few months later—on Christmas Day—he died at the age of twenty-four. Most historians cite the cause as either tuberculosis or pleurisy, but golf lore lists it as a broken heart.

Following the Morrises were the Parks (Willie Sr. and Jr., good for six Opens twixt them), not to mention the Dunns, Philps, McEwans, and Forgans, all of whom knew not only how to wield clubs but how to craft them as well. A century later, St. Andrews was still brimming with dads and lads who played together regularly (not to mention a few father-son-grandson three-balls).

Indeed, sometimes the whole town seemed to be divided into two generations. When the university was in session, nearly half the inhab-

itants were under twenty-five, while the other half—the resident population—appeared to be alarmingly over sixty. In St. Andrews you
were either in the bloom of youth or long in the tooth. And so it was
totally appropriate that once each spring several dozen additional fathers and sons arrived for the mother of all tournaments.

Nine different countries were represented in the field that Scott
and I joined and we spent our four days playing side by side with duos
from Germany, England, Scotland, and the U.S. The winners were a
pair from Taiwan.

In some cases the fathers had brought college-age sons as I had,
and there were even a few high-schoolers in the field, but most of the
teams were comprised of young-adult sons and their senior-citizen
dads, on a last fling together, perhaps inspired by Jim Dodson's
poignant memoir, *Final Rounds.*

The venues, in keeping with the spirit of things, were a mixture of
old and young courses. After a practice round on the Duke's Course
(opened in 1995), the tournament unfolded at Kingsbarns (2000), the
Devlin Course at St. Andrews Bay (2002), the New Course (1895), and
the Old Course (c. 1300), arguably the five best playgrounds in town.

Scott, a 3-handicapper, hadn't played much golf when he arrived,
but once the bell rang he turned it on with a 75 in high winds at Kingsbarns, as his father struggled to finish the 18 holes without hurting
himself. Oh, how old and mortal I felt that day, watching my son out-
drive me consistently by 50 yards. But our better-ball tally of 41 Stableford points (roughly 40 of them from Scott) staked us to a share of
third place among the fifty or so teams.

The next day the wind gusted close to 50 miles per hour, but I finally joined the squad and we partnered for a two-day total of 76
points that kept us among the leaders. I also won the long-drive prize
that day. Okay, it was the Dads Only division and most of my co-
competitors were on Metamucil, but hey, a win's a win. Besides, there
was a big headwind—that 183 yards was much longer than it looked.

I'd figured Team Peper would make its move on the New and Old
Courses, and we did—backwards—slipping to fifth place after three

rounds and finally into a tie for eighth, comfortably outside the prize list.

We were dejected, for about fifteen seconds. Over those five days, we'd had way too much fun. In addition to the golf, there had been several lunches and dinners with the other fathers and sons, rife with intergenerational ribbing, not to mention a malt whisky tasting and a kilt-fitting demonstration during which one brave father and son had volunteered as models, immediately becoming the butts of ribald cat-calls.

For the awards banquet, all one hundred of us got decked out in full Scottish regalia. Scott, who had scoffed at the prospect of donning a plaid skirt, took one look at himself in the mirror, resplendent in kilt, waistcoat, sporran, and shiny black shoes with laces crisscrossing smartly up white knee socks, and said, "Hey, Mom, don't you wanna take a picture?" She did, and it became an instant classic of the family album.

Scott left the day after the tournament, and it would be many months before he and I would play again. But the week had left me with some fond and indelible memories, one in particular. It was during the last round, on the elevated tee of the par-3 11th hole of the Old Course. As is often the case on that hole, play had backed up a bit. Scott stood on one side of the tee making mini–practice swings, taking the club back a few feet and checking his backswing plane. I stood on the other side, watching him and thinking thoughts that, for me, were uncharacteristically warm, fuzzy, and fatherly. Suddenly, as if he'd heard me, Scott stopped his fiddling and looked over at me. We held each other's gaze for a moment. Then he gave me a sheepish, knowing smile and I smiled back, neither of us saying a word.

Golf just doesn't get any better than that.

19

Pedo-phile

I n St. Andrews, motorized carts are about as abundant—and esteemed—as tennis players. Whether with a trolley, a caddie, or the bag over one's shoulder, golf is played on foot.

Oh, a couple of those insufferable "buggies" (pronounced "boo-gies") do exist, but they appear to be reserved for the royal family and double-amputees. Everyone else walks. And not just on the golf course but everywhere. Eighty-year-old ladies trundle daily to town and back, university students hustle through a circuit of classes, dining halls, dormitories, and pubs, sightseers meander through the harbor and ancient ruins, dog walkers parade down the gorse-lined paths within the Old Course (and sometimes help you find your ball), and couples and families stroll along the beach.

But most significantly, each day five hundred or so people head off the tees of the six town courses. You see, the canny Scots know a thing or two about golf that we Yanks are still learning. First, walking is the most efficient way to play. Whether you're carrying your own or accompanied by a caddie, you stride purposefully toward your ball and your ball alone (in St. Andrews it's strictly one caddie per bag—no double loops). There's none of that insane tacking and zigzagging from one cart partner's shot to another. As a result, even when a course is packed, the average round takes less than four hours (assuming it's packed with locals—during the summer, when half the play comes from visitors, figure on four and a half to five). One morning at the nearby Elie Golf Club I played in a three-ball that finished in just over three hours. However, the guys in front of us—a four-ball of septuagenarians with bags over their shoulders—left us in the dust.

Second, the price is right. We'd moved to St. Andrews, in part, because as a card-carrying resident of this town I was entitled to an entire year of unlimited play on the Old Course and five others for roughly one half of what it would cost me to play one round of golf at Pebble Beach. And there's something very pleasing about knowing that, once that annual fee is paid, there are no hidden extras (such as cart fees).

Or, for that matter, caddie fees. Although the St. Andrews caddies are justly celebrated for both their knowledge and their entertainment value, $80–$90 was to my mind an absurd amount to hand someone for toting my featherweight bag and telling me to aim at a distant steeple. Still, I was always pleased when one of my companions hired a caddie for the brogue-laced banter that invariably ensued.

All the natives carried their own, and while a few of them took trolleys (pull carts), the great majority shouldered their clubs. (On the Old Course, trolleys aren't even allowed until the afternoon.) In contrast to the Americans sporting steamer trunks crammed with haberdashery, groceries, and pharmaceuticals, the Scots travel light, most of them favoring the double-strap kickstand bag and a few opting for a glorified fly-rod case that holds half a dozen clubs, four or five balls, and nothing else. Upon being paired with one of the latter, a chap in his forties who appeared hardy enough to handle something more substantial, I inquired as to his preference for minimalism.

"Oh, it improves my game," he said.

"How so?"

"Aye, well, consider having to blast out of a pot bunker when your most lofted club is a 9-iron. Or tough out the last few holes in the pouring rain when you have no umbrella and your only glove is soaked. Or hit over a broad stand of gorse when you're down to your last ball. Either you find a way or you pay a price." And no self-respecting Scot wants to pay a price.

Thirdly, the people in the cradle of golf know that buggies are extremely dangerous. You see, in the first moment or two after hitting a particularly execrable shot, a seething Scot should not be allowed to sit in close proximity to another human. He needs some time and space to himself. Walking solitarily from shot to shot provides a cooling-off period during which he can put his troubles behind him and get a feel for the next assignment to be botched.

Truth be told, I'd always hated the exercise of walking. One of my heroes, Winston Churchill, said, "Never stand if you can sit, never sit if you can lie down." I just wish the old boy had added "never walk if you can ride." After all, during the last century or so, we have developed something called the automobile. Why would anyone plod painfully over terrain that could be covered in a fraction of the time while sitting in a climate-controlled, CD-equipped, GPS-guided, leather-lined, carcass-warming 200-horsepower marvel?

There's also the bus, subway, streetcar, cable car, monorail, minivan, motorcycle, and if you must, the bicycle. Not to mention rickshaws, dogsleds, bobsleds, palanquins, pickup trucks, motorbikes, dirtbikes, skateboards, Rollerblades, and Segways. Why, I always wondered, would anyone walk anywhere? Oh, I'd heard the arguments—it's all about the aerobic exercise, the fresh air in your lungs, the noble fun of a good stroll. Sorry, strolling did nothing for me. Strolling was for rheumy-eyed, tweed-jacketed old men, homing inexorably toward the sunset, hands clasped behind their backs.

I was no pedo-phile. Even on the golf course, I'd allowed myself, over the past few years, to be enticed by the motorized cart. After all, most private clubs and resorts in the U.S. don't allow you to tote your own, even fewer offer caddies, and when given a choice between a caddie and riding, I'd increasingly begun to plop my ample butt be-hind the wheel.

Once in Scotland, however, free of American constraints—and excesses—I'd joined the legion of walkers. The transition wasn't with-out difficulty. The first few rounds left me with aching calves and hamstrings that occasionally cramped up in the middle of the night, with the result that Libby was jolted from slumber by her husband's unique interpretation of *Riverdance.*

I also had a bit of trouble finding the right bag. My back was too weak to bear anything remotely weighty—even the kickstand models were too much for me. On the other hand, most of the Sunday bags were too tiny—and I wasn't about to shortchange myself, I wanted the full allotment of fourteen weapons.

One of the happiest days of my golf life came on the morning I discovered a Ping Moon Bag in a St. Andrews golf shop. It was essen-tially a six-inch-diameter tube with room for fourteen clubs (and not one more) plus two small pockets—just enough space for a few balls, a couple of gloves, and my tightly wadded Galvin Green rain suit (the manufacturer claims you can actually stuff the top and bottom into a pair of golf ball three-packs).

At the time, I was trying to decide between two sets of irons I'd brought over with me, one steel-shafted, the other graphite. When I realized the graphite set was palpably lighter in the bag, that decision was made. The whole kit now weighed in at just seventeen pounds (yes, I actually put it on the bathroom scale).

So it was that I converted to the ranks of blissful, if somewhat self-righteous, golf pedestrians—bag on my shoulder, wind at my back, lilt in my step as I traversed the linksland. There was indeed a certain no-bility to it all. Yes, with apologies to Mark Twain, golf is a very good walk—in fact, it's the only good walk.

20

Playing Backwards

O dd as it may seem, the 1st green of the Old Course is actually the last green. By that I mean it's the youngest, the last one to have been designed and added. On this links estimated to be more than six centuries old, the green at number 1 is but a child of 135.

Up until 1870 the 1st hole shared its green with number 17, the Road Hole, in the same way that—even today—the 2nd hole shares with the 16th, the 3rd with the 15th, the 4th with the 14th, the 5th with the 13th, the 6th with the 12th, the 7th with the 11th, and the 8th with the 10th, each of the front-9 holes having a white flag, each of the back-9 holes (with the odd exception of 18) a red. (Note how each pair adds up neatly to 18.) Today, the only single-hole greens on the Old Course are the 1st, 9th, 17th, and 18th.

The two-holes-in-the-same-green idea arose in 1832 in response to a sharp increase in play on the Old Course. Before that time, the same cup had been used by groups heading outward on the front 9 and groups coming home on the back—a situation that can be assumed to have produced some awkward, perilous, and I daresay nasty moments among the tweed-coaters. So to relieve the congestion, they added a second flag to the greens.

Another oddity—up until 1870, when the 1st green was installed, the Old Course was played backwards—or left-handed, as the locals refer to it. Instead of playing down the right (seaside) edge of the property and then turning counterclockwise for the homeward route down the left corridor as we do now, golfers played from the 1st tee to the current 17th green, then played from the 18th tee to the 16th green, the 17th tee to the 15th green, and so on, working their way up the left side of the course before making a clockwise turn into the homestretch.

But when some land freed up on the west side of the Swilken Burn and keeper of the green Old Tom Morris slotted in the new target for number 1, light bulbs went off under the tam-o'-shanters. "Auch," they said, "we now have an option—we can play the course either clockwise or counterclockwise!" For the ensuing seventy years or so, that is exactly what they did, switching between the left- and right-handed courses on alternate weeks. In the estimation of many, the reverse course was just as good as—and more difficult than—the course we all know today. The 1896 British Amateur was played on the lefty layout.

Eventually, however, sanity prevailed. The left-handed course called for golfers teeing off at the 1st hole to crisscross with those finishing at the 18th. With the advent of harder, faster golf balls, things became a bit dangerous. After World War II, the reverse course was used only sporadically, and eventually abandoned.

Then a few years ago, as a way of encouraging increased play in the early spring, the Links Trust brought the backwards course back, for three days a year. On April 1, I was one of the lucky fools who secured a tee time. Having barely reached a point where I was comfortable courting the old lady, I was suddenly face-to-face with her schizophrenic twin.

Holes 1 and 2 became one of the most difficult starts in golf. The first played from the same tee in front of the R&A clubhouse but now headed 399 yards diagonally across the 18th fairway. Out-of-bounds beckoned on the left, and the approach called for a long-iron shot over both the Swilken Bridge and the Road Bunker. The (17th) green was so narrow and so acutely angled to the line of play that it begged to be attacked with a fade, but any shot that failed to fade would be in the road, any fade that faded too much would find the infamous pit. I roaded myself and started with a 6.

Number 2, now a par-4 of 452 yards with OB down the entire left side, called for a big drive and then a slinging hook around the corner of the Old Course Hotel. After another 6, I decided to forget about making a score and just enjoy the novelty.

A true revelation was the 7th played from the traditional 13th tee along the fairway of number 12 to the raised green of the par-3 11th hole. (Confused yet?) Four fairway bunkers, invisible on the right-handed course, are suddenly very much in your face on this tee shot, and the approach shot must be played over the dreaded Hill Bunker to a green that is about as friendly as a Parisian waiter.

I'd never seen so many blind shots. At number 12—played down the fairway of traditional number 7—a good drive left me just a wedge to the green, but I didn't know where my shot had finished until I'd strolled around the acre or so of gorse that stretched to within a few yards of the putting surface (the stuff that lurks behind the 6th green of the right-handed course). Another adventure came at 13, where, in order to get to our flag (the usual 5th) we had to play our approach shots directly over the heads of some nice people putting out at the 5th (the usual 13th) green.

Indeed, there seemed to be far greater potential for traffic accidents with the reverse course. Happily, to my knowledge, there were no casualties over the three days, but something extremely bizarre did happen, and I was privileged to witness it.

Since the course was jam-packed, play had backed up to the point that at most holes we were able to get an up-close view of the tee shots played by the four guys in the group in front of us. They were average golfers, but one of them was a big, strong dude with Popeye arms and a windmill swing. When he made solid contact, he hit the ball a very long way, but he rarely managed to get all his vectors aligned for a proper launch.

The final hole called for a tee shot from the usual 2nd tee diagonally across the 1st fairway toward the 18th green. Now, as many of us are prone to do on that final hole, our man went for a big hit—but he caught the ball a couple of dimples thin, and it shot out at ankle height, straight at a wooden footbridge over the Swilken Burn, perhaps 50 yards off the tee. Like a bullet it pinged into one of the bridge's metal supports and ricocheted straight back, striking our big friend squarely in the crotch.

It all happened so quickly that, for a split second, there was nothing but shocked silence—then, as Bluto bent over in groin-clutching agony, his entire foursome, my entire foursome, plus half a dozen or so caddies and assorted onlookers doubled over in laughter. He had just felt the full visceral thrill of the Old Course in reverse.

21

Having a Wee Flutter

illie and I were in the middle of one of our early-morning walkies and had reached a point just beneath the expansive front windows of the Rusacks Hotel dining room—a spot where, incidentally, Millie had demonstrated an uncanny proclivity to deposit the steaming excreta of her evening meal just as the surveillant hotel guests were tucking into their breakfast sausages—when a gray sedan careened left off Golf Place and headed toward us at alarming speed.

Happily, it slowed down or Millie would not have been the only one with a contribution to the Ziploc bag. In fact, it stopped smack in front of us and out popped Professor David Malcolm, known to everyone in town as Doc.

"I've just spent two days in the library at Edinburgh University," he said excitedly, "and in the old newspapers I uncovered the most marvelous information." Malcolm, a man of sixty-five years with a great shock of white hair and a unique mid-Atlantic burr that betrayed an education from both Cambridge and California, was a research scientist and lecturer with a specialty in genetics. But like most people in this town, his true passion was golf, and Doc's, like mine, extended to writing about the game. For the better part of two decades he'd been researching and writing the definitive biography of Old Tom Morris, and rumor was that the manuscript had grown to nearly a thousand pages.

"It seems that as early as 1850 people were gambling rampantly on the game," he continued. "All those exhibition matches involving the Morrises, the Parks et al had hundreds of pounds riding on them. Hundreds!"

I'd known that, back then, the citizens of towns along the east coast of Scotland were fiercely supportive of their home boys, but this, according to Doc, was the earliest proof of organized betting in golf.

It made sense. The Scots, I'd discovered, will bet on just about anything, and have been doing so for decades. When Bobby Jones won the Grand Slam in 1930, he didn't earn a penny, but Bobby Cruickshank cleaned up. A canny Scot if ever there was one, Cruickshank had played with Jones in a tournament earlier that year which Jones had won by 13 strokes. Immediately, Wee Bobby wired a few quid to his bookie, with long odds on Jones winning all four national championships. When the final putt fell in the U.S. Amateur at Merion, Cruickshank potted $60,000, a sum that in today's dollars would exceed the gross domestic product of several African nations.

These days, street-front betting parlors are everywhere in the U.K., there's a multimillion-pound business through Web sites, and it's all legal. At the Open Championship, if a player's feeling the magic he can nip into the local bookie and place a few quid on his own head before teeing off. Indeed, five-time champion Tom Watson admits he has augmented his winnings over the years, and several small fortunes were made in the competitors' locker room at Birkdale in 1985 when Ian Baker-Finch came through against 50–1 odds.

I remember well my one and only flight on the Concorde, a return trip from the 1983 Open Championship. I was seated in front of Peter Jacobsen and Andy Bean. Andy had placed a few bets on himself that week, including an elaborate win-place-show thing, and he'd finished tied for second with Hale Irwin, a stroke behind Watson. I'm not sure whether he had trouble computing the odds, was flummoxed by the pounds-to-dollars conversion, or just couldn't deal with numbers of such size, but he seemed to take fully half of that three-hour flight calculating his winnings, which were substantial.

In 2003, if surprise winner Ben Curtis had had the prescience to put a thousand pounds on himself at the start of the championship, he would have banked more than he did by winning the title. Curtis's opening odds were 750–1, and first prize was £700,000.

I must say, the U.K. bookies made it fun. The morning I entered the Ladbrokes parlor on Bell Street, I was looking to have a wee flutter on the 2004 Masters, but my attention was immediately diverted by other opportunities, one of which I should have snapped up: 20–1 odds on London getting the 2012 Olympics. There was also the chance to bet on what color hat the Queen would wear to the Ascot races, whether Tony Blair would grow a mustache before the end of his term (66–1), whether the Beckhams would divorce (10–1), and— another missed opportunity—whether Charles and Camilla would tie the knot (12–1). Anyone meteorologically inclined could bet on the possibility of a white Christmas (15–1), not to mention a white Wimbledon (200–1).

You can even bet on yourself. In January a fellow named Arthur Best had collected £6,600 on a £100 bet he'd placed ten years earlier at 66–1 odds that he would live to be 100 years old.

In the golf area, the options are similarly rich. You can of course bet on any player in the field. There is also the option of picking the winner with Tiger Woods in the field or without; if you bet on a player to win "Without Woods" and he finishes second to Tiger, you win. Another way of hedging is to bet on a player to finish among the top five places. In that case you get one fourth of his odds. If, for example, you put a first-five bet on Sergio Garcia at 20–1, then no matter whether he finishes first, second, third, fourth, or fifth, you get paid at 5–1.

Head-to-head bets are very popular. Say Davis Love and Chris Di-

Marco are paired together. You can pick one of them to beat the other (odds are offered on each guy). Then there are the "six-shooters." The bookie gives you a group of six players and you pick the top finisher.

If all that's too complicated for you, then you can pick the top American, the top Euro, the top Scot, or the top player from the rest of the world. And John Daly is a bookie's bonanza. In addition to the traditional bets, you can get odds on whether he'll make a score of at least 10 on a single hole.

At the counter, I looked at a sheet of odds, took a £20 note out of my pocket, and filled out a little slip, putting all of it on Phil Mickelson at 25–1. I'd been watching him in the early events and he seemed to be controlling his irons better than in years past. He was also hitting his driver like Tiger—long and straight—while Tiger seemed to be hitting it like Mickelson—long and crooked. I just had a hunch this would be the week Phil broke through for his first major.

Twenty pounds at 25–1 odds translated to £500—about $900. With that at stake, I should have felt some excitement as golf's rite of spring approached. But the truth was, I was feeling a bit depressed, thanks to a case of Pre-Masters Post-Partum Syndrome.

Not familiar with it? Well, it's relatively rare. PMPPS, also known as Doug Ford's Disease, is a virulent affliction that strikes in the early spring, descending on a small, pathetic group of mature adults who, having attended a chest-thumpingly long string of Masters tournaments, suddenly face their first April without Augusta. Typical symptoms include irritability, a tendency to wheeze and cough when exposed to dogwood or azalea, and a perverse craving for pimento cheese sandwiches. In the most extreme cases, the sufferer projectile-vomits green.

My own record of perfect attendance had begun in 1976. The last time I'd missed a Masters, Gerald Ford was president and Tiger Woods was an embryo. Now not only would I not be in Augusta, I'd be three thousand miles away. Not only would I have to watch the Masters on television, I'd have to watch it at night! Given the five-hour time difference, my Sunday at Augusta would begin just about when the actual Sunday at Augusta ends—at 7:00 P.M.—and would probably extend past midnight.

That was simply unacceptable. I'm a morning person—there was no way I could stay awake that long, not in a place where darkness sets in at teatime. Hell, by seven o'clock, my thoughts typically had turned to flannel jammies and a glass of warm milk.

I'd considered writing a letter to Masters chairman Hootie Johnson, showing the absurdity of the situation, and suggesting the obvious solution: Send the leaders off at 8:00 A.M. EST instead of 2:00 P.M. That way the East Coast folks could have *Breakfast at the Masters,* watch the full show, have a proper lunch, and still get in an afternoon 18. Meanwhile, all of us on the other side of the pond could play our morning four-ball, have a pint or two, and plop in front of the telly at a civilized hour. Everyone wins except the religious right, who would surely claim that church attendance would suffer. The truth, of course, is that the only absentees would be the same heathens who play golf religiously every Sunday anyway. Oh, and I suppose TV ratings on the West Coast might dip, but that's actually a good thing—given the state of California's economy, they should conserve electricity.

So it was the perfect solution. I knew I had no chance with Hootie though, so I resigned myself to my fate. Instead of watching the telecast, having dinner, and going to bed as a normal human should, I would do the opposite—sleep-eat-view.

Happily, I had two options. Plan A was to nap all afternoon, storing up my viewing stamina, have a light dinner—no booze, plenty of coffee—and then lock in for the five hours, hoping for a riveting back-9 battle. But I doubted that would work. A year earlier, Libby and I had made a pre-renovation visit to St. Andrews during the week of the U.S. Open. On Sunday evening I'd said good night to my wife at nine and walked up to the Dunvegan pub just in time to see Jim Furyk make the turn at Olympia Fields. Now, granted, that championship presented the world of golf with a deadly confluence—a dull guy, pursued distantly by other dull guys, on a dull course. Still, by the 14th hole, I was facedown in my Carlsberg.

So I was resolved that, unless the 54-hole lead was seized by Arnold Palmer, I would go to Plan B—record the Sunday telecast and watch it Monday morning with my coffee and yum-yum. My ideal scenario, in fact, was for the tournament to end in a tie, for the sudden-death playoff to extend until darkness prevented further play, and for everyone to have to come back the next morning at nine. That's 2:00 P.M. U.K. time, which would give me just enough time to view the recording, have some lunch, and flip on the BBC for live coverage of the conclusion. Then, assuming the drama and quality of play had inspired me, I'd do something I'd always wanted to do in the moments following a major—I'd head out for a quick round.

That was the plan, but when my man Phil got himself into the hunt going into Sunday, I knew I'd have to hang in there with him. And when Mickelson's putt on 18 hit the cup, I jumped into the air even more clumsily than he did. I was a bit groggy the next morning but perked up considerably when the clerk at Ladbrokes handed me my £500.

Yes, so delighted was I with my first betting experience, and so convinced was I that this was the beginning of a big roll for Mickelson, that I bet on him to win—at appreciably shorter odds—each of the next *six* majors—and lost everything I'd won and more. It was eighteen months before I finally gave up on him and went with Tiger—just in time for Phil's return in the PGA at Baltusrol.

22

21 Ways to Get on the Old Course

The current daily green fee at the Old Course is £120—about $216. That represents some rampant inflation. In 1970, when I played it the first time, I paid 40 pence (then about a dollar). The price today simply reflects the law of supply and demand—a limited supply of tee times and a huge demand to play.

During the peak season there are not enough spaces to accommodate all the locals and all the tourists. That is the reason for the ballot—a daily lottery for Old Course tee times—a forbidding, tense, and potentially exasperating experience for any visitor who has traveled a long distance and has just one day, one chance, one hope to play the legendary links.

In its bureaucratic complexity the Old Course ballot is similar to the U.S. tax code. Its myriad intricacies are understood only by veteran St. Andreans and those with an aptitude for advanced multivariable calculus. For instance, two blocks of times—one in the morning and one in the afternoon—are reserved for balloting by local people.

On Thursday and Saturday, however, the local times extend to include every alternate tee time in the afternoon. There is only one ballot for each day except for Saturday, when locals have two ballots and in August and September when the R&A has its own block of times for members to vie for, so that in effect there are three ballots.

You sign up either by phone or in person by 1:00 P.M. the day before you want to play (you must be in a group of at least two—no singles— and the handicap limit is 24 for men, 36 for women). You hear your fate by 3:00 P.M. The results are posted at several locations in town as well as on the Web at www.linksnet.co.uk/barononline/ballot.aspx.

Remarkably in this digital age, the actual pulling of the ballots is done entirely by hand, much in the manner of the TV ladies who snatch floating Ping-Pong balls for state lotteries. It all happens in the offices of the St. Andrews Links Trust, where each morning five members of the reservations staff have a little lottery of their own. At nine o'clock they assemble in a room along with a sixth person—not a member of the reservations staff. In front of them is a little black bag containing five golf balls, numbered one to five, each ball corresponding to a different staff member. Once everyone has arrived, the sixth person reaches into the bag and pulls out a ball. The reservations staffer whose number was chosen thereupon assumes responsibility for the day's ballot.

This little drill became necessary a couple of decades ago when the former system was found to be fraught with corruption. In those days, there was one omnipotent ballotmaster. His office was a little hut behind the 18th green, now used as a retail shop. All ballots were submitted to him, all tee times were allotted by him. He was above reproach, but not above bribery.

At the same time, certain residents—mostly university students and caddies—worked the system. During the prime season they signed up for local times, then repaired to the local pubs where they sold their spots to any tourists willing to pay a few quid. (In those days, there was no system for checking the validity of things.) All in all, the ballots were about as clean and tidy as the ones in Florida for the 2000 presidential election.

But that has all changed. Now, at two o'clock each afternoon the designated balloteer sits down and painstakingly determines the list. First all the cards are examined for irregularities—were the blanks filled in correctly, were there any duplicate names, did everyone list a handicap, and were all handicaps within the prescribed limits? Just as important, did any name appear on two different ballots—either by accident or in an attempt to subvert the system? Each day several cards are disqualified for one reason or another.

Next the ballot cards are divided into four stacks—local players, those requesting early times, those requesting late times, and those willing to play at any time.

The locals come first. The stack of cards is shuffled and then the card on top is drawn—that becomes the earliest of the local times. The second card becomes the second tee time, and so forth. If the block of local times is not filled by local requests, the drawmaster goes to the stack of cards from people willing to play at any time, shuffles, and selects as many cards from that stack as needed to fill out the local times.

The same process is repeated for the early-times requests and the late-times requests—the first card drawn from the early people gets the earliest of the early times, the second gets the second earliest. In each case, the anytime people fill in times not used. The whole process takes about half an hour, after which the ballot is released to the public. As a visitor, your chances of success vary depending on the time of year. In season (mid-April through mid-October) the prospects are about 35 percent; off season better than 95 percent.

The system is 99 percent legitimate, but when pressed, the Links Trust people will admit it can be rigged. "There's little question that if the king of Morocco were to apply through the daily ballot, a tee time would be found for him," said one trust official. Indeed, throughout much of our first year of residence, a raging controversy surrounded J. P. McManus, one of Ireland's richest men. It seems that one fine summer morning he and three friends had played the Old Course in one of the times reserved for local golfers. They were recognized by a couple of members of the St. Andrews Golf Club who checked the ballot and saw that the lead name in that time slot belonged to an employee of the Links Trust. The issue was raised publicly and the fellow whose name was on the ballot, one of the course marshals, was sacked. But he didn't take it lying down. He claimed he'd been unfairly treated by his superiors, took his case to court, and got his dismissal reversed, while embarrassing both McManus and the Links Trust.

The good news, I guess, is that even a few billion dollars won't get you preferential treatment on the Old Course, at least not without some public humiliation. Happily, there are other ways to get on—twenty other ways, to be exact—some of them, admittedly, more bona fide than others. As a public service they are delineated here, along with the prospects and costs you can expect.

1. Ride a Local's Coattails: If you can befriend a resident of St. Andrews or a member of one of the town's five golf clubs (three men's, two women's), you have the right to enter the ballot as part of his/her group. This will put you in the blocks of starting times allotted solely for locals (specifically, 8:00–9:00 A.M. weekdays and 8:00–10:00 A.M. Saturdays all year round plus 1:00–2:00 P.M. in the winter and 5:00–6:00 P.M. in the summer on Mondays, Tuesdays, Wednesdays, and Fridays and every alternate afternoon time on Thursdays and Saturdays). Guests are allowed to take part in these times, as long as the local folk play in the group. And if your host is feeling insanely generous, he may even let you use four of his twenty-four annual "guest concession" points, meaning your green fee will be reduced by almost two thirds. Your prospects: 80 percent in season, 99 percent off season. Your cost (based on $1.80 per pound): $77 in season, $36 off season (assuming you get to use the points).

2. Walk on as a Single: If you're on your own or don't mind splitting up your group, you can join the predawn queue at the starter's box next to the 1st tee of the Old Course. Depending on the time of year, your wait could be as little as a few minutes or as long as a few hours. Your prospects: 80 percent in-season, 99 percent off-season. Your cost: $216 in-season, $106 off-season.

3. Book Way in Advance: The St. Andrews Links Trust accepts advance applications for specific dates and tee times (by e-mail, fax, or letter), beginning the first Wednesday in September for the year to follow. Allocation is on a first-come, first-served basis, and you'll get a reply within six weeks of receipt of your application. Contact: Reservations Office, St. Andrews Links Trust, Pilmour House, St. Andrews, Fife KY16 9SF Scotland; tel: 011 441 334 466 666, fax: 011 441 334 477 036 (www.standrews.org.uk). Your prospects: 40 percent. Your cost: $306 in-season (includes a second round on either the New Course or Jubilee Course).

4. Call the Old Course Experience: This golf tour operator has an exclusive contract with the Links Trust for roughly 800 starting times per year. The good news is that by booking with them you're guaranteed a tee time, pretty much on the day you want it; the bad news is that it's extremely expensive. Your prospects: 100 percent. Your cost: $1,908–2,206 (includes a round on the New or Jubilee plus two nights at a top hotel, daily breakfast, one dinner, transfers to courses, and assorted other goodies. See www.oldcourse-experience.com).

5. Move to St. Andrews: A 1974 Act of Parliament guaranteed any resident of St. Andrews a Links Pass, allowing them full privileges on all six of the town's courses for an annual fee that is currently $203. Unfortunately, you must be a certified tax-paying, voting resident—and show multiple evidence of same in the form of signed affidavits by local clergymen, schoolmasters, solicitors, and so on. Your prospects: 70 percent. Your cost: $200,000–$3,000,000 for a home, plus $203.

6. Move Near St. Andrews: People who live in northeast Fife (but not within the confines of St. Andrews) may buy a Links Pass at twice the price St. Andreans pay. Unfortunately, due to the large number of people now retiring to the Auld Grey Toon, there's a lengthy waiting list for the ticket—and there are absolutely no exceptions. Mary Thomson only recently got her ticket after a multiyear wait—not extraordinary except that her husband is Peter Thomson, five-time winner of the Open Championship. Your prospects: 100 percent (eventually). Your costs: $100,000–$3,000,000 for a home, plus $406 for the Links Pass.

7. Join the Royal & Ancient Golf Club: Okay, they're not exactly on a membership drive, but hey, you never know. With your annual dues you get free playing privileges. Your prospects: less than 1 percent. Your cost: If I told you I'd be drummed out of the club, but rest assured, it's very reasonable, especially by American standards.

8. Join the St. Andrews Golf Club or the New Club: You must be proposed and seconded, but both clubs welcome overseas members. Unlike the R&A, membership (for Americans at least) does not bring with it free access to the courses, but you may buy a Links Pass (at three times the prevailing price). Your prospects: 10 percent. Your cost: $100–$200 per year, plus $609 for the Links Pass.

9. Enroll in the University of St. Andrews: Granted, you may be a little old for school, but once you're in you qualify for a pass. Your prospects: less than 1 percent. Your cost: roughly $30,000 for first-year tuition, room and board, plus $203 for the Links Pass.

10. Join Rotary International: The Rotarians have been playing an annual tournament at St. Andrews every June for over fifty years and it includes one round on the Old Course and one on the Eden Course. The tournament is open to all members worldwide and is limited to 360 spots, but it rarely sells out. Your prospects: 100 percent (once you get into your local Rotary club). Your cost: Rotary dues, plus a $475 entry fee.

11. Join the Royal Air Force and Get Stationed at Leuchars: If you can get yourself assigned there—even as an American serviceman—you'll be eligible for a Links Pass at two times the locals' rate. (And if you can make it to base commander, you'll be eligible for membership in the R&A.) Your prospects: less than 1 percent. Your cost: $406 for a Links Pass.

12. Play in the Dunhill Links Championship: The European Tour's version of the AT&T Pebble Beach Pro-Am, this annual October event gets you onto the Old Course, Carnoustie, and Kingsbarns, playing in a two-man team alongside a tour pro. Throw in practice days and you get six rounds of golf—seven if you're one of the twenty teams to make the cut for Sunday's final round on the Old Course. Your prospects: 40 percent. Your cost: $7,500.

13. Buy the Last Spot in the Dunhill Links Championship: Each year the Dunhill spots sell out, but there is still a way to guarantee yourself a berth—go on the Internet and make the highest bid in the St. Andrews Pilgrim Foundation charity auction that takes place two weeks before the event. Of course, you'll pay a bit of a premium—over the last few years winning bids have averaged about $30,000. But it's all for a good cause that preserves and protects the historic buildings in town (see www.pilgrimfoundation.org). Your prospects: 100 percent. Your cost: whatever it takes.

14. Give Your Father (or Son) a Treat: Play in the annual St. Andrews Father-Son Tournament (see chapter 18). Your prospects: 100 percent. Your cost: $7,000 entry fee for two.

15. Play in the St. Andrews Links Trophy or St. Rule Trophy: These are the two big men's and women's amateur events held each summer. The men play three of their four rounds on the Old Course, the women two of their three. Of course, to be eligible for the Links Trophy you'll need a handicap of scratch or better, for the St. Rule (Annika is a former champion), 6 or better. Your prospects: less than 1 percent. Your cost: $100 entry fee.

16. Get a Job in the British Golf Media and Join the Association of Golf Writers: Every five or six years, when the Open returns to St. Andrews, members of the AGW are invited to a media day that includes a round of golf on the Old Course. Your prospects: less than 1 percent. Your cost: nil.

17. Get a Job at the St. Andrews Links Trust: The organization employs roughly 200 full-time workers and one of the perks is a free Links Pass. Who knows, you may even become one of the five ballotmasters. Your prospects: less than 1 percent. Your cost: nil.

18. Get a High-Level Job at the R&A: All members of the senior staff—about ten of them—get links privileges. Your chances: less than 1 percent. Your cost: nil.

19. Qualify for the Next Open Championship at St. Andrews (expected to be 2010): Pull that one off and you'll get an entire week of play on the Old. Your prospects: less than 1 percent. Your cost: $200 entry fee.

20. Win the Open on the Old Course: All champions at St. Andrews are granted the Freedom of the Links, entitling them to a lifetime of gratis green fees. Your prospects and your cost: nil.

23

A Different World

There's a story the Old Course caddies love to tell about the Texas rancher on his first visit to St. Andrews. One day, after a morning round of golf, he hops into his rented Jaguar for a cruise through the countryside. A couple of miles out of town he happens upon an elderly farmer plowing a field.

"Howdy," says that Texan, "is this your place?"

"Aye, it is, sir," says the farmer.

"Nice little spread you got. Whaddaya grow?"

"Oh, mostly wheat and barley for the distilleries, and some hay for the animals."

"Hmm," says the Texan, "ya know, back home I have me a farm, and I can get up at the crack of dawn, hop on my tractor, drive it in a straight line all day long, and when the sun goes down, I'm still not at the end of my property."

"Aye," says the farmer, "I know exactly what you mean."

"You do?" says the Texan, a bit surprised.

"Aye, sir, I once had a tractor like that."

The story may be apocryphal but its point was one that Libby and I had begun to feel with increasing frequency. We'd arrived in a different world, a much smaller, slower, simpler world than the one we'd left eight months earlier.

To a certain extent we'd girded ourselves. We knew that by exchanging our four-bedroom home for a two-bedroom flat we'd done some serious downsizing. And I'd realized that my days of conspicuous consumption had ended—freelance writers tend to live close to the bone.

For me, the most painful transition had been the change of wheels. My last car in the States had been a Lexus SC 430, a sleek two-seater convertible with a hard top that, at the push of a button, folded flamboyantly into the trunk. It was loaded with elaborate electronica, including a GPS system voiced by a sultry cyberwoman whose mission, it seemed, was to tell me in dulcet tones exactly what she'd like me to do with her. That car was a totally impractical, utterly self-indulgent purchase—the ultimate midlife crisis machine—but I loved it. Libby did not share my rapture—SC in her mind stood for Stupid Car.

Now I was suddenly at the helm of a 1.4-liter, standard-transmission, 85-horsepower Honda Jazz that rocketed from 0 to 60 in about 97 seconds. It was, however, admirably fuel-efficient, and in the face of the side-splittingly high U.K. petrol prices, the only line on the window sticker that had interested me was the one that read "50 mpg." Gas had ended up costing about the same as for the Stupid Car.

In choosing that car, our location was also a consideration. On most days I parked alongside the white fence that defines out-of-bounds on the 18th hole. Within a week of taking delivery of the car, I'd suffered my first golf ball pockmark, within a month, the back-right window had been smashed in, and within six months, every metallic blue panel had the complexion of Manuel Noriega.

Being one of those deeply complex guys whose self-esteem at any given moment relates in large part to the opulence of the car he's driving, I'd steeled myself for a period of auto-induced depression. Blessedly, that never happened, for the reason that, in St. Andrews, as in most of the British Isles, 90 percent of the population drives dumpy little cars.

Again the main reason is fuel consumption. Filling the large tank of a full-size Mercedes or BMW will run you $125 or more and you'll have to refill it just as frequently as you would a Ford Focus or VW Polo. Another issue is maneuverability. Roads in the U.K. are far narrower than in the U.S., and the parking spaces are tiny—a Lincoln Navigator would need two or three of them.

Fundamentally, however, I think the Brits favor small cars for the same reason they favor small refrigerators and small golf bags—they don't want or need anything more. Besides, ostentation is sort of a national no-no. Small is standard, medium is large, and large is obscene.

And so I'd puttered around in my little ball-battered Honda with a kind of ascetic pride, a feeling I'd never experienced in the leather and mahogany cockpit of the Lexus. That spartan nobility extended to our telecommunications setup, where for the first time in a decade, neither Libby nor I had a cell phone. Nor did we own a fax machine or a copier or a phone with speed dial or call waiting. We'd stopped buying CDs and instead listened happily all day to Classic FM, a marvelous station that played everything from Beethoven to John Williams. We'd also curtailed our book buying—instead we'd joined the public library. It was simply what people in St. Andrews did.

We'd come from the global center of materialism, class consciousness, and social climbing, and landed in a place where those things, although they existed, were far more subdued, far less important. Even inside the austere R&A, I'd come to appreciate a remarkably egalitarian spirit. Early on, a long-standing member who had sort of adopted me said, "There are chaps here who are billionaires and other chaps who don't have two nickels to rub together, but you'd never know who is who. No one in this club has anything to prove to anyone else." That news had been enormously comforting, since I doubted there were many R&A members I could embarrass in a résumé-matching contest.

The kindness and gentleness of the citizenry surely had helped make St. Andrews a very safe place to live. Certainly we'd known that by trading suburban New York for the East Neuk of Fife we were leaving a prime terrorist target for a place that was unlikely to be on Osama bin Laden's hit list. The worst crime I'd witnessed was the wedge shot on number 1 that hit the green and spun back into the Swilken Burn.

On my first visit to the local constabulary, the doors were locked and the lights were off—apparently, the cops didn't see a need to open up shop until after 8:00 A.M. On another occasion, back when we were renting our flat to students, one of our tenants had vanished in the middle of the year, without paying his second semester rent. No one knew where the kid had gone—not the university, not the solicitor who'd drawn up the lease, not even the lad's mother, who was distraught. All the local and national authorities had been alerted. The kid was a certified missing person. That summer we'd visited the flat, and while cleaning out one of the closets I'd come upon a box full of letters left by the boy—letters to a male friend with whom he'd apparently had a relationship. Sensing that this could be useful evidence, I took the box to the police station.

This time the place was not only open but busy. I got in a queue just behind a tiny, earnest-looking Scotsman of at least eighty years, clad in a dark suit, white shirt, and tie. When he reached the window he said, "I have found something and I'd like to turn it in."

"Yes, of course," said the officer on duty. "What do you have?"

"This morning, at about 9:30, near the corner of Bell and Market streets, just in front of the Oddbins Bottle Shop, I happened to look down at the pavement, and I saw this!" At that point, he reached into the pocket of his suit coat and produced what I thought at first was a piece of paper but after snooping over his shoulder I saw to be cash—more specifically, a single bill—a one-pound note, worth at that time approximately a dollar and a half.

"Aye, sir," said the officer. "And you'd like to file a formal report."

"Yes, of course," said the little chap.

"Right then, sir. You'll have to supply some information now. If after three weeks no one has come in to claim the property and identify it as theirs, you are entitled to return here and claim it for yourself. Do you understand?"

"Yes, I do."

"Okay," said the officer, "this will take several minutes." At that point, he looked over the wee man's head to me. "I hope you don't mind, sir, this is a matter we need to take care of right now."

"Oh, no problem," I said, almost laughing. After all, I only had material evidence in a nationwide missing person's case—a case that might have been kidnapping, murder, who knows what. That certainly could wait while this little geezer with the common sense of a spaniel filled out a twelve-page report on his found pound!

I'd come to learn, though, that St. Andrews was full of such people—kind, thoughtful, caring folk. People who dropped by your home with flowers for no apparent reason, who invited you for drinks on the spur of the moment, who offered to pick up your cleaning or walk your dog or water your plants. And I'd also realized that these people lacked nothing in the way of intelligence; rather it was I who lacked a few things—things like patience, an active interest in others, and a willingness to make sacrifices. St. Andrews had begun to teach me lessons I would never have learned in New York.

In fact, Libby and I had begun to wonder what our adventure had become. The cradle of golf had turned out to be a broader sort of a cradle where we'd found a purer, more innocent kind of life, and our sojourn in St. Andrews had in that sense become not just a hiatus but a retreat, a chance to regenerate ourselves—a life mulligan.

24

Happy Anniversary

was awakened early one spring morning by an unaccustomed sound—the loud, repeating clank of metal on metal.
One clank per second, it was—clank one thousand one, clank one
thousand two, clank one thousand three—Chinese hammer torture.
Further slumber being impossible, I staggered to the bay window to
see what was afoot.

Overnight, two dozen trucks and a small battalion of workmen
had encamped on the Bruce Embankment, the green sward just north
of the 1st tee of the Old Course, and an ambitious project had begun,
the erection of a structure that would be the second largest of its kind
ever in Scotland—one enormous room with a fifty-foot ceiling and
total floor space of over 64,500 square feet. When fully fitted with
plumbing, electricity, and air-conditioning, it would comfortably accommodate 1,200 people. And three weeks later it would disappear.

His Royal Highness the Duke of York would christen it the Wigwam—but no Native American and few members of the royal family
had ever entered such a tent. This magnificent marquee would be-

come the focal point for sixteen days of celebration—the longest, most lavish party St. Andrews had ever seen—the 250th anniversary of the R&A.

Little had Libby and I known when we decided to take our leap that our timing would be so propitious. Oh, in the recesses of my pre-Alzheimerian brain I recalled receiving a message, nearly two years earlier, something about the club having commissioned a vintner to produce an anniversary claret and did I want to reserve a case for delivery to my door (at a transatlantic shipping cost Baron de Rothschild might have found reasonable but I did not). After that I'd put the whole 250th thing out of my mind.

Then, a week or so before we left for St. Andrews, a huge packet arrived from the R&A, describing what was planned for the upcoming spring—half a dozen black-tie dinners, an equal number of golf competitions for men, women, and children, a fireworks display, a pipe and drum concert, an exhibition of aerial acrobatics by the RAF's Red Arrows, and, in the middle of it all, the 109th British Amateur Championship on the Old Course. Invitations had been sent to nearly seven thousand people, including Her Majesty the Queen, who was expected to speak at one of the dinners.

My, my, I'd thought, what a nice way to welcome the Pepers to town. A few months later, I'd had another thought—maybe I should help. Shortly after our arrival in September, I'd written a letter to R&A chief executive Peter Dawson offering my services. I knew of course that it was the eleventh hour of a project that had been in the planning for several years, but the way I saw it, someone had to be there at the end to take the credit. Besides, I figured if I could wangle a visible job of some kind—maybe serving champagne and smoked salmon at one of the galas—I'd be able to meet and ingratiate myself with a few R&A members.

In the course of our first six months I'd made some progress learning the secret handshakes and tribal rituals of the club. I'd discovered, for instance, that there was a "monthly medal"—a stroke-play competition among R&A members played on the New Course the third Friday of each month, and that if you wanted a good starting time (in my case, one of the earlier ones), you were well advised to sign up on the first day of the month, when entries opened. I'd also learned, after a notably unballetic jeté, that the bottom step on the club's main staircase was a bit steeper than the others. And after weeks of close observation I'd cracked the clubhouse dress code—jacket and tie were required in parts of the first floor, all of the second floor, and none of the third floor. Most importantly, perhaps, I'd learned that if you wanted to enjoy several gin and tonics without being transformed into a blithering fool, you ordered a "club measure," and when a chap was said to have gone to "the House of Lords," it meant he was relieving himself. Still, I hadn't met too many members. I just wasn't very good at cold-calling British aristocrats to set up games of golf. So I saw the opportunity to make this 250th anniversary my coming-out party.

Peter Dawson had sent me a prompt, polite reply, thanking me for volunteering and assuring me that someone would be back in touch as the celebrations drew nigh. Then in early March I'd received a call from Charles Philip, the member in overall charge of the celebration.

"Yes, as it happens, we could use another good soldier on the golf front," he said. "Could you make a meeting on Tuesday at ten?"

That meeting lasted nearly five hours, and when I emerged from it I was numb. Good soldier, hell, I'd just been made a full bird colonel and sent to the front lines. Somehow, I'd been appointed the "lead member" in charge of four of the six anniversary tournaments, including one that involved simultaneous play on four courses and another where the field was comprised of 143 two-man teams representing twenty-three nations.

Meet members? Oh, I was going to meet some members, all right. The first thing I was handed at the meeting was a sixteen-page list of names, addresses, and phone numbers of R&A guys who lived locally and had volunteered to help with the various tournaments as starters, stewards, score recorders, and so on. My primary job was to marshal those marshals—orchestrate duty rosters and ensure that each guy hit his mark.

Mind you, I knew less about the workings of the club than any of them. As if that weren't intimidating enough, a quick scan of the list revealed that about half of my recruits were OBEs and the other half had names prefaced by "Supreme Air Marshal," "The Right Honourable," and "His Exalted Worthiness." And I was just George.

But they all sounded nice enough on the phone. In fact, several of them chatted me up, possibly intrigued by the American accent. Filling in the duty rosters was blessedly glitchless.

The first event was called the Local Clubs Competition. As a way of reaching out to the town of St. Andrews, the R&A had invited all members of the other clubs—the St. Andrews Golf Club and the New Golf Club (like the R&A, men only), and the St. Rule Club and the St. Regulus Club (ladies only)—along with the lads at the Leuchars air base golf club to enter a one-day competition with silver bowls awarded as prizes across three handicap divisions. The ladies' event was held at Kingsbarns and the men's (which I ran) was at the Torrance Course of the St. Andrews Bay resort.

The first tee time was at 7:00 A.M. I arrived, after a sleepless night, at 5:45 to find the clubhouse deserted and locked tight. No other human appeared until 6:30 and for the half hour after that I and an intrepid trio of early-shift marshals scrambled to put together the registration table and assemble goodie bags containing course guides, rules sheets, commemorative ballmarkers, and sleeves of Titleist Pro V1s bearing the R&A Centennial logo, barely finishing as the first contestants arrived.

There were one or two minor snafus—a couple of no-shows (or "scratchings" as they are known and reviled in the U.K.) and a few guys who had gotten their tee times confused—but we managed to get everyone safely around 18 holes and they all seemed to have a good time. In the process, I was able to meet and greet nearly two hundred of the town's most passionate golfers, not to mention the first dozen members of my volunteer army.

The following evening everyone who had played in the competitions was invited, along with a guest of his or her choice, to the first of the black-tie dinners in the Wigwam. Now, as impressive to behold as the Wigwam was from the outside—a football field in length and two stories high—few who entered it on that first night were prepared for what was on the inside. A reception area displayed dozens of anniversary gifts the R&A had received from clubs and associations around the world: original oil paintings, bronze sculptures, crystal and silver trays and bowls of every shape and size, plus a collection of exotica from the more remote outposts: a piñata, a wooden variation on Rubik's Cube, and three different objects incorporating the figure of a rhinoceros.

From there everyone was ushered up a flight of stairs to a gallery level that ran the circumference of the tent. It was there that cocktails were served from half a dozen bars, although one scarcely needed to seek a drink, as a squadron of waiters and waitresses circulated constantly with silver trays bearing glasses of champagne, whisky, and wine, while others floated by with an assortment of hot and cold hors d'oeuvres.

What was most striking, however, was the ambience of the place. Bear in mind, we were within a couple of weeks of the longest day of the year, and in Scotland that means bright daylight until well past ten o'clock. To mask that, the tent had been draped with 4,200 meters of blackout lining. Then, through a display of lighting and special effects that would have made George Lucas jealous, the place was transformed into something resembling the Starlight Roof of the Waldorf-Astoria. When I first beheld the main floor—120 tables glittering with crystal, china, and silver and individually illuminated in deep indigo—I half expected to hear a voice from the beyond say "Good evening, ladies and gentlemen, and welcome to the 76th Academy Awards." I'd never seen a more magnificent ballroom.

Our dinner table was a fun-loving group, none of whom I'd met before that evening but all of whom became fast friends during the next three hours. All the guests were in a great mood, having had the golf, drinks, and dinner all laid on by the R&A, and all the hosts were relieved finally to have the anticipation over and everything in motion.

This, in the consensus of those who attended all the dinners, would be the most festive of them all.

The food was as good as in a fine restaurant, and the service was remarkable—each course arrived and departed at precisely the right moment, neither too soon nor too late—thanks to some meticulous planning. The R&A had recruited two hundred boys and girls from nearby schools, decked them out in snappy uniforms, and schooled them to perform a caterer's *Swan Lake*. But the true secret, I learned later, was the team of commandos deployed in the overhead gallery, wearing headsets, eyeballing every seat at every table, and barking orders to the kitchen staff: "Table 67 needs more butter . . . Table 12 is finished with their salad . . . Some clown at Table 33 just spilled claret all over his wife . . ."

The speeches were marvelously entertaining, particularly the one by Emil Pacholek, a St. Andrews Golf Club member and publishing executive from Dundee who, if he chose, could make a very nice living as a stand-up comedian.

Wine flowed freely throughout the evening, and as dessert was served each table was presented a bottle of the R&A's specially commissioned 250th anniversary single malt whisky. This I found to be an extraordinary gesture, both for its generosity and—coming at nearly midnight—its excess. Of course, I was quick to fill my snifter, as was the vivacious young lass sitting next to me, Julie Farmer, the daughter of local golf professional Jim Farmer. Everyone else stuck with their port and coffee. As the evening broke up, I looked over at the bottle of scotch—still three-quarters full—and thought what a shameful waste. Yielding to a lowly impulse, I crammed the bottle into the breast pocket of my tuxedo and ripped off the R&A.

However, I wasn't the only one to do so, as I learned several months later when I tried to purchase a couple of bottles. (Inasmuch as it was available only at the R&A, was priced reasonably at £25, and had an attractive label featuring the club symbol and an ornate "250," the commemorative malt made an impressive gift to take back to friends in the States.)

"Could I get three bottles of the 250th single malt?" I asked Evelyn, a friendly and always accommodating member of the catering staff.

"Oh, no, I'm afraid we're all out, Mr. Peper," she said.

"Really?" I said, looking crestfallen I suppose.

"Well," she said, "actually, is it for yourself?"

"One's for me, two are for friends," I said.

"Do you mind if the seals are broken?" she said.

"Not really," I said.

"Well, then we have lots of bottles."

Having been burned on that first night, the R&A had responded at the five ensuing dinners by delivering the post-prandial bottle with its seal broken and its cork removed, thus discouraging all thieves except those who truly could hold their liquor.

The Queen never made it to the celebration but the King did—Arnold Palmer spent several days in town and spoke emotionally at one of the dinners. Palmer, who did so much to raise the profile of the Open Championship, is an honorary member of not only the R&A but the St. Andrews Golf Club and the New Golf Club as well, although his appearances have been infrequent. One afternoon he was strolling down the links, past the entrance to the St. Andrews Golf Club, when one of the older members hailed him. Arnie, ever obliging, chatted amicably with the chap for a few minutes, then realized he was running late for an appointment.

"Can you tell me where the New Club is?" he asked.

"Aye," said the old fellow, "but you should bloody well know how to find it, you've been a member there since 1973!"

Former Open champions Peter Thomson and Tom Weiskopf also were in town for the big show and the contingent of American R&A members included former USGA presidents Will Nicholson, Sandy Tatum, and Bill Campbell (Campbell is one of only three Americans to have served as an R&A captain) and PGA Tour commissioner Tim Finchem.

Our houseguest for the week was one of my oldest and dearest friends, USGA executive director David Fay. David and I had roomed together as a couple of bachelors in New York City, had been best man at each other's weddings, and had led essentially parallel lives, married with two children. In fact, the younger of his two girls was at Princeton, two years ahead of our Scott. Weddings and grandchildren will surely be the next of our shared life passages. David had made two prior trips to St. Andrews, staying at our place both times, and Libby had named our spare bedroom the David Fay Room.

"This time I'm not coming for meetings," he said, "so let's play lots of golf." And so, while the British Amateur unfurled outside our door, David and I absconded, first to Crail, where he took my money, shooting a 74 off his 13-handicap. (The truth is, his golf skill is no worse than mine, maybe a bit better. Thirty years earlier we'd paired together in my club's member guest and had led the field of qualifiers when David—then a supposed 7 or 8—had twirled a 69 on his own ball. For someone responsible for the world's largest handicapping system, David is a shameless sandbagger!)

Granted, the next day at the New Course he did shoot 90 but I'm convinced at least half a dozen of those shots were struck solely for the purpose of restoring credibility in his 13. On another day we joined up with *Golf Digest* editor Jerry Tarde and one of his executive editors, John Barton, for 36 holes at St. Andrews Bay. Jerry and I had been friendly but intense rivals for two decades and it was nice to get together simply as friends. Our handicaps were the same, and on that day he and I competed as closely as ever, each of us shooting 80 in the morning, 81 in the afternoon, but the Fay-Tarde team nipped the Peper-Barton squad twice, because of you-know-who.

Jerry was supposed to have joined me, David, and USGA president Fred Ridley the next day at Kingsbarns, but he stood us up. "I hope you understand," he said. "I've been invited to play with [PGA Tour commissioner] Tim Finchem, [IMG president] Alastair Johnston, and Arnie." I did understand and was insanely jealous.

So I drafted the ever-ready-to-play Gordon Murray, who partnered with Fred against me and David. It was a horrible day—rain and wind so heavy that Arnie et al packed it in after 9 holes—but the four

During the 1984 Open Championship the *Golf Magazine* banner hung, somewhat ostentatiously, from our bay window. *Author's collection*

Then and now: the flat as it looked when the renovation got under way, and the kitchen today. *Author's collection*

The regular Saturday game: David Sandford, Bryce Hogarth, Gordon Murray, and myself. *Iain Lowe*

A happy quartet on the Swilken Bridge—Michael Bonallack, Pedro Dos Santos, myself, and Gordon Murray—the day I finally shot even par on the Old Course. *Author's collection*

Wee Raymond Gatherum starting another round of par or thereabouts on the Old Course. *Iain Lowe*

In the footsteps of royalty. HRH the Duke of York leads the way to one of the 250th Anniversary galas. The fellow in the tux bringing up the rear is yours truly. *Author's collection*

Gordon Murray—the only Old Course caddie who lives on the 18th hole and keeps his caddie bib in the trunk of a Mercedes. *Iain Lowe*

The notorious Road Hole bunker on 17. Millie carefully observes my technique. *Iain Lowe*

Fairway mats are an Old Course fact of life from November through March. *Iain Lowe*

Post-round drinks with the Thursday Club "partisans" in the lounge of the St. Andrews Golf Club. *Iain Lowe*

My always friendly neighbors Eric and Margaret Reid, on their balcony overlooking the 17th green. *Iain Lowe*

I may not be able to write like the late Herbert Warren Wind, but as inspiration I have the nameplate from his R&A locker. *Iain Lowe*

My son Scott looks much better in a kilt—and in everything else—than I do. *Old Course Experience*

The R&A clubhouse with the North Sea in the background and the first tee of the Old Course just to the left. *Author's collection*

The front bay window of the R&A's Big Room, with its magnificent view of the Old Course. *Royal & Ancient Golf Club*

The captains' balls are on constant display at the R&A but are kissed only once a year. *Royal & Ancient Golf Club*

Surely three of the most coveted trophies in golf: the Thursday Club Decanter, the Orthopod Plate, and the Wedge-Away Cleek.
Iain Lowe

The view from our bay window. Who could give this up?
Author's collection

The four Pepers together for Christmas: George, Scott (and Millie), Tim, Libby.
Author's collection

of us went the distance. Fred, I'm afraid, did not play like the guy who had won the 1975 U.S. Amateur, and David and I dusted him and Gordon on the 15th hole. But when Gordon suggested we play the 18th for the first round of beers, his partner rose to the occasion with a closing birdie.

Inside the clubhouse, we exchanged greetings with Arnie and his group, and of course Gordon knew all of them personally. Indeed, it turned out he'd attended grade school in Aberdeen with Alastair Johnston. "He's a Celtic [European football team] fan," said Rangers supporter Gordon as they shook hands, "but I won't hold it against him."

There was another formal dinner that evening and I had the good fortune to be seated next to the fellow who, along with Johnny Miller, is in my view golf's best TV commentator, Peter Alliss. Like Palmer, he was an honorary member of the R&A and he, too, had spoken at one of the dinners. (Professional golfers such as Palmer and Alliss may not become regular members of the R&A, but over the years the club has invited several of them into membership. The current group also includes Roberto De Vicenzo, Tony Jacklin, John Jacobs, Kel Nagle, Jack Nicklaus, Gary Player, Peter Thomson, Lee Trevino, and Tom Watson.)

We had a lovely chat (it's difficult to have anything but a lovely chat with Peter Alliss) and toward the end of the evening, after we'd each done our part to deplete the club's wine cellar, I asked him to confirm a story I'd always enjoyed.

As it goes, Alliss and Henry Cotton are doing a live broadcast of the Women's British Open at Sunningdale. This is sometime back in the 1980s, and they're sitting in one of those television production trailers where half a dozen or so screens show various views of the action.

Now, what the two of them *think* the viewers are watching is an aerial view of a short par-4.

"Lovely little hole here," says Alliss, to which the venerable three-time Open champion Cotton replies, "Yes, but it was a good deal tighter in my day."

What the viewers, in fact, are watching is a rear view of LPGA player Marlene Floyd as she bends over to mark her ball.

It all seemed just too perfect to have really happened, so having recounted my version, I asked Alliss, "Is that really true?"

He looked at me for a moment with a sly, omniscient smile. "Every word."

Meanwhile, amid all the celebration, some serious golf was in progress. Two hundred and eighty-eight players had converged to compete for the British Amateur, which began with 36 holes of qualifying on the Old and Jubilee Courses. Eighty players had gone on to the match play stage, led by Kevin McAlpine, a twenty-year-old Scot studying at Colorado State who had set a new competitive record of 62 on the Old Course, sparked by consecutive birdies on holes 2 through 8, for a 29 on the outward half. It was just the second time he'd played the golf course. (Apparently, those with sufficient talent need less time unraveling the mysteries of the old lady.) He shared the qualifying medal with England's James Heath, whose score of 63 was even more impressive, as it set a new record for the Jubilee.

Also among the qualifiers was nineteen-year-old Walker Cupper Matthew Richardson of England, fresh off victory in the prestigious Brabazon Trophy. His caddie for the week: Gordon Murray. "Yeah, a pal of mine told him I knew the course," said my ubiquitous neighbor. "I quite fancy his chances, the way he's playing."

Representing America's highest hopes was a several-time Winged Foot club champion named Andrew Svoboda. In the weeks prior to the tournament, I'd been contacted by five different friends from the States alerting me to Andrew's arrival and asking me to help him feel at home. It turned out my services weren't needed because our neighbors, Winged Footers Tim and Cindy Hultquist, had long ago decided to be in residence that week and had invited Andrew to stay with them.

Andrew arrived the weekend before the championship and Tim kindly invited me to join the two of them for a practice round on the Old Course. Andrew struck the ball beautifully, and despite it being his first round on a links he navigated the 18 holes without incident. Part of the reason was his caddie, Neil Ogston. One of the most respected veterans in the caddie corps, Oggie, as he was known to everyone, was a no-nonsense kind of guy who knew every inch of the links. He'd owned the Dunvegan Hotel for many years, was a member of the St. Andrews Golf Club, and, like Gordon, caddied largely for the exercise. His wife, Liz, worked in the shop at Kingsbarns, their son, Neil Jr., owned a couple of fish-and-chip shops in town, and one of their grandchildren, fourteen-year-old Frazer, had just won his division of the Scottish Boys Championship. They were the kind of solid citizens who made St. Andrews a fine place to live. Oggie had been hooked up with Andrew by—who else—Gordon.

Surprisingly, Gordon's own loop didn't get past round two, but Svoboda made it all the way to the semifinals. By that point he'd created quite a stir back in the States, specifically in the offices of the Metropolitan Golf Association in New York, where the person manning the Web site was a summer intern named Scott Peper, who had enlisted me as his on-site reporter. Dutifully, I took David Fay and Millie out to watch the last 9 holes of the semifinal match, which went all the way to 18, where Svoboda lost to a birdie. The fellow who beat him, one of England's top players, Lee Corfield, lost the 36-hole final match the next day to Stuart Wilson.

All four semifinalists were invited to the Championship Dinner the following evening but Svoboda had not brought a tuxedo. Moreover, his return flight was scheduled for that evening and there was a hefty rebooking penalty. Enter Gordon, who scared up a monkey suit, gave Andrew a pair of black shoes, and alerted Charles Philip, who graciously agreed to absorb the rebooking fee as part of the anniversary budget. Andrew not only attended the dinner but went, along with his guest Gordon, to a champagne reception in the R&A clubhouse.

With the Amateur completed, there remained only one major event on the 250th anniversary calendar—the International Foursomes tournament—and that was my show to run or ruin. Entries had been received from virtually every major private club in the world—

Pine Valley, Augusta National, and Shinnecock Hills led the American field, Royal Birkdale, Muirfield, and Sunningdale were among the large British contingent, and there were numerous teams from continental Europe, South Africa, and Australia.

It was a two-day Stableford event—competed in foursomes (alternate shot) over the New Course and the Old. Happily, thanks to the volunteer army of R&A members, everything went well. As the first day closed, I watched the final group play 18 on the Old Course in perfect fashion—a drive up the left-center of the fairway, an approach to about 20 feet, and a birdie putt that hit the center of the hole. As it dropped, the assembled gallery erupted into applause and the younger of the two team members leapt into the air with a shout of glee.

"You two certainly are crowd pleasers," I said, rather boldly, as they entered the scorer's hut. They were the R&A team of Peter Thomson and Prince Andrew, and they'd combined for a very respectable 32 points, 7 adrift of the Zimbali Country Club from Kwazulu, Natal, and Royal Guernsey from the Channel Island of the same name.

I was happy for them, but standing this close to His Royal Highness made me a bit nervous, because of an assignment I'd been given that afternoon. I'd been asked, actually told, that on the following evening I'd be taking the podium in the Wigwam to present prizes to the winning teams—I would announce the winners and Andrew would hand out the silver. The specific instructions were "Take a moment or two to say a few words but then get right to the presentations. It wouldn't be right to have HRH standing there too long with his hands in his pockets."

That was fine with me. Although I loved the notion of sharing the limelight with a member of the royal family, I also had a phobia about public speaking. So when the time came I kept it short, opening with the anecdote that had become my standard when giving a speech:

"I'm honored to be announcing the winners this evening, especially to such a large and distinguished group. Usually, the only scores I get to report are my own, and the only audience is my wife.

"Just last week I began to regale her with my exploits on the Old Course. 'I parred the first, bogeyed the second, birdied the third, parred the fourth and fifth, bogeyed—'

" 'Wait a minute,' " she said, 'you've got me mixed up.'

" 'Oh, sorry, dear,' I said. 'I'll start again—I parred the first, bogeyed the second—'

" 'No, that's not what I meant,' she said.

" 'Well then, what did you mean?'

" 'I meant you've got me mixed up with someone who gives a damn.' "

The winning team (Merion Golf Club) and runner-up (Royal Liverpool) serendipitously offered fodder for a bit of reflection. In 1930 those two courses, along with the Old Course, hosted three of Bobby Jones's four Grand Slam victories. When the trophies had all been distributed, Andrew and I took our seats, he at Table 1, I at Table 93.

A couple of days later, it was all over. Several thousand people boarded planes home, and the clank, clank, clank meant the dismantling of the Wigwam. I was delighted to have had a role in it all—not for what I'd contributed but for what I'd gained: a lengthy list of new names and faces—new friends. During two very busy weeks, I'd been forced into close if brief contact with more than two dozen fellows I'd never met: Walter Alexander, Peter Bairsto, Jamie Barber, Kit Blake, Peter Bucher, Alf Cattanach, George Cunningham, Peter Forster, David Goodsir, Jack Haines, Neil Henderson, Jim Hulme, Colin Kennedy, Lachlan Macintosh, Alf Mackie, Jim McArthur, John Mills, Angus Mitchell, Arthur Morris, Phillip Mould, Angus Ogilvie, Ian Sandison, Gordon Senior, Robin Singer, Ken Smith, Aubyn Stewart-Wilson, John Sullivan, Ian Syme, Eric Thain, and Doug Tully. These and others I was soon to meet were the great and good men of the R&A, and at last I was beginning to feel comfortable in their company.

25

Other Courses, Other Charms

With the celebrations concluded, Libby and I had roughly a month to catch our breath before the first of our summer visitors were due to arrive. Nearly three dozen American friends had booked bunks with us between June and September.

I took advantage of the downtime to do some reading—actually rereading—of the works of a fellow who was arguably the first great golf writer, Horace Hutchinson. In addition to being a fine player (British Amateur champion in 1886 and 1887) and a keen student of human nature, Hutchinson was an inveterate St. Andrews man. Back in 1890 he captured the magic of the place with words that still ring true:

"When two stranger golfers meet upon some neutral ground, one of the first questions that will pass from one to the other will most certainly be 'Have you been to St. Andrews?' and should the answer be in the negative the questioner will immediately deem himself justified in assuming a tone of patronage which the other will feel he has no right to resent."

I'd read those words before, but it was particularly pleasing to read them while looking out my window at the course in question. Not long afterward, I picked up a copy of *Golf Digest* that had found its way across the pond and noted with a smile that they'd begun rating the best golf courses outside the U.S. For over forty years they'd been rating America's Best 100 Courses, but never foreign ones, and back in 1979, as a way of getting *Golf Magazine* into the course-rating game, I'd started a list of the Top 100 Courses in the World. Now, twenty-five years later, *Golf Digest* had found a way to start another ranking.

I was amused also because the course that had finished at the very top of the *Golf Digest* list—a list compiled from the votes of more than eight hundred experts around the globe—was the Old Course at St. Andrews. The panelists had been sent a ballot of over a thousand courses from 184 countries and had been asked to consider several factors, among them shot values, resistance to scoring, design variety, memorability, aesthetics, conditioning, ambience, and walkability.

Maybe it was my competitive instinct resurfacing, but I was flabbergasted to see that result. Granted, the Old Course was my own favorite—and granted, also, Bobby Jones, Jack Nicklaus, and Tiger Woods had, in various ways, called it their favorite. But the best course in the world? I don't think so.

I tended to agree with my neighbor Eric Reid, who was fond of noting that "the Old Course is not the best course in the world, it's not the most beautiful, and it's not the most difficult . . . it is simply the most *famous* course in the world." In fact, a near-year in St. Andrews had led me to the view held by many of the locals, that the Old was neither the best course nor the hardest course *in town*! Those distinctions belonged, respectively, to the New and the Jubilee.

The New Course—new by St. Andrews standards at least—was designed by Old Tom Morris in 1894 at a fee of £100 per hole, paid mostly by the R&A. It was built in response to increasing demand for golf from both the locals and the growing number of visitors coming to town on the railway that had been constructed. It opened officially the day after the 1895 Open Championship when the champion, J. H.

Taylor, and twenty other competitors had a crack at it, none of them scoring better than 85.

The New lies side by side with the Old and runs more or less parallel to it, but it is more strictly a 9-out-and-9-back design with no loop in the middle as on the Old. It's also a far sterner test of accuracy than the Old, both off the tee and into the green, with thick stands of gorse tightening most of the drive zones—rather severely at holes such as the 4th and 6th—and smallish greens (there is only one shared green, at the 3rd and 15th).

Many local competitions—and all of the R&A monthly medals—are held on the New. While not as fascinating as the Old, it is also far less quirky—fewer blind shots, invisible bunkers, hidden humps and hollows; it's about as straightforward and honest as St. Andrews golf gets.

Stretched along a narrow strip of land between the New Course and the sea is the Jubilee, opened in 1897 to commemorate the Diamond Jubilee of Queen Victoria's reign—sixty years on the throne. Back then it was a 12-hole layout, but it soon expanded and has since undergone a series of renovations including a complete facelift in 1988 by golf architect and R&A member Donald Steel, who raised many of the tees and created several new green sites.

Because of its position near the sea, the Jubilee is the most exposed to the elements of any St. Andrews course and because of the thin sliver of land on which it is plotted, its fairways are the narrowest. Those factors combine with 18 artfully contoured greens to make it the consensus toughest test in town. It is also the longest, at 6,742 yards, although a set of bronze tees, used by many locals throughout the winter, cuts that by nearly a thousand yards. Believe me, on a frigid, blustery February morning, 5,800 is plenty.

When I couldn't get a tee time on the Old, I played the New, and when the New was packed, I went to the Jubilee. Of the three, it held the least appeal for me, largely because I intensely disliked one of the new holes—number 15—a short but absurdly tight par-4 to a volcano of a green that pitched away steeply at the front and sides with instant-lost-ball gorse at the back. It's the kind of hole that looms in your consciousness the entire round, especially when you're trying to make a score. On more than one occasion I'd come to that hole just a couple of strokes over par and left it foaming at the mouth. I just couldn't come up with a strategy, apart from putting the ball in my pocket and walking to the next tee. At one stage I decided to play a 5-iron off the tee, hoping that would leave me another 5-iron into the green. Trouble is, I'm rarely capable of hitting two straight and solid 5-irons in a row. My average score on number 15 was somewhere between 6 and infinity, and I don't think I ever broke 80 on the Jubilee.

When I couldn't get on the Jubilee, either I went outside town to play or I didn't play at all, despite the fact that there were three other courses within a thousand feet or so of our door—the Balgove, the Eden, and the Strathtyrum. The Balgove eliminated itself immediately on the basis of being a 9-holer for beginners. As for the Eden, it wasn't my cup of tea—too many short par-4s, stone walls, blind drives, and OB stakes, not to mention a halfhearted little water hazard in the middle of the back 9—a man-made pond on a St. Andrews links. For Pete's sake!

The Strathtyrum, built in 1993—the first new golf course in St. Andrews for almost eighty years—plays from the tips at 5,620 yards. That, in the words of R&A historian Bobby Burnet, is "insultingly short." It has only fifteen bunkers but the rough lining its fairways is typically taller than on the other courses. In a stiff wind, I found it to be an excellent place to lose golf balls. The other thing I didn't like about it was that it wandered so far away from the town—when I stood at the 13th tee, the westernmost extremity of the course, I always felt as if I'd walked halfway to Leuchars. And when you're having an off day, or playing into a headwind, the road home can be a long slog. The Eden and Strathtyrum were very popular with the locals—especially the lady and elderly players—and I was delighted for them to keep those courses to themselves.

There is one other course in St. Andrews, typically overlooked by visitors, but an absolute joy to play. The second oldest in town, it was established in 1867 and designed by Old Tom Morris on a plot of land just north of the second tee of the Old Course. A relentlessly engaging 18 holes with a par of 36 and a total distance of approximately 500 yards, it is the Ladies' Putting Course, known affectionately as the Himalayas.

There is actually a Ladies' Putting Club to go with it, founded by a group of R&A members who wanted to provide some recreation for their daughters (who in those days were relegated to archery and croquet). Back then the course was near the site of the present Rusacks Hotel, just up the street from our flat. By the turn of the twentieth century it had moved to its present location, a delightfully humpy half acre of linksland.

The club is independent of all others in town and boasts an enthusiastic membership of 217, one of whom was our neighbor Margaret Reid, who putted with grim determination in the weekly Wednesday tournaments. Men may not join, but if sponsored by a member they may become associate members. A fresh course is laid out each week, and except for a few hours a week that are member-only times, the public is welcome to play. The Himalayas averages about 50,000 rounds per year at a green fee of 70 pence ($1.25).

Some of the most enjoyable golf matches I've ever played have been on the Himalayas—both with visiting friends from America and our neighbors in St. Andrews. Invariably, such games were coed and were both preceded and followed by a cocktail or two. On a couple of occasions, we added an element of difficulty by taking Millie along and tethering her to the flagsticks. She never even sniffed at the balls, just sort of sat there until we made it clear that she was obstructing our second putts, but canny competitors knew how to make strategic use of her body and leash.

Most of the important club competitions in town are played on either the Old or New Course with occasional visits to the Jubilee. There is one exception, however: the R&A's Winter Foursomes, a relatively informal match play event that extends from October through

April, with an unusual twist—after each round, new partners are drawn out of a hat. If you and your partner win your opening round match, you split up and play with new partners in round two. If you win again, you get another new partner for round three, and so on, right to the semifinals, where if you and your partner win, you oppose each other (each of you partnering with one of the guys who'd won the other semi) in the final.

Since the members' winter schedules are difficult to align, the organizing of the matches is left rather loose—you're asked to complete your first-round match by November 1, your second by December 1, and so on. One member is designated the convenor of the match, meaning it's his responsibility to pick a time and place and ensure that everyone can make it.

I'd entered the previous winter and my partner and I had managed to squeak out a first-round victory on the 18th hole. For the second round I was pleased to see that I'd drawn Iain Donald as a partner. First of all, he was one of the few members I knew—Iain had been my solicitor (sort of a combined lawyer/real estate agent) for twenty years and I'd always liked him. Secondly, I knew him to be a fast-improving golfer. He had recently retired, had been playing lots of golf, and his 16-handicap was coming down quickly. Third, he was a big fellow—around six foot three—very fit, and intimidatingly long off the tee.

Indeed, a month or so earlier Iain had made history. At the par-4 12th hole of the Old Course, while playing in a casual game, he'd hit his tee shot 316 yards onto the green and into the cup for a hole-in-one. Since he'd had a handicap stroke on that hole, his net score was 0—4 under par on one hole!

And therein was a conundrum. A letter to the R&A members secretary began, "Iain Donald's remarkable feat at number 12 leaves us with both a problem and an opportunity. What does one call such a score? As we all know, one under par is a birdie, two under is an eagle, and three under is an albatross. But there is no term, avian or otherwise, for four under par. However, given the name of the fellow who has done the deed, it would seem there is one obvious choice. Surely any score of four under par must henceforth be called a Donald Duck."

With Iain as my partner, I figured I could play like Minnie Mouse and we'd still win. I was especially pleased to see we had drawn against a team of relatively high handicappers, an 18 and a 22. The 22 was Dr. John Mills, a delightful fellow with a waggish sense of humor. He'd been designated the convenor of the match and one morning he phoned me.

"Can you make it on December 14, George?" he asked.

"Absolutely," I said.

"Wonderful, that's all four of us set. We'll be playing the Strathtyrum."

"Uh . . . okay . . . see you on the 14th then."

I wasn't sure why any sane individual would want to play the Strath-freaking-tyrum when the Old was wide open all winter—but I had a suspicion.

That day, as John and his partner, Robin Singer, bunted merrily down the fairway, Iain and I blasted a succession of riotously wayward tee shots that cost us hole after hole. On the 16th green it was all over, 3 and 2.

An hour later, over lunch in the clubhouse, Mills looked at me, a twinkle in his eye, and said, "Now George, I bet you don't know why we played the Strathtyrum today, do you?"

"Well, yes, John, as a matter of fact, I think I do."

"No, I don't think so," he said.

"You chose it to neutralize the distance advantage that Iain and I had over you guys," I said.

"You're right," he said, "but that's not why we played the match on the Strathtyrum. We played the match on the Strathtyrum because the Himalayas wasn't available!"

Until moving to St. Andrews, I'd always thought that the city with the finest array of golf courses was New York. Four U.S. Open layouts—Winged Foot, Baltusrol, Shinnecock, and Bethpage Black—are within two hours of the Empire State Building, as are another half dozen or so courses that rank within the top 100 in America. Philadelphia, Chicago, and Columbus, Ohio, also have fine collections of courses within their extended city limits, and then there is of course Pinehurst. But if one truth had become evident to me in the time we'd been in Scotland, it was this: No city in the world can match the assembly of courses within easy reach of St. Andrews.

In addition to the six operated by the Links Trust, there is Kingsbarns, in the nearby town of the same name, where designers Mark Parsinen and Kyle Philips transformed 250 acres of farmland into a majestic seaside test that, since its opening in 2000, has ranked among the top fifty courses in the world.

Two fine layouts adjoin the St. Andrews Bay Hotel, which sits on a hill above the town. The resort's founder, Dr. Donald Panoz (founder of Mylan Laboratories and inventor of the nicotine patch), wanted two courses that would be sharply different from each other, and he got exactly that in the Devlin and the Torrance, named after designers Bruce and Sam, respectively. The Devlin is an American-style course, with a couple of ponds in play on the opening holes, major elevation changes throughout, large, sloping greens, and panoramic views of the sea and the town, while the Torrance is more linkslike, a walkers-only course whose holes wind through low-lying dunes and occasionally thick stands of fescue rough. Like Kingsbarns, these courses are twenty-first-century additions to the St. Andrews portfolio.

Dotted along the coastline to the south are four classic links, named after the towns in which they lie: Crail, Elie, Lundin, and Leven. To the other side of St. Andrews are four inland charmers—the Duke's Course, Scotscraig, Ladybank, and just across the Tay Bridge in Dundee, Downfield, where a meandering stream and hundreds of towering fir trees evoke North Carolina or Colorado more surely than Scotland.

Now, if you start with the Old, New, and Jubilee Courses in town, then add the three modern courses, the four old links, and the four parkland beauties, that's fourteen fine golf courses within half an hour of St. Andrews—a different course every day for two weeks. And if that's not enough, another half hour west is Gleneagles (with three scenic and formidable courses) and Blairgowrie, described by Old Tom Morris as "the finest inland green I have ever seen," while another half hour north are the links at Panmure, Monifieth, and mighty Carnoustie. That makes three weeks' worth of golf—twenty-one courses—within an hour's drive. Meanwhile, six of the world's most renowned links courses—Muirfield, Gullane, and North Berwick to the south, and Royal Aberdeen, Murcar, and Cruden Bay to the north—all are easily doable as day trips. Essentially, for the traveling golfer, St. Andrews is one-stop shopping, the only place you need to hang your hat.

The parade of hat hangers chez Peper began the first week in June, and brought a sudden role change for Libby and me, from know-nothing newcomers to seasoned tour guides. As I squired the men around the smorgasbord of courses, Libby took the ladies castle-hopping to Stirling, Falkland, Crathes, Banchory, and Blair, to woolen mills in Kinross, seaside lunches in Anstruther, and shopping trips to Edinburgh. At times, we felt as if we were running a bed-and-breakfast, but it was great to see familiar faces from America, and we loved showing off our new home.

It was nice knowing that friends were always heading our way, but occasionally it was the impromptu—out of nowhere—visitors who were the most fun. There was Colin Sheehan, the young American golf writer who just knocked on our door, introduced himself, and ended up sharing most of a bottle of Macallan with me. There was Israel Horovitz, a prominent American playwright who had just come from Paris where one of his works had been performed at the Comédie-Française. "Are you George Peper?" he asked me on the street. That led to a long golf conversation and, later, a round of twilight golf on the New Course with our sons. His boy, Oliver, was a film studies major at Harvard and was caddieing on the Old Course. A budding writer, he somehow managed to get an article published in the Open Championship edition of *Sports Illustrated Golf Plus*. Oliver and Scott became golf and drinking buddies for much of the summer.

And there was the early morning I was on the treadmill at the Old Course Hotel spa when an attractive woman in spandex said, "George?" It was Mary Lou Bohn, director of advertising for Titleist, in town to supervise the filming of three commercials for the NXT golf ball, starring John Cleese.

But the oddest bump-into of all came while I was playing golf. On the Old Course one Tuesday afternoon, I was putting at the 3rd hole when I looked across the double green at the group putting out at number 15. One of them was unmistakable—the monochromatic outfit, navy slacks and V-neck sweater over a white golf shirt, the jet-black hair and dark, dancing eyes. But what was he doing here?

I walked a few yards closer, just to be sure. When there was no doubt, I made my way toward his group and caught his eye.

"Seve! Welcome back to St. Andrews," I said.

"Yorsh!" he said, as surprised to see me as I'd been to see him.

Twenty-six years earlier, on the evening after the final round of the 1978 Open at St. Andrews, I'd driven to the nearby town of Strathkinness, where, in a little white shepherd's cottage, twenty-one-year-old Seve Ballesteros had stayed for the week with his agent, Ed Barner. That night I'd met him for the first time, chatted with him a bit (he could barely speak English), and learned that, beginning the following year, he'd be joining the PGA Tour. I'd stayed less than an hour but before I left Barner and I agreed on an exclusive contract for Seve to become a playing editor for *Golf Magazine*. It was an association that would span more than a decade and include all five of his major championship victories, two wins in the Open Championship at Royal Lytham, two Masters jackets, and fittingly a fist-pumping victory at St. Andrews in 1984.

"What are you doing here?" he asked.

"I live here now," I said.

With an incredulous look he asked the question I'd heard a hundred times. "All year round? How do you stand the winter?"

"Well, it ain't Spain," I said, "but it's bearable."

He rolled his eyes, bade me good luck, and we headed back to our respective groups.

Seve had had a tough couple of years, simultaneously struggling with his game, separating from his wife, and feuding with the European Tour. I later learned that he'd come to St. Andrews on a one-day-appearance gig for a wealthy American celebrating his fiftieth birthday.

One of the prime benefits of showing first-time visitors around the Old Course was the air of self-assurance it instilled in yours truly. Invariably it led to good golf. One June morning, playing with my life-long friends Ed Grant and Semo and Fran Sennas, I was so carefree that I brought Millie along, tethering her to my bag. I spent more time scooping poop than thinking about my golf, with the result that after 16 holes I was even par. Then I found my game, finishing bogey-bogey for a 74.

Still, I seemed to be rounding into form. Two days later, on a morning of constant rain, I posted fifteen pars, two bogeys, and a birdie for a 73—that made it thirty-six holes at 3 over par. I was certain now that I would hit my par-or-better goal—I'd come too close for it not to happen. In the meantime, I was experiencing the joyous thrill of repeatedly coming close.

26

Rifts and Schisms

ore than a hundred years ago, the man in charge of golf at St. Andrews, Old Tom Morris, decided that the links should be closed for play on Sundays. "The course needs a rest," he said, "even if the golfers don't."

And so it remains. On Sundays, the Old Course reverts to a public park, just as it was in 1123 when King David gave the land to the town. Families stroll up and down the 1st and final fairways, some of them spreading blankets to picnic. Kids kick soccer balls and fly kites, dogs chase after seagulls and hares, and everyone poses for photos on the Swilken Bridge.

I'd begun to look forward to early Sunday mornings. At about seven o'clock, before anyone else arrived, Millie and I would head out the door and hop the white fence, just the two of us out there in the middle of our big beautiful backyard. While Millie raced around, I'd stand there and take it all in with a sort of slow-motion pirouette— from the broad sandy beach and the rolling waves of the North Sea, up to the R&A clubhouse and the Scores, back along the row of gray townhouses to the Swilken Burn, and down across the endless, billowing links. To be there alone on a fine spring morning was to feel a serenity bordering on the spiritual.

I'd come to learn, however, that St. Andrews was something less than a garden of perpetual peace. Under the surface brewed several conflicts—conflicts that strained the relationships of friends, neighbors, and families. In every pub, club, and coffee shop in town you could find a debate—sometimes two or three—and while the specific topics varied, the overarching issue was always the same—a battle for the very soul of the town.

The 800-pound gorilla of day-to-day St. Andrews is neither the Old Course nor the Royal & Ancient Golf Club, it is the university. In recent years that gorilla had bulked up substantially, with the enrollment having more than tripled since 1980—from 2,000 to 7,000—and that expansion had brought a more than commensurate increase in complaints of all-night partying and drunken, boorish behavior. One of the off-campus residences, John Burnet Hall, was across the street from us, just outside our bedroom window, and Libby and I had been less-than-amused witnesses to a string of nocturnal revelries, including two toga parties, a naked wheelbarrow race, and an impromptu mass frolic in the burn. But in truth I rather preferred the vitality of St. Andrews during the academic year. Besides, there were major benefits—the university generated £100 million of commerce and 2,500 jobs each year.

The more critical problem was housing. The University of St. Andrews had operated for half a millennium as a residential seat of learning—all students ate and slept on campus—but that was no longer possible. An ever-higher proportion of students had been forced to rent flats and homes from absentee landlords. With a limited supply of such places, rental fees had risen sharply. I'd seen this firsthand (delightedly in fact) over the two decades we'd rented our place to students.

As a consequence, a growing number of parents of St. Andrews students had begun buying properties in the town, figuring that if they had to pay extra for housing that payment might as well be in the form of a mortgage that allowed them to build some equity. Many of them planned to keep the places as vacation/retirement homes after their children graduated.

The seaside location and the charm of the medieval town had long made St. Andrews one of the most popular holiday destinations in the U.K., with the biggest draw of all being the high-quality, low-cost golf. However, to qualify for a low-cost Links Pass one must live strictly within the municipal boundaries—anyone residing even a foot over the line not only must pay two or three times as much for the Links Pass (depending on how far away the residence) but must go on a waiting list. The list had grown to over 900 and the wait was running close to four years.

Not surprisingly, residential construction in St. Andrews had accelerated dramatically—an average of seventy-five new homes each year since 1998. That is a lot for a small town to absorb, and there had been growing pains in the form of increased traffic and insufficient parking in the town center.

Many of the longtime residents resented the way the university had begun to dominate the town. A by-product of the influx of new residents had been a shift in the town's demographics and a growing division between the incumbent middle class and the wealthier new-comers, many of them from London and the south of England. As more and more people sought summer homes in St. Andrews, the prices of those homes had gone up and up. The locals had in effect been priced out of their town with the sad consequence that their children could not afford to buy homes there. There was no small antipathy toward the carpetbaggers.

As a natural adjunct to the population growth, commercial development had expanded. Since 1983 when we'd bought our home, several buildings had popped up around the town: At the edge of the water, just a few yards behind the R&A clubhouse, came the St. Andrews Sea Life Aquarium (a tourist attraction whose location was marked for many years by a fiberglass electric-blue sailfish so enormous that Old Course caddies used it as an aiming point for their golfers from as far away as the 15th tee) and next door to it, bizarrely, the Seafood Restaurant. Along the same shoreline rose the British Golf Museum, the Links Clubhouse, and the Visitor Centre at the castle ruins. Meanwhile, on the edge of town, St. Andrews's first American-sized supermarket had arrived. The university had erected several new residence halls and classroom facilities and even the R&A had expanded, converting a home on Golf Place into offices and annexing the top floor of a building across from the 18th green for extended member dining and entertainment facilities.

Most intriguing was the abortive Gateway Centre, a three-story glass-sided hockey puck erected just in time for the 2000 Open Championship. Standing "a well-struck 7-iron from the famed Road Hole," it billed itself as the home of the St. Andrews Golfing Society, an international golf club with a $1,450 initiation fee and annual dues of $550 (corporate memberships could be had for $8,700). Trouble was, the SAGS had little to offer beyond its cavernous headquarters. No one joined, the club disbanded, and the building was sold to the ever expanding university.

Other developers had had more success. The most prominent was the St. Andrews Bay complex, a mega-resort with two courses, 200 guest rooms, an elegant spa, five restaurants, and conference facilities for 600, all just three miles outside town. In 2006 it was bought by the Fairmont Hotel chain. Meanwhile, another group had asked to develop 300 acres for a golf course and 600 residential units. That proposal was rejected but resurfaced two years later as the St. Andrews International Golf Club, a private club with a Tom Weiskopf golf course and forty luxury suites for members. Over the protest of many townspeople, it was passed by the Fife Council in March of 2004. Construction began in late 2006.

The major force in opposition to all this was the St. Andrews Preservation Trust, a nonprofit group supported by local citizens and founded with the aim of preserving the buildings, character, and history of St. Andrews and its environs. The trust's planning committee reviews all applications for new developments and attempts to influence their scale and design. Since 1995 the trust had fervently supported the creation of a green belt around St. Andrews to protect the town's character and landscape setting. Numerous meetings had been held, but nothing final had taken shape.

Libby had met a couple of ladies involved with the trust and had joined it. Meanwhile, I'd become involved with the St. Andrews Pilgrim Foundation, whose goals were much the same.

Almost unavoidably, there was an awkwardness with regard to the R&A. The exclusiveness of the club, the prominence of its clubhouse, the celebrity of its international membership, and the substantial income it derived from the Open Championship spurred a mixed reaction among the locals—pride, yes, but a bit of envy and resentment as well.

In recognition of all that the R&A has done over the past century or so to further the interests of the game and the town, all R&A members—even those residing outside the U.K.—get lifetime privileges on all the golf courses. Meanwhile the locals—even the members of golf clubs—must annually pay for their Links Passes. In fairness, fewer than ten percent of the R&A's 2,400 members play more than a dozen or so rounds per year in St. Andrews, and the R&A makes a substantial lump-sum payment to the Links Trust to cover those rounds. Still, there were a few disgruntled souls who argued peevishly that the sum didn't cover the lump.

The over-the-top generosity of the 250th anniversary celebration had done a great deal to quell such antipathy, and most of the hundred or so R&A members who lived locally got along very well with their fellow golfers in town—indeed, several were also members of the St. Andrews Golf Club and the New Golf Club—but in August and September, when the R&A took control of a huge block of tee times on the Old Course, certain members of those two clubs were less than pleased.

Thus, on occasion, when in the presence of my non-R&A-member friends I felt a bit ill at ease. I rarely mentioned being an R&A member, and although they knew I was, they rarely brought it up. In fact, I suspect most of them were neither impressed nor resentful—they didn't much care one way or the other. Nonetheless, I was sufficiently paranoid that, whenever clad in blazer and club tie and walking the two hundred yards up the road to the R&A, past the bay windows of the other two clubs, I tended to keep my eyes to the ground.

But even within the R&A there was a bit of social stratification. Many of the local members, who during most of the year enjoyed a tacit satisfaction at being at the top of the food chain, experienced a bit of a cold shoulder when certain members from the south of England arrived.

I discovered this while playing in a three-ball during my first Spring Medal, a one-round stroke-play event played in threesomes on the Old Course. My two companions were a Scottish farmer who had been a member for decades and an Englishman from London, a member for only a few years. Each of them was affable and pleasant to me, but they barely spoke to each other.

I knew the local guy a bit, so at the 8th hole, after he'd sunk a fine par-saving putt (with no "well holed" coming from our third), I pried a bit.

"Oh, he's just one of those London toffs," said the local. "There are hundreds of them in the club—more Englishmen than Scots, we have—and most of them only show up for the spring and autumn meetings when they assume this air of superiority. They hang together like a rugby scrum, never give anyone else the time of day."

I knew there had been a bit of history between the Scottish and English elements of the club, reflective of the immense rift that has always existed between the Scots and English in general. In fact, at one point in the past century, there had been quiet talk, though it was never documented, about moving the R&A headquarters to London. Most of the last hundred or so R&A captains had come from the south, most of the members of the General Committee that runs things were non-Scots, and with regard to the Club Committee—a group that oversees the day-to-day operations—someone at some point had seen the necessity to impose a caveat that at least two of the eight members be residents of the town of St. Andrews.

I had to admit that our third, who had described himself on the 1st tee as a "merchant banker" (it sounded like a job from the Magellan era but was Britspeak for stockbroker), was a bit reserved, but I'd figured that was just routine Englishness. On the inward nine, I was about to pry a bit with him when he suddenly opened up.

"So how are you enjoying life in St. Andrews?" he asked.

"It's been wonderful," I said. "My wife and I have been given a warm welcome by the Scots. I think they're sort of amused by us Americans."

"Hmm . . . well, I'm sure you're getting a much better reception than an Englishman would."

"Really?"

"Oh, yes, the Scots and English have long had a sense of mutual, shall we say, chilliness."

"I had no idea," I said, and until that day I hadn't.

"Yes, there's an old joke, you know, about the Scot who has a gun with two bullets in it. He walks into a room where there is a German, a Frenchman, and an Englishman. What does he do?"

"I don't know . . ."

"He shoots the Englishman twice."

So there Libby and I were in St. Andrews, watching it all—the university and the town, the locals and the carpetbaggers, the rich and the middle class, the developers and the preservationists, the town golfers and the R&A, the Scots and the English. Yes, serene little St. Andrews wasn't quite as serene as it seemed, and at times it made us wonder just how much we wanted to be a part of the whole scene.

27

A Matter of Trust

Contrary to popular belief, the Royal & Ancient Golf Club does not own—or manage—the Old Course. Those who labor under this misconception may be forgiven, however, because the title and stewardship of the ancient links were a matter of some dispute for more than two hundred years.

Use of the land for sport and recreation was always deemed to be the birthright of the citizenry, the first written evidence coming in 1552 when Archbishop Hamilton signed an ecclesiastical decree that confirmed the right of the St. Andrews community to play golf on their land. Old Hamilton, mind you, was not the most savory character. He was hanged in 1571 for complicity in the death of Lord Darnley, the dashing husband of Mary Queen of Scots (an occasional golfer herself).

The golf ground remained in the happy hands of the St. Andreans until the late eighteenth century when a bunch of incompetents got onto the town council and ran the place into enormous debt. In 1797 their backs were so hard against the wall that they resorted to a real estate fire sale, ceding part of the linksland to a farmer for the sum of £805, surely one of the best deals since the Dutch bought Manhattan. One of the conditions, however, was that the citizens' right to play golf be maintained, "that no hurt or damage shall be done to the golf links nor shall it be in the power of any proprietor to plough up any part of the said golf links in all time coming but the same is reserved entirely as it has been in all times past for the comfort and amusement of the inhabitants and others who shall resort thereto for that amusement."

In those days, amusement on the links included everything from archery to croquet, cricket to pony rides. Among the hardworking housewives, carpet beating and clothes washing in the burn were popular pastimes. But the big draw was golf.

Unfortunately, the chap who bought the land, a Mr. Erskine, sublet it to a family of farmers, the Dempsters, who, in complete disrespect of the golf caveat, established a sizable rabbit farm. Their game plan was to sell the fur and meat, but the rabbits did what rabbits do best, and before long the links were overrun. So flustered were the members of the R&A that they added a rule of play allowing free relief to any player whose ball had come to rest in a rabbit scrape. At one point an infuriated mob of town golfers invaded the links and shot, clubbed, and snared the rabbits wholesale, igniting a feudal feud that would rage for the better part of a century.

In 1821, one of the members of the R&A, James Cheape, took matters into his own hands and bought out the Dempsters, banishing most of the rabbits and allowing golf to be played in peace once again. By 1848, however, the town council was again in debt—this time a crippling £10,000—and so it sold an even bigger plot of the land, also to the Cheape family. The price was £5,683 and the purchase this time included the parcel of ground on which the Old Course lay (which fetched £1,805).

Things ran well enough for the next forty years or so, but by the end of the century golf had grown in popularity and the links were becoming crowded. The R&A members had become concerned about their safety, especially in the area of the High Hole (number 11) where golfers' tee shots crossed over the heads of players on the fairway of number 7. Their aspiration was to redesign the Old Course while at the same time building a new one to accommodate the increased play. In 1893 they approached the Cheapes and offered £5,000 for the land they wanted.

When the townspeople got wind of this they arose in opposition and appealed to Parliament. In the face of that protest, the R&A tactfully withdrew their offer, and an 1894 Act of Parliament put the land back in the hands of the town of St. Andrews (which by this time had gotten its fiscal act together sufficiently to make Mr. Cheape a fair offer). Thus, nearly a hundred years after losing control of the Old Course the citizens got it back.

One of the stipulations of the act was the formation of a joint green committee, comprised of two representatives from the town and five members of the R&A, charged with the operation and maintenance of the links. A few rabbit farmers, still plying their trade, were allowed to keep going as long as they curbed their cottontails—those who strayed onto the links would be deemed pests, legally slaughterable by whatever means the aggrieved golfers chose.

The Cheape family did all right, too. Among the conditions of the sale was the family's right to dig shells from pits at the mouth of the Eden Estuary. (It's unclear why this shell digging was so important to the Cheapes—possibly they had a fondness for bouillabaisse or were contemplating a craft shop offering native jewelry.) The family was also allowed playing privileges in perpetuity on the Old Course and any other courses that might in the future be built. In fact, on the Old Course they were accorded six tee times a day—three in the morning and three in the afternoon.

That was a big deal. Do the math. Six tee times per day times four golfers per tee time times 313 days a year (remember, the course was closed on Sundays). That's over 7,500 rounds per year—at today's green fees, a value of over a million dollars. Furthermore, these times gave them the right to disrupt whatever competition might have been in progress. Imagine the scenario: "Uh, Tiger, I'm afraid you and Vijay will have to wait a few moments before playing the final round of the Open Championship. Bertie and Oswald Cheape have the tee."

Happily, the Cheapes weren't keen golfers; they never used the times. However, as the game continued to expand and St. Andrews became a major tourist destination, a worry arose that if the family ever were to sell their estate—and the golf rights with it—the new owners might be less blasé. At one point a rumor circulated that a Japanese consortium was about to buy the Cheape estate solely for the sake of the starting times. In 1992, after protracted negotiation, the family ceded its playing rights in exchange for a payment of £245,000.

The 1894 Act of Parliament might still be in effect today had it not been for a reorganization of the Scottish government in the mid-1970s. The St. Andrews town council was being disbanded in favor of a larger and more distant government, and the fear among the locals was that they'd once again lose control over their golf lands, which by this time had grown to include five courses. So once again they appealed to Parliament.

The result in 1974 was another Act of Parliament, which created the St. Andrews Links Trust, a self-financing charitable body with full responsibility for managing all aspects of golf on the town's courses. The staff members of the trust report to the Links Management Committee—comprised of eight representatives from the town's golf clubs—who oversee the operation and maintenance of the courses—while the Links Trustees, an octet comprised of both golfers and government officials—make the important decisions.

Under the three decades of Links Trust management, the overall condition of the St. Andrews courses had improved immeasurably, as had most aspects of the golf operation. However, in recent years the trust had become a lightning rod for controversy, both within the town and around the world of golf. Since our arrival, major articles had appeared in golf publications—*Bunkered* in the U.K. and *Golfweek* in the U.S.—taking the trust to task.

The central issue was that the trust had exceeded the prerogatives given to it by Parliament, had become too big and powerful, that the nonprofit entity was generating too much income and spending its money without sufficient advice and consent from the populace.

In the five years between 1998 and 2003 the trust's general and administrative budget had doubled, reaching nearly £1 million. Granted, both before and during that time they'd made some major improvements to the golf landscape, most prominently the Links Clubhouse, which serviced the New and Jubilee Courses, a place—at long last—for visiting golfers to park their cars and change their shoes. But the more strident of the locals claimed the building was bigger than it needed to be, that its services were of questionable legitimacy, notably a pro shop and dining room that competed with local merchants, and that it was rented out for weddings, private parties, and functions having nothing to do with golf.

The protests had grown louder and wider when the trust announced that it planned to spend several million dollars to build a seventh golf course, just outside town, to keep up with what it claimed was unmet demand by local and traveling golfers. Opponents countered that the current courses, apart from the Old, weren't overcrowded, that in any case there were a dozen other fine courses within easy reach, and that the trust was simply looking for ways to spend its fortune and build its empire.

However, the move that brought protest from all corners was the exclusive arrangement the Links Trust made with one of the major golf tour operators—the Keith Prowse Agency, owners of the Old Course Experience—a deal that allowed Prowse to purchase 800 tee times—3,200 rounds—a year on the Old Course and resell them for whatever price they wanted. Prowse packaged these rounds with ground transportation, vouchers for meals and merchandise in the Links Clubhouse, an additional round of golf on one of the other courses, and rooms for two or three nights at the best hotels in town. When the à la carte costs of all the other goodies were extracted, the amount remaining—effectively the charge for one round of golf on the Old Course—was a shocking $1,800 (assuming three nights in season at the Old Course Hotel).

In fairness, only about ten percent of the people who play the Old Course pay this kind of money (and they are people who have chosen to do so). Other visitors—about a quarter of the play on the Old—pay the £120 in-season fee, while the lion's share of rounds comes from the locals using their Links Passes, the best deal in golf. Indeed, it should be remembered that with so many local residents paying so little, the upkeep of the courses needs to be financed in some way. The widespread feeling, however, was that the solution was not to allow a situation wherein one round of golf—for one person—costs $1,800, nearly four times the fee at Pebble Beach.

Among the local merchants there were additional repercussions in that the Prowse packages included only a limited number of hotels and the vouchers for food and merchandise induced visitors to spend their money in the Links Trust's own facilities rather than in the town. There was also resentment that the Links Trust had called itself the only purveyor of "official" St. Andrews merchandise.

"My store has been around here for over one hundred years, which is a hell of a lot longer than the Links Trust," said Bob Millar, owner of Auchterlonies golf store, in the *Golfweek* article. "Where do they come off saying they're the only ones with official merchandise?"

Golf tour operators also felt the pinch, either being unable to offer customers a sufficient number of advance tee times, or having to buy such times from Prowse (at a premium) in years when Prowse was unable to sell its full allotment to consumers.

Among the most vocal locals, however, was a fellow with no particular axe to grind, my neighbor Gordon. The article in *Bunkered* magazine was presented as a face-off on the subject of the seventh course, asking whether it was needed. The yes answer was written by the managing director of the Links Trust, Alan McGregor, and the no came from "St. Andrews resident Gordon Murray," the range of whose discontent extended beyond that of the local merchants to more practical golfer concerns such as pin sheets not being ready for the early tee times, illegible yardage markers, the absence of refreshment facilities at the turn until after 9:00 A.M., and ineffectiveness of marshals in improving the pace of play. He also wondered how the Links Trust could charge visitors as much as they intended to during the coming winter (£55) when most of the bunkers on the Old Course would be out of play, being refurbished in preparation for the Open Championship. Gordon's feeling was that the trust had taken its eye off the ball, that in the course of exploring questionable expansion ventures it had abrogated its central responsibility to provide world-class facilities to all.

The trust did not appreciate Gordon's take on things. First of all, as a part-time caddie, he was expected to be part of the team. At one point, in fact, they intimated to him that his further services might not be required. But the Old Course caddies do not work for the trust, they are independent agents—a point that the trust emphasized in 2004 when they began charging the lads £5 for every 18 looped, another bone of contention.

But as the trust saw it, Gordon did have an axe to grind. Since he often made the floor below his flat available to visiting golfers, they saw him as another disgruntled tour operator, and they closely monitored his bookings of the Old Course, suspicious that he was leveraging his local-resident privileges to secure tee times for his boarders, thereby depriving other locals of games, a no-no in the St. Andrews scheme.

Gordon did occasionally use his local times in that way, but he claimed that he was not alone. In truth, many of the locals had benefited at one time or another from their ability to get friends and associates onto the big ballpark, whether the return gift was a bottle of wine or a business contract.

The Keith Prowse issue would come to international attention when *Golf Digest* published a five-thousand-word piece entitled "A Scalping at St. Andrews." It condemned the $1,800 green fee and beseeched the Links Trust not to renew the deal when the contract comes up. They calculated that the Prowse deal brought the trust roughly a million dollars in revenue and that the trust could recover that money simply by charging a $91 fee for each of the 11,000 rounds that were pre-booked each year.

That made a lot of sense to me. In fact, I'd been thinking along the same lines for months, although I'd spread out the burden across the board. I'd thought of it as my $25 plan: 1) Charge the locals $25 more for their yearly Links Pass. This, I realized, was a suicidal suggestion among my fellow townsmen, who viewed golf as their birthright. 2) Raise the Old Course green fee $25 (it would still be lower than Kingsbarns). 3) Add a $25—instead of *Golf Digest*'s $91— pre-booking fee.

I hope the Links Trust sees a way to do something like this. I know they do good work, I appreciate the fine condition of the golf courses, and contrary to Gordon, I have no problem with the services (sure, play on the Old Course could move faster in the summer, but hey, there are worse places to be stuck—besides, slow in St. Andrews means four and a half hours, not five to six hours as in the States).

My view comes more from a sadness, a sadness that in this town where Everyman has traditionally been king, where everyone has had equal access, where for five hundred years no one paid a cent to play golf, and where, as recently as 1970, the visitor's green fee was less than a pound, that anyone at any time for any reason should pay a fee of $1,800. That is a shameful situation, and for the sake of St. Andrews's good name, it needs to stop.

28

Did It—with Sir Michael!

In the town of St. Andrews there is no more highly regarded figure than Sir Michael Bonallack. The finest amateur golfer of his time—and a rare example of an outstanding player who remained an amateur all his life—he won five British Amateur Championships, five English Amateur Championships, and four English Stroke Play titles, and played on nine Walker Cup teams, captaining the 1971 squad that defeated America for the first time in thirty-three years. He was also the low amateur in two Open Championships, finishing in eleventh place in 1959.

From 1984 to 1999 he was secretary of the R&A and upon his retirement he was named captain. He also served as chairman of the PGA of Great Britain and Ireland, chairman of the British Golf Foundation, president of the English Golf Union, a director of the European PGA Tour, and chairman of the World Golf Rankings. In 1971 he received an OBE for his services to the game, in 1998 he was knighted by the Queen, and in 2000 he was elected to the World Golf Hall of Fame. Other than that, he didn't accomplish much.

I'd had the privilege of knowing him for twenty years, although our friendship had been based largely on brief hellos, usually at the Masters or Open Championship. In 1999 I'd drafted Michael onto a panel to help select the 500 World's Best Golf Holes for a book *Golf Magazine* was publishing, and that summer, during the Open Championship at Carnoustie, he'd met with me and half a dozen others to hammer out the final list.

Since moving to St. Andrews, I'd bumped into him once or twice at the R&A, and at a couple of parties Libby and I had chatted with him and his wife, Angela, whose accomplishments as a golfer were almost as impressive as her husband's—a two-time English ladies champion, member of six Curtis Cup teams, and winner of the national amateur titles of Sweden, Germany, and Portugal. In contrast to Michael, who is soft-spoken and rather shy, Angela is one of the most outgoing and engaging people in the world, always working to make people feel comfortable. She and I had an instant bond—each of us had had a double hip replacement—but it was Libby who interested her.

"Now, you two are members of the Duke's Course, aren't you?" she said.

"Yes," I said, "but I'm afraid we haven't been there yet."

"Oh, I know you haven't," she said. "You see, I'm the lady captain of the Duke's. But we're going to take care of that. Libby, I know you're not a keen golfer, but we're going to take care of that, too. Next week we're having a special golf clinic and luncheon for lady beginners, and you will be coming as my guest."

One does not say no to Lady Angela, and so, despite huge apprehensions, Libby had dusted off her Callaways and headed to the Duke's. I was nervous, too. More than anything, I'd wanted her to love St. Andrews as much as I did, and to me, that meant getting into golf the way so many of the women had. I knew I couldn't be the one to make that happen—there were just too many issues in husband-wife golf, mostly the fact that she knew how desperately I wanted her to play well and get hooked, and that pressure was just too much. So I hoped Angela would be the answer.

I was sitting at the computer late that afternoon when Libby returned.

"I played golf, and I won!" she said.

"Ohmygod, you're kidding," I said. "I want to know all about it."

"Well, I played nine holes, I was terrible, then we went in for lunch and I won third prize in the raffle."

"Oh . . ."

The good news was that she'd played a few holes with Angela, who had given her plenty of encouragement. In return Libby had promised to take a series of golf lessons. There was hope.

Ironically, Libby had played golf with Angela, but I had not played with Michael. Angela, however, had taken me aside at a party and said, "You must invite Michael out for a game. Now that he's retired, he barely plays anymore—just walks the dogs on the West Sands—and he can't bring himself to call people up and arrange games. You must do it."

That was not going to happen. In a shyness-about-calling-people contest, I could give anyone a run. Too bad, too, because as intimidated as I was by the notion of playing with Sir Michael Bonallack, I was curious about how his game had held up. He was listed as a 4-handicap, and I figured he played to it. I'd asked him whether he'd shot his age (sixty-nine) yet and he'd said no, adding with typical modesty that he expected Angela, the same age, to do the deed before he would. In any case, I figured that unless Michael and I drew each other in some sort of R&A competition, I would never play with him.

Enter Gordon Murray. One of his summer lodgers was a delightful Portuguese fellow named Pedro Dos Santos, who was the general manager of the Ritz-Carlton Club in Chicago. Years ago, Pedro had somehow become friends with Sir Michael (probably through Gordon), Gordon now was hoping to put the two of them together for a game on the Old Course, and would I be interested.

"Sure," I said. "Will you call Michael though?"

"Sure," said Gordon, "I know Michael well." Of course he did; Gordon knew everyone. "I'll also get him to put us in for the ballot.

Not that I distrust my good friends at the Links Trust, mind you, but I suspect that if they see Sir Michael as the lead name we'll have a better chance at getting a time."

So there we were at 10:30 A.M. on the first tee of the Old Course, the international four-ball of Gordon, Pedro, Michael, and George, with me feeling more nervous than at any time since my opening round when I'd skied a tee shot of thirty paces.

Pleasantries were exchanged, including a bit of light banter between Michael and Pedro's caddie, Andy Christie.

"It's nice to go round with a good golfer for a change," said Andy, a veteran who had traversed the links a few thousand times. "How are you, Sir Michael?"

"I'm well, Andy, and you?"

"Just fine—quite a bit better than I was during the Town Match."

Each September, the members of the R&A take on the golfers from the rest of St. Andrews in a day-long competition that involves about two hundred matches on the Old and New Courses. It turned out Sir Michael and Andy (handicap 8) had drawn each other a year earlier, with the R&A side emerging victorious.

"Aye," said Andy, a twinkle in his eye, "he's a clever lad, Sir Michael—waited until I was eighty to take me on!"

It was Gordon, of course, who organized our match. "Let's see, I'm a 13; Michael, you're a 4; George, 7; and Pedro, 16—looks like it should be George and I against you two." At that moment, the voice of the starter came over the speaker: "Ten-thirty game, play away, please, gentlemen." Gordon flipped a golf tee into the air and it hit the ground pointing to me. Our team was up and I was batting.

And thank goodness for that. Generally speaking, on the 1st tee of a golf course, the more time I have to think about my drive, the less likely I am to hit it squarely—and on the Old Course that's doubly true.

Steeling myself to swing as slowly as possible and stay behind the ball, I made unconsciously good contact and sent a bullet down the left-center of the fairway, well over 250 yards. I'd barely heaved my sigh of relief when Sir Michael said, "Do you hit them all like that, George?"

In truth, I'd been playing fairly often, and I was just about at the peak of my game, particularly with the driver. I'd also reached a comfort level on the Old Course that had instilled in me a kind of mystical confidence. Still, I was glad to have that tee shot over, and very appreciative of Sir Michael's comment. It told me I didn't have to worry about proving anything to him.

Everyone else got off the tee nicely as well, Michael's compactly efficient swing producing a low burner dead down the middle. For a big man—over six feet and over 200 pounds—he wasn't a long hitter, but he surely knew how to put the clubface on the ball. On this day, he would not miss more than one fairway and two or three greens.

Neither, as it turned out, would I. After a routine par at the 1st I made my worst mistake on number 2 when my approach found a bunker and I fatted the explosion shot, leaving it in the sand for a double-bogey. But birdies at the 3rd and the par-5 5th, where a big drive allowed me to reach the green with a 6-iron, got me back to even par. A bunker off the tee cost me a bogey at 6, but I drove the par-4 9th and 2-putted for birdie. Out in 36, even par.

Gordon had played well also—our better-ball score for the front was 2 under par gross, 7 under net—and we were 1 down! Michael and Pedro, after going 1 down through the first five holes, had played the 6th through 9th in 3-3-2-3. After tapping in for my birdie on 9, I thought we'd halved the front side, but I should have known better as Michael stepped up to his 25-footer for birdie. Bending into the wide, severely crouched stance that was his trademark, he took a couple of steely-eyed looks at the hole and then stroked his ball straight into the center for a tying birdie and the first leg of our one-pound Nassau. Gordon and I looked at each other and shook our heads, joining a half century of Bonallack victims.

The inward 9 went much the same way. Michael birdied 10, but I made the first 2 of my life at 11 to get us back, and thereafter we settled into a string of halved holes. I was playing remarkably error-free golf—strong drives into the fairways and wedge approaches to the greens of holes 12 through 16. But Sir Michael was playing very tidily as well—sneaky long drives and softly penetrating iron shots that plopped onto the greens. He was 1 or 2 over par—and Gordon and I were still 1 down on the match—as we came to the 17th.

We should have won that hole, but I choked. The flagstick was located behind the gaping Road Bunker, and I yanked my 4-iron approach so that I was left with a very difficult flop shot over the pit to the pin. Happily, there was some cushioning grass beneath the ball and my brief but blessed imitation of Phil Mickelson left the ball 4 feet from the pin. Everyone else had bogeyed the hole, so I needed that putt for a par to square the match. It never touched the hole. When we made four pars at the 18th, the match was over and the team of Bonallack and Dos Santos had won, 1 up.

I don't think I've ever been so deliriously happy after a loss. The reason is that in the midst of this pitched battle, something else had happened. When my 3-foot putt for par hit the hole on 18, I'd posted a 36 on the inward half for a total of 72. I'd done it—shot 72 on the Old Course! Four birdies, two bogeys, a double, and eleven pars—and one of the witnesses had been Sir Michael Bonallack.

When we shook hands on the final green he said, "George, that was a very well played round of golf." No sweeter words had ever touched my ears.

29

Nice Measurements

When George Bernard Shaw said Britain and America were two nations separated by a common language, he was just scratching the surface. I'd found the height of transatlantic lunacy to be evidenced not in spoken words but printed numbers—specifically, in measurements. Consider the evidence.

Time: The Brits have a perverse love of the twenty-four-hour clock. I can only assume this has something to do with their unfortunate northern location. In the dead of winter, when the sky begins to blacken in mid-afternoon, it's vaguely comforting to think of the hour as 15:30 instead of 3:30.

Date Notation: Christmas Day in the U.S. is written 12/25. In the U.K. it's 25/12. Truth be told, their way is more logical—but despite a year of practice I'd been unable to catch on, as evidenced by a burgeoning collection of hilariously misdated bank checks.

Weight: We Americans measure weight in pounds—the Brits measure prices in pounds (all too many of them) and they can't seem to decide how to measure weight—in pounds, kilograms, or stone.

My weight the day before I came to Scotland was 185 and the next day was 185, 84, and 13.2.

Motoring: The idiocy is not that they drive on the left side, or that their stoplights change from red to yellow before going green. No, the real question is why they enforce speed limits through an Orwellian network of roadside cameras—and why my dusty little Honda hatchback had proved to be one of the most photogenic cars in Great Britain.

Petrol: Standard unleaded gas is dispensed not in gallons but liters. In one sense, that's a blessing as it makes it damnably difficult for an American to calculate how much he's Shelling out. Out of masochism, I did, and the answer came to just under $7—and that's for the cheap stuff.

Electricity: I've never been too smart about watts and amps and such—I can barely put the batteries in a flashlight. All I knew when I arrived in the U.K. was that those nifty little three-pronged adapter plugs had always done the trick with my computer. Then I tried one on one of our standing lamps from the States and nearly blew up the house. American TVs don't work in Britain, either—something about lines of resolution that can't be resolved.

But I'd come to live with and even embrace all this British eccentricity. In fact, there was only one system of measurement that I couldn't abide—the standardized stupidity they refer to as their "golf handicap scheme."

It's administered by something called CONGU, which, if it didn't stand for Council of National Golf Unions, would be short for Confusion Guaranteed.

Since arriving, I'd done a little experiment, tracking my handicap simultaneously according to the CONGU system and the USGA method. The result: two handicaps that were *seven strokes apart.* Let me explain—or at least try.

In the USGA system golfers are expected to post a score for every round they play. The course rating is subtracted from the score to get a differential. The ten lowest of the twenty most recent differentials are averaged, and then (for a mysterious reason the USGA has never adequately explained) that average is multiplied by 96 percent to get a decimal number known as the Handicap Index. (When I arrived in St. Andrews I had a USGA Handicap Index of 6.5.)

In Scotland, I'd been fortunate to play most of my golf on the Old Course, where, as I've said, I'd begun to learn how to navigate without major disasters. The Old Course had a rating of 71.2, which in my mind was generous, especially during the winter months when the tees were moved up and the course played at about 6,300 yards. So it was no surprise that nine of those ten lowest rounds used to compute my handicap had come from the Old and that the resulting index was 4.3.

I could never have returned to America with that handicap—neither my ego nor my wallet could have stood the beating. Happily, though, I didn't have to, because my official handicap had become a matter for CONGU.

In the CONGU scheme handicaps are established only in competitions, and those competitions don't occur very often—in the typical club, just once or twice a month. This is partly because the Brits love match play and hate slow play. In their matches, once the hole has been won, lost, or tied, everyone picks up and heads for the next tee (instead of grinding out their 3-footers for scores, as many Americans do).

So there are the monthly medals. Only three scores are needed to establish a handicap that is the average of the three differentials (the scores made minus the course ratings). It's actually a bit more complicated—involving something called a Competition Scratch Score—but the main point is that it takes just three scores. Also, there's no "slope system" as the USGA has, to allow you more or fewer strokes for harder or easier courses—if you're a 12, you're a 12 from the tips at Carnoustie and a 12 from the fronts at Pittypat Heath.

Now, because it's all but impossible to commandeer a block of starting times on the Old Course, the monthly medals in St. Andrews are played on the New Course, which for me plays about four strokes harder than the Old. It's the same length but its par is 71 and its course rating is 71.9. That's point number one.

Point number two is that I'm a congenital choker. In my first medal, shaking with terror for most of the round, I shot 88. The next month I did battle with a couple of gorse bushes and came in with an 85, and the third time I managed a 79. The average of those three was 84. After subtracting the Competition Scratch Score ratings for the three days (which averaged 73) I had a CONGU handicap of 11. If I had tried to return to America with that handicap, I would have been stopped at the border and arraigned on charges of international sandbagging.

But that 11 wasn't my actual handicap—it was just the handicap from my experiment, the handicap I would have had if I'd alighted from an alien spaceship and tried to establish one from scratch. The reality was, I was allowed—indeed, required—to start out with my imported 6.5 and go from there. But after those three undistinguished scores, my Handicap Index went up only two tenths of a stroke, to 6.7, over the course of three months. That's the way CONGU works— you can go up only a tenth of a stroke each month. (You can go down a few tenths of a stroke, but only if you shoot the lights out.) What's more, there's a buffer zone—ranging from one stroke for the lowest handicappers up to five strokes for the highest—and if your score falls within that zone you don't move at all. It can thus take years to see your handicap budge as much as one stroke.

So the bottom line was, my handicap had gone down 2.2 USGA strokes while simultaneously going up .2 CONGU strokes. Which system did I like? Neither.

30

Victoria's Vase

n September of 1886, Daniel Shaw Stewart became the
129th Captain of the Royal & Ancient Golf Club. His term
of office the following year was an event of no significance except that
it coincided with the fiftieth anniversary of Queen Victoria's ascension to the throne. (Victoria, a sturdy old gal, sat for sixty-three years,
longer than any British royal, although Elizabeth II—fifty-five years
and counting—is giving her a nice run for her monarchy.) Mr. Stewart, having a fine sense of history, offered to commemorate the anniversary by presenting a silver cup to be played for annually. The club
accepted his gift and so was born the Queen Victoria Jubilee Vase, a
single-elimination match play tournament contested among the
members of the R&A.

The Vase (pronounced voz and only voz) takes place during
the second week of a three-week period in September when nearly
five hundred R&A members converge for the Autumn Meeting. The
first week is devoted to the Calcutta Cup, another single-elimination
match play event, but for foursomes (two-man teams playing alternate

shot). The third week is the Autumn Medal—one round of stroke play on the Old Course (it takes four days for everyone to get off the tee).

Although I'd been a member for seventeen years, I'd never entered either of the match play competitions and had played in only one medal. While I was living in the U.S. it was just too big—and uncertain—a time commitment. Potentially, the Cup or the Vase could go on all week—the opening round matches were on Monday and the final—seven matches later—was on Saturday. Of course, there wasn't much chance of my getting to the final. Far more likely was the probability of my losing in one of the first three rounds, meaning I'd be golf-idle the rest of the week. Also, the whole notion of an extended mingle with the lords and gentlemen had always intimidated the hell out of me.

Now, however, I had a couple of things going for me. Number one, to get to the golf course I didn't need to cross the Atlantic, just the street. Number two, I'd met enough of the R&A members to feel at least vaguely comfortable among them. Truth was, I kind of liked them. So I entered all three events.

My partner in the Calcutta was to be an old golf writing colleague, Malcolm Campbell. A 5-handicapper from nearby Lower Largo, Malcolm had been editor of Britain's *Golf Monthly* when I was at *Golf Magazine*. He'd also been editor of the *St. Andrews Citizen* as well as a couple of smaller publications. He was fond of saying, "I'm the ex-editor of so many things, you can just call me Malcolm X." We'd played a few times together, our games seemed to fit together well, and we both had sarcastic senses of humor that I figured would serve us nicely. I also knew Malcolm was one of the best match players in the club—he'd been runner-up in the Calcutta Cup once and in the Jubilee Vase twice, on one occasion losing at the final hole to Sean Connery.

Then I realized the Calcutta Cup was the first week of September. There was no way I could be in St. Andrews that week—that was when Scott headed to Princeton.

It turned out to be one of the greatest breaks Malcolm Campbell ever got—after I canceled, he called K. C. Choo, a 3-handicapper from British Columbia, and they went all the way. It was sweet justice for Malcolm, not only because he'd come close so often but because another golf writer, the great Bernard Darwin, had won the Cup precisely seventy years earlier.

Truthfully, any regrets I had about missing the Calcutta Cup were tempered by a relief at not having to compete on the New Course— the New and I still hadn't quite made friends. I was able to make it back for the Vase, however, and the venue for the Vase was the Old Course, where my year of study had brought me to a game plan that seemed to be working.

Over the first four holes, I just tried to stay out of trouble—keep it left off the tee, take extra care with the planning of the approach shots, and work hard to save four par-4s. Over the next eight holes—except for nasty little number 11—I took a more aggressive tack, basically trying to get as close to the par-4 greens as possible (hoping to drive at least one or two of them) and expecting to reach the short par-5 5th in 2 (assuming the wind was benign and the tees weren't back). I'd come to feel that any day I didn't cover that soft midsection of the course in par or better, I'd screwed up. Then, on the finishing stretch, I returned to damage control, keeping the tee shots safely left (except at 17, where for some reason I'd become comfortable taking an aggressive line to the right, biting off a big chunk of hotel property).

Like any game plan, it fell apart now and then, and I still hadn't learned how not to fall apart with it. But when it worked, it worked well. During July and August, I'd played the best sustained golf of my life—my eight most recent rounds on the Old Course had been 74-73-73-81-72-73-72-73. Throw out the 81 and I was a scratch—and yet according to the blessedly sluggish CONGU handicap system I remained a 7. Sure, the chance of my winning the Jubilee Vase was one in 256, but as the R&A Autumn Meeting approached, I was optimistic. In the words of captain Ben Crenshaw on the eve of the final round of the 1999 Ryder Cup (when his team was behind 10 to 6 with 12 points to be played for in the singles on Sunday), I had "a good feeling about this."

And an unaccustomed feeling it was. I almost never have positive vibes on the eve of golf competitions, probably because I have a long history of catastrophic collapse. But this time I was imbued with a serene confidence—the stars just seemed aligned.

The only aspect that gave me pause was the schedule—a potential 144 holes of golf in six days—18 holes each on Monday, Tuesday, and Wednesday, 36 holes each on Thursday and Friday, and the 18-final on Saturday. My wimpy constitution wasn't used to that much walking and lifting. On the other hand, there was some encouragement in the certainty that roughly 200 of the 256 guys in the field were either older, fatter, or frailer than I was. Nonetheless, on the morning of my opening match I packed light, loading my Ping Moon Bag with fourteen clubs, one glove, a dozen tees, and four balls.

My opening-round opponent was Richard Rose, a companionable 9-handicapper from Toronto who seemed much less nervous on the 1st tee than I was.

"I've never played in this before," I said as we walked down the 1st fairway, "have you?"

"Oh yes, I wouldn't miss it—this is, I think, my seventh time. We have a big group from the Toronto Golf Club who come every year—at least a dozen of us are here this year. I really enjoy the competition."

"Have you had much success?" I asked (and I shouldn't have).

"Yeah, last year I won five matches, made it to the quarterfinals."

Clearly, I was going to have my hands full. We played fairly evenly until I birdied the 5th and then the 7th to go 2 up. At the 9th tee, feeling confident, and in the heart of my aggressive stretch of the course, I took a big swing and pushed the shot so dramatically it missed not only our fairway but the adjacent 10th fairway and embedded in a patch of impenetrable gorse. I figured the hole was likely over, but since match play is unpredictable, I teed up a second ball, knowing that if I could hit it onto the green I might still save par. This time I swung even harder—and duck-hooked it into the gorse on the left.

The two shots didn't really fluster me, nor did the act of conceding the hole on the tee of the easiest par-4 on the course. What flustered me was the fact that, in the space of two minutes, I'd used up half of my ammunition quota. I now had only two balls in the bag, and there was plenty more gorse to hurdle on the way home, beginning with a sizable patch on the very next hole. What a jerk I'd been to bring only four balls!

I thought immediately of Tiger Woods at the 2000 U.S. Open. Leading by a record 11 strokes after 53 holes, he'd stood up at the 18th at Pebble Beach and yanked his tee shot into the Pacific (uttering a very audible obscenity for which he was later fined). At that point his caddie, Steve Williams, handed him another ball and said, "Tiger, let's cut our losses—hit the 2-iron."

"No, Stevie," said Tiger, "I'm gonna rip one down the middle, get home in 2, and make no worse than a 6."

"Tiger, I really like a nice stinger 2-iron here," said Williams.

"No way—just give me the driver."

Tiger did rip it down the middle, did make birdie on the second ball, and of course went on to win that Open by a record 15 strokes. A couple of weeks later he and Williams were at another tournament. Walking down one of the fairways, Williams said to him, "Remember when I wanted you to hit the 2-iron on 18 at Pebble?"

"Yeah," said Tiger, "I've been meaning to ask you what that was all about."

"Well, now I can tell you," said Williams. "Tiger, if you had hit another ball into the water, we would have been out of pellets."

Woods, sitting on an 11-stroke lead, would have had to withdraw from the tournament—or so Williams thought—because of the pro tour's one-ball requirement (you must finish the round with the same make and model of ball you used to tee off). The truth is, had he pumped another ball into the Pacific, he could have borrowed a ball of any make—from a fellow competitor, a spectator, anyone—played the final hole, and incurred only a 1-stroke penalty for breaking the one-ball rule. Although it was Williams's fault for not knowing they were fully equipped on the 1st tee, there were extenuating circumstances. The prior evening, Tiger had gone to the practice green, taking a wedge, a putter, and a few balls from his bag. As always, he'd attracted a crowd and when he was finished practicing he tossed the balls to kids in the gallery.

Now, not being Tiger Woods, and having a lead of one hole rather than 11 strokes, and having a very hazy familiarity with the Rules of Golf, I stood up to my tee shot at number 10 with something less than buoyancy. All I could think of was, "If you hit this in the gorse, you're down to one ball." Somehow I necked it into findable territory, but I knew I had a problem that wasn't going away.

My opponent, of course, had no idea of my plight, and I didn't want him to find out, although I suspect he was befuddled when, instead of walking down the fairway to my tee shot, I worked my way up the left rough, threshing my club desperately through the fescue. Blessedly, amateurs aren't forced to observe the one-make-of-ball rule as the tour pros are, so all I needed was something round—any brand or color would do.

As Richard was playing his approach to the 10th, I hot-footed over to the 11th tee and explained my situation to the two fellows playing the match ahead of ours. "Is it within the rules for me to buy golf balls from you guys?" I said.

"Sure," said one of them, "but you don't have to buy them. Here," he said, handing me a three-pack of Maxfli Noodles. "If you lose them, you can buy me a drink, otherwise just return them."

The comforting knowledge that I had four balls in reserve was enough to restore some fluidity to my swing, and Richard and I halved the next five holes. He was playing well—we both were a few strokes over par, but at 15 he bogeyed to my par, and when the same thing happened on 16 the match was over, 3 and 2.

My opponent the next day turned out to be the fellow who had so kindly lent me the golf balls. Roderick Hutchison, a Brit who had expatriated to France, was a few years older than I and had a handicap that was a few strokes higher, but he'd been so kind to me the day before that I felt one down to him before we ever teed off.

It must be said, however, that Rod was at a major disadvantage inasmuch as his selection of fourteen clubs did not include anything longer than a 3-iron. As a result, he would be ceding a seventy-five-yard disadvantage off the tee of all but the two par-3s. I got off to a good start, he did not, and after three holes I was 3 up. We remained that way for the next three.

At the 7th I had two putts from twenty feet for another win, but as I was addressing the first of them I had some bad luck.

"Did you see that?" I said. "My ball just moved." Rod hadn't seen it, but that didn't matter. My ball clearly had shifted a quarter turn or so toward the hole, and I was in violation of the rules. I picked it up. "Your hole," I said.

I was now only 2 holes up, but my gesture had given me an inner-peace-through-self-righteousness that carried me to another 3-and-2 win.

On Wednesday morning I came up against another Canadian, Douglas Leith of Ontario, and unbelievably, for the third day in a row, there was a rules issue involving a golf ball. At the 3rd hole, Doug had pulled his approach some eighty feet left of the pin—he was actually closer to the flagstick location at number 15 than at the 3rd. I'd pulled my shot, too, but not as badly, perhaps 30 feet beyond the flag. Doug had a couple of major humps and hollows to negotiate and his approach putt veered viciously off the wrong side of one of them with the result that it careened smack into my ball.

I wasn't sure of the rule, but he seemed to be. "That's your hole," he said with disgust. It put him 2 down, and he never recovered, allowing me a 6-and-5 win. In the clubhouse later I learned that Doug had been wrong—whereas in stroke play there's a penalty, there is no penalty in match play when one ball struck from the putting green hits another ball that is also on the green. I felt retroactively guilty for not having been able to correct him. On the other hand, I doubt it would have affected the outcome of the match.

So I'd made it through three matches, had four to go. The starting field of 256 was now down to thirty-two, but the opponents were getting tougher. On Thursday morning I faced yet another Canadian, Jack McDonald from British Columbia. The good news was that for the first time I was getting handicap strokes rather than giving them. The bad news was that Jack was a scratch player and according to one of the guys he'd vanquished he was playing to it.

He was close to scratch against me as well, but on that morning I played some of my best golf. It was windier than on the first three days and at the par-5 5th hole after a good drive I still had a shot of well over 200 yards to the pin, which was on the extreme right side of the green. It was the perfect situation for a shot I'd been getting away with all summer, a driver off the deck, and the moment club met ball I knew the result would be good. The ball shot out low and toward the left side of the green with a gentle fade. I could only see the first bounce, a nice jump to the right. When we got to the green there it was, 5 feet from the hole. With a handicap stroke, I was lying net 1 and didn't need to putt it. That put me 1 up.

We battled closely for the next 9 holes, but somewhat uncharacteristically, I managed to make every short putt I faced and that kept me ahead. For the third time in four matches it ended at the 16th, 3 and 2.

In the clubhouse locker room, I ran into Malcolm Campbell and another golf writer friend, Colin Callander, who had been Malcolm's successor at *Golf Monthly*. I knew that each of them had won his first three matches.

"Well," said Colin, "are we three has-been editors now also three has-been Vase competitors as well or are you still alive?"

"Alive for the moment," I said, "but oh do my legs ache, and I have to go back out there this afternoon."

"Oh, stop your complaining," said Malcolm. "We both got

thrashed this morning so we have nothing to do now but drown our sorrows at lunch."

"That actually sounds delightful," I said. "It's supposed to be wet and cold out there this afternoon and I'm the last match off. I think I'm going to go home and have a hot bath."

The weather was indeed worsening, and my next match was not due to head out until 3:20. If it went the distance, we'd be racing darkness. Eric and Margaret Reid had invited us to a cocktail party that evening—there was no chance I was going to make that before 7:30.

"So you'll get there when you get there," said Libby as I stumbled through the kitchen, shucking layers of clothing en route to the tub. "We'll survive without you for an hour." Then she looked at me oddly. "You really think you can win this thing, don't you?"

"Boy, you can read me like no one else," I said. "Yeah, it's funny but all week I've had this sort of premonition that it would go my way, and so far everything's humming right along. I haven't really had a hard match. I know it sounds ridiculous, but I really do think it might somehow be in the cards."

"Peper luck?" she said skeptically. It was an expression I'd often used to describe the good fortune I'd had in life, and one that Libby never liked hearing. "I know you believe you have good luck, George," she said, "but it sounds like you're bragging. Just remember, no one's luck lasts forever."

I took my bath, Libby gave me a bowl of soup and a sandwich, I popped three Aleves to go with the three I'd taken in the morning, and headed out to the tee for opponent number five.

He didn't look particularly formidable, a shortish, gray-haired, bespectacled fellow of seventy years—but oh could he play. Jim Cook was a 4-handicap from Muirfield and he'd been one of that club's best players for decades.

He had one of those classic British swings—short and tidy. Although not long off the tee, his drives were always struck on the button, and his gently drawn iron shots rarely settled far from the flag. When he made a rock-solid par at the 1st and I missed my putt from 6 feet I was behind in a match for the first time all week. When I found sand at the 2nd I was 2 down, and when I found more sand at 7 I was 3 down as Jim reached the turn in 1 under par.

A birdie at 10 got me one back and then I struck my best shot of the week, a 6-iron that stopped 4 feet away at 11 for another birdie—back to 1 down. I gave one back with a bogey at 13 but my handicap stroke came to the rescue at the par-5 14th, where my 5-net-4 was a winner.

The early-evening wind had freshened dramatically—I'd never seen it more in the face on the back 9—and the temperature had dropped about 10 degrees. We both bogeyed 15, neither of us able to reach the green. Then at 16—a hole that I'd played most of the summer with a driver and a short iron—I hit back-to-back drivers to reach the green, only to 3-putt for a halve. With two holes to go, I was still 1 down.

It was past seven o'clock and the skies had begun to thicken with rain clouds. All the other matches had been won or lost and Jim and I were the only guys on the course. We both played 17 cautiously off the tee, but he fluffed his second shot and I was able to get a 3-iron just short of the green and run the pitch close enough for a conceded 4 that put us all square with the 18th to play.

As we walked off the 18th tee after a pair of solid drives, I glanced over at the picture windows of Eric and Margaret's house. The party was in full swing. I hoped someone might look out at us, so that I could signal the status of the match. No one did, but the fact was, even if they had looked out they might not have been able to see much. It was very dark and the rain had begun.

Jim and I both reached 18 in 2, both putted to about 2 feet, and when we conceded each other's pars we looked ruefully at each other. There was nothing to do but keep playing. As we walked across to the 1st tee, we looked inside the bay window of the R&A, where the cocktail hour was going strong. A few of the members, incredulous at seeing there was still a match on the course, drew closer to the window to watch us tee off.

Ten minutes later I stood over a 6-footer for par to win the match, and jerked it left. Ten minutes after that, Jim Cook stood over a 10-footer for par to win the match, and left it on the lip. It was now 7:45, raining harder than ever, and darkness had all but closed in. As we played the 3rd hole, the only light came from the illuminated bays of the practice range a thousand yards to the east. An R&A official had kindly come out in a cart to escort us back when the match ended—if it ever ended.

The front 9 was now playing straight downgale so my tee shot finished on the front edge of the 3rd green, about fifty feet from the pin. Jim was only a bit shorter, but he hit a poor second to the back of the green and then putted to about 10 feet. I putted my second shot to 5 or 6 feet. As I marked my ball he said, "That's good."

"Whoa," I said, "are you sure? If you make and I miss, we're still tied."

"Yes," he said, "but you won't miss that. Besides, thirty-nine holes of golf is enough for me and I don't want to miss the rest of the cocktail hour. Good match," he said, and shook my hand.

It was more than a good match, it was one of the best matches of my life. I almost ran home, took a speed shower, and fairly skipped across the street to the party. I'd reached the quarterfinals, down to the last eight guys, and having survived the likes of Jim Cook, I was surer than ever that this was my week.

Early the next morning before my match, I headed into town on a couple of errands. At the newsagent, I bumped into one of the Old Course caddies.

"Hey, nice going, you're still in it, man," he said.

"Thanks," I said. "Are you working for anyone this week?"

"Was until yesterday. We lost on 18. Want a caddie today?"

"No thanks, I don't want to change anything."

"Understood. Good luck," he said.

"Yes, good luck indeed," said Joyce the lady behind the counter. "I've been watching your progress."

"Gee, thanks," I said. "I had no idea so many people followed the matches."

"Oh, it's sort of a tradition here, the Vase. The results appear in the *Fife Courier* every morning and lots of us pay close attention."

Walking home, I bumped into the wife of one of the R&A guys.

"Well done, George," she said. "Now keep it going."

It felt awfully good to know that people cared about the progress of the tournament, and even better to be the one whose progress they were still following.

An hour later, as I walked to the tee, I was stopped in my tracks by the sight of the club's highest-profile member. There standing alone next to the starter's hut was Sean Connery. A formidable competitor, he had won the Vase in 1991, but this year had been eliminated in an early round.

We had a mutual friend, another R&A member named Chris Goodwin, who was also a member of the Lyford Cay Club in the Bahamas where Sean lived and played for much of the year, and a few years earlier I'd played a couple of very enjoyable—and very competitive—matches with Sean prior to playing in the Lyford Cay Four-Ball Invitational with Chris.

I didn't think he'd recognize me, but I couldn't resist the chance to reacquaint myself with him.

"Sean, how are you? I'm George Peper . . . you may recall, we played some golf together with Chris Goodwin a couple of years ago."

He looked at me quizzically for a moment, then arched one of his world-famous eyebrows. "Ah yesh, the magazheen guy. Are you still in it?"

"For the moment."

"Well, good luck to you."

With those words of encouragement to spur me, I stepped onto the tee and shook hands with my opponent in the quarterfinal, Al Nicholson. This, I knew, would be a difficult match. An 8-handicap from Florida, Nicholson had reached the finals of the Vase two years earlier. How did I know that? His innkeeper for the week was the man for whom there is never more than three degrees of separation, Gordon Murray.

Al turned out to be a delightful guy and a pleasure to play with, if a bit deliberate. One of his earlier victims, knowing I was a fast player, had warned me to either throttle down or prepare to be throttled.

When, at the 1st green, he pulled out a long putter, I thought, Fine, he'll have his hands full if he leaves himself a 90-footer. Wrong. I was to bear witness to as fine a display of long-distance putting as I'd ever seen.

Through five holes we were all even. At the 6th we both hit good drives and wedges to the vicinity of the pin. By this time, due to Al's pace of play, we'd fallen more than a hole behind the match in front of us. But give him credit—he knew how to catch up. When we reached our balls, each about 10 feet from the hole, Al looked at mine, looked at his, looked at me, and said, "Good-good?"

"Are you serious?" I said.

"Sure."

"Okay, why not." We picked up the balls and laughed our way to the 7th tee, having saved two or three minutes of lining up and stroking.

At 7, Al left his approach 60 feet away and I got mine to within 8 feet.

"Good-good?" he said again, a big grin on his face

"Pass," I said.

I probably should have taken him up on it. He came closer to making birdie than I did. We were all square through 9 but over the next six holes he sank a couple of 10-footers and stroked four approach putts—averaging 50 feet—within gimme range. Over the same stretch, I putted like an arthritic sumo wrestler and fell 2 down. At the 16th hole, when my approach shot settled against the face of a deep bunker, the match was over. I was 3 over par (albeit with the 10-foot gimme at 6), but I'd lost 3 and 2 to a guy with a handicap 1 stroke higher than mine.

Al went on to win again in the afternoon and the next day in the final he faced Peter Bucher—the same person he'd lost to in the final two years earlier. This time their match went to the 19th hole, but the result was the same.

As for me, well, it had happened so quickly I was numb for an hour or so. Having won five matches, I had trouble accepting that I hadn't won the sixth and wouldn't be winning the seventh that afternoon and the championship the next day. Of course, I should never have felt such golf entitlement—the game never owes anyone. Nonetheless, it had been a wonderful week of camaraderie and competition. I'd made several friends and played just as well as I'd hoped I would.

There is something magical about the newness of doing anything for the first time—whether it's the first day of kindergarten, the first day of driving a car by yourself, your first sexual encounter, whatever. The experience brings a heightened sense of reality, of exuberance, and leaves memories that last forever. The Jubilee Vase had been my first big R&A tournament, and the day after it was over, I was already looking forward to doing it again.

31

On His Majesty's Secret Service

Roughly a month and a half before the Autumn Meeting, I'd gotten a phone call from Aubyn Stewart-Wilson, the R&A members secretary. Through my involvement with the 250th anniversary, I'd gotten to know Aubyn fairly well and had nothing but the highest regard for him, both as an administrator and as an individual. He oversaw the day-to-day operations of the club with remarkable dedication and efficiency but was also a likable chap with an easy sense of humor and a genuine interest in the lives of the members.

However, I must admit that when Libby handed me the phone and whispered, "It's Aubyn Stewart-Wilson," my reaction was mystification tinged with worry. Aubyn had never called me at home, and my sense was that it was not good news, that perhaps another member had reported me as having done something scandalous.

Had I failed to wash my hands before leaving the House of Lords? Had I parked my Honda in a forbidden sector of the club lot? Had I signed the wrong line on my scorecard in the monthly medal? Had my last column in *Links* revealed more about the club than it should have? All those things—and worse—raced through my mind as I took the receiver.

"Aubyn," I said, "how are you?"

"I'm well, George, thank you." His tone was even more serious than usual, and a bit officious. "George, I'm sorry to call you like this at home. Do you have a few moments to talk?"

"Uh, sure." Now I knew I was in trouble.

"George, this is a matter you need to keep in complete confidence. Are you familiar with the Club Committee?"

"Uh, y-yes, a little," I said. The Club Committee! No opening words could have been more ominous.

A year earlier, the club had separated rather historically into two entities, a public body with committees responsible for the Open Championship, the rules of golf, equipment standards, and so forth, and the private members' club—run by the eight members of the Club Committee—with a General Committee overseeing both sides. The division had been made, in large part, to protect the members from a mega-million-dollar lawsuit from an equipment company. Prior to that, had Callaway or Titleist sued the R&A for $100 million over an equipment regulation, each of the club members would have been personally liable.

The Club Committee, in the parlance of an American private club, was a combination of the house committee, golf committee, and entertainment committee. Now I knew I'd committed a cardinal sin—probably something to do with the last members' dinner, when I'd been a bit over-served with after-dinner port.

"George," said Aubyn, "I've been asked to sound you out on something. Each year, two vacancies open up on the Club Committee, and your name has been advanced as a possible candidate to fill one of them."

"You're kidding," was all I could come up with.

"Not at all. Your work on the 250th anniversary was noticed."

My God, not only was I not the club reprobate, I'd fooled people in high places. In a flash of self-indulgence, I envisioned Prince Andrew, at the head of a General Committee meeting, muttering, "Yes, that Peper chap, fine lad, hmm . . ."

"Well, I'm very flattered, I . . ."

"Well, this is not an invitation, George, it's a bit more complicated than that. In fact, at this point, it is just exploratory and as I say, very confidential. I must ask that you mention this conversation to no one."

"Of course . . ." Was this what they meant by His Majesty's Secret Service?

"For now, assuming you're interested, what would be most appreciated is if you could send or e-mail me your résumé, with special note of any participation you've had in golf club committees or golf associations. The committee is considering several candidates, and will make a decision on the final two at the next meeting, in a couple of weeks. If you're chosen, your name will be proposed to the General Committee for approval, and if they approve, then your name and résumé will be posted on the club bulletin board and the club Web site two weeks before the Autumn Meeting, to give the entire membership a chance to review and comment. During that time, other members may choose to offer themselves as alternative candidates. If that happens, there will be a general election. If no one else runs, and if there are no negative reactions to your candidacy, you will be elected at the Autumn Meeting of the club, at the Scores Hotel at 6:00 P.M. on the Wednesday afternoon of the third week of September."

"Wow," was all I could muster.

"George, this is not an assignment you should take lightly and for that reason you might want to give it a day or two of thought before giving me your decision. There are five or six Club Committee meetings each year plus you'll be assigned to at least two subcommittees, each of which will meet several times a year. It's all rather time-consuming, I'm afraid."

"That's all right," I said. "Once I get past the book I'm writing I'll be relatively free, and my deadline isn't far away."

"Fine. But there is one other thing that you should be aware of—

appointment to the Club Committee is for a period of four years. We need to be sure that you'll be staying in Scotland for at least that long—through 2008."

"Right . . . well, I . . ."

"George, why don't you give all this some thought and give me a call—the end of the week will do."

"Yes," I said. "Thank you, Aubyn, and please give my thanks to the committee for considering me."

When I told Libby she seemed delighted. "But it's a four-year deal," I said.

"Well?" she said.

"Well? I don't know—how do you feel?"

"You know I like it here—we've only been here a year, but I like the whole feel and pace of things here much more than back in the U.S., especially with the way Bush is mismanaging the U.S., he's lying to everyone about Iraq, I'm afraid Scott and Tim may get drafted, gas prices are going through the roof, Bush is going to get reelected and then we'll probably invade every country *except* Great Britain."

"Yeah, yeah, but do we really want to stay here for four years . . . or more?" I said.

"I don't know," she said. "I don't think we can make that decision now. But I think you should tell Aubyn yes."

"Me, too. Heck, if we stick to our plan and leave a year from now, what are they going to do, kick me out of the club? I can always come up with a semi-legitimate reason for having to return. And if we do stay, well, I think it will be four years well spent. I also think I can contribute something."

"Then it's decided," she said. "You'll say yes and we'll think maybe."

Six weeks later—almost a year to the day after we'd arrived—I became the first American elected to the Club Committee of the Royal & Ancient Golf Club.

32

The Night I Kissed the Captains' Balls

he R&A's Autumn Meeting traditionally concludes with the Annual Dinner, a black-tie affair attended by five hundred or so members. As I headed up to the club that evening, I reflected harrowingly on the only other time I'd attended the dinner, fifteen years earlier. At roughly ten o'clock on that evening, had you bellied up to the urinal next to mine in the men's room of the St. Andrews Town Hall and then turned your head indecorously to the right, you would have beheld a balding, middle-aged man in a state of abject terror.

It was intermission—halftime in a marathon of bibulous fellowship ritually culminated by the presentation of the Calcutta Cup, Jubilee Vase, a dozen or so other awards, and the delivery of four speeches. That night, as I pulled up my zipper and pushed down the plunger, the relief in my bladder did nothing to quell the turmoil in my stomach, the tightening of my esophagus, or the tympanic thumping in my chest. All of the evening's medals and trophies had been presented, and two of the four speeches had been given. Two remained, with the second of them—the evening's universally anticipated barn-burner, knee-slapper oratorical climax—scheduled to be delivered by George Peper.

It had all begun a month or so earlier, with a phone call from Sir Michael Bonallack.

"Delighted that you'll be heading over for the Autumn Meeting, George," he said in his distinctive British tenor. "If I'm not mistaken, this will be your first trip since becoming a member."

"That's right, Michael," I said. "Happily, I've been able to combine it with a trip to the Ryder Cup the next week." I was, at that moment, becoming very suspicious of this call.

"Yes, yes, you'll have a grand time, I'm sure. Now, George, on be-half of our current captain, Sandy Sinclair, I have the honor of asking you to undertake an important assignment."

"Really . . ." I said, wariness tempered now with curiosity. After all, what service could I possibly perform for the R&A—a quick copy-edit of the dining room menu?

"George, at the Annual Dinner we'd like you to give the Reply to the Toast to the New Members."

Gulp. Brain spin. Full-body sweat. Momentary blackout.

"George?"

"Yes, sorry. Do you mean a speech?"

"Not just *a* speech, George, *the* speech. It's an R&A tradition that dates back nearly a century. Each year at the dinner, one of the long-standing members gives a speech that concludes with a toast welcoming the members who are attending the dinner for the first time. Then one of those new members accepts on behalf of his cohorts."

Suddenly I felt like a character out of Kafka. *"As George Peper awoke one morning from uneasy dreams, he found himself transported to a podium facing five hundred black-tie-clad members of the Royal & Ancient Golf Club."*

Wasn't there anyone else they could have tapped for this? Was it too late for me to propose Billy Crystal for membership? Would they let me prerecord it on videotape? Did they have the faintest idea what they were doing to me?

I can think of nothing in this world that frightens me—not death, snakes, IRS audits, three-foot putts, or proctologists—more than public speaking. The mere mention of the word "speech" makes my throat go dry.

"Do I have the option of declining this invitation?" I asked Sir Michael, adding a laugh to my voice to mask the panic.

"Yes, but I'm afraid that if you decline, the penalty will be loss of membership," he said, with a laugh of his own. "You'll do fine, George. It's only twenty minutes or so and—"

"Twenty minutes!"

"Half an hour tops."

"But what do I talk about for that long?"

"Well, golf would be good. The important thing is to be entertaining. Generally it works best to keep things light until the last couple of minutes, then close with a serious word or two as you raise your glass.

"By the way, we're expecting quite a crop of new members to attend this year—forty or fifty from around the world. And, of course, after your speech you'll lead them all in a procession to the front of the hall, where, one by one, you will kiss the captains' balls."

"Right . . ." Now I knew it had to be a joke. For a split second, in fact, I thought, This isn't Michael Bonallack at all, it's one of my jackass golf buddies messing with me. I was about to call his bluff when I vaguely remembered something about ball kissing. (Among the R&A's most prized possessions are three sterling silver replica putters, each festooned with dozens of sterling silver replica golf balls, each ball commemorating the investiture of a club captain. In what I suspect is some sort of nod to the pre-Reformation era—when St. Andrews was run by dangerously repressed Catholic prelates—the members have enthusiastically embraced the ritual of kissing other men's balls.) Yes, this was in truth Michael Bonallack, he was indeed asking me to make *the* speech, and whether I wanted to or not, I was bloody well going to do it.

Over the next four weeks I paid little attention to family, friends, and job. Every spare moment was spent working on and worrying about the speech. Writing for print, I'd found, is immeasurably easier than writing for oration, for the simple reason that the writer does not have to look his reviewers in the face. As people read my books and articles, I suffer none of their sneers or snores. So I put far more work into writing a twenty-minute speech than a twenty-page article—just to get myself feeling semi-comfortable.

But this would be the biggest speech of my life, and with a week to go I remained in near-suicidal terror. Then I had the misfortune to receive another phone call, this one from Bonallack's counterpart at the USGA, my supposed friend David Fay.

"Hey, I heard you're giving the speech on behalf of the new members this year," he said. "That's huge."

"Yeah, ginormous," I said, telephone cupped under my ear as I scribbled notes into the margins of draft number thirty-seven.

"No, I mean it. They only ask big shots and great speakers for that one. Alistair Cooke gave it recently and I think Eisenhower did it back in the 1950s."

"Great, maybe Ike would like to do it again. He'd have a better chance of pulling it off than I do."

"Oh, don't worry—you'll be fine. Nothing like that guy they had a couple of years ago . . ."

"What guy?"

"Haven't you heard about it? They found some guy from Philadelphia I think it was—I have no idea what his claim to fame was, but he got up there and bored everyone senseless for forty-five minutes, droning on about amateur status or the Stableford system or something. And, as I'm sure you've been told, it's a tough crowd."

"Uh, no I hadn't . . ."

"Some of those old coots in the back tables, when they get a few belts in them, feel compelled to express themselves, and there's apparently a tradition that when a speaker has overstayed his welcome, it's okay to spoon him."

"Spoon him?"

"Yeah, one of the geezers starts to rap his dessert spoon loudly and rhythmically on the table—rap . . . rap . . . rap. Then another guy picks up the beat, and then another and another and within fifteen seconds or so the place is a cacophony of silver on mahogany. They spooned Mr. Philadelphia right off the podium."

"Wow . . ."

"But you'll be great. Just go and have fun with it."

"Yeah. Fun."

On the eve of the big day, I decided on a strategy to keep my nerves at bay: sleep late and drink early. By four o'clock the next afternoon, breakfast barely digested, I was into my first beta-blocking single malt.

Successful prep-oratory drinking is an underappreciated art, the object of which is to strike a delicate balance—consume just enough alcohol to quash your terror but not so much as to make you a blithering idiot. I liken it to the tachometer on a car. You want to get your rpm's up as high as possible without blowing the engine. I use the same strategy to gird myself when I think I might be asked to play the piano. Totally sober, I'm too self-conscious to play even Chopsticks, and when blotto drunk, I can't find the keys. Ah, but when I'm on that red line—when I've had just enough (and equally important, when my listeners have had just enough), I'm Van freaking Cliburn.

Normally, the right number is between three and four shooters, but I'd sensed that this evening—my adrenaline and perspiration pumping hard—might call for extra sedation. So even before I made my way to the R&A clubhouse I had two Macallans working for me. Big ones.

At least two hundred members had assembled in the club, spreading through the front lobby, the bar, the hallways, and the Big Room. Everyone was dressed in black tie except a dozen or so of the eldermost, decked out in white tie and tails—red tails to be exact, or morning coats as they are known. These were the living captains of the club, clad exactly as every R&A captain has been clad for this dinner since the middle of the eighteenth century.

I was just inside the front door, patting the breast pocket of my tux to be sure my thirteen pages of double-spaced, nearly memorized hilarity and insight was still with me, when I felt a tap on my shoulder. Turning around, I beheld a total stranger. The tallest man in the room, he was easily six foot five. And he was dressed in red.

"Are you George?" he said, bending downward with a kind, almost shy smile.

"Yes, I am."

"Hello, I'm Michael Attenborough. I'm the incoming captain. I'm so glad to meet you. Are you all set for tonight?"

"Well, I'm not sure . . ."

"Are you as nervous as I am?"

"Yes!"

"What a relief to hear that. Let's have ourselves a drink, shall we?" he said, taking my arm and steering us to a quiet corner of the room, where he signaled to one of the waitresses.

"Whisky all right?" he said.

"Whisky's perfect," I said.

"Two please, and better make them doubles," he said, giving me an "okay with you?" glance, which I returned with a vigorous nod in the affirmative.

Michael Attenborough turned out to be just the soulmate I needed at that moment. Not only was he a fine gentleman, he'd spent most of his career in publishing, rising to the directorship of Hodder & Stoughton, one of London's most highly regarded book publishers. He even claimed to have bid on the British rights to a book I'd written a few years earlier.

Barely had we finished our drinks when the hall porter approached us.

"It's time to go to the town hall, sir," he said to my new friend.

"My coach awaits," said Attenborough, rolling his eyes. "Would you join me? It's just a minibus, actually."

And so off we went, a dozen or so blocks across town, to the only building in St. Andrews capable of hosting five hundred people for dinner. Seating was prison-style—only about a dozen tables, but each of them a hundred feet long. At the far end of the room was a raised gallery with another dozen or so tables, shorter in length. (It was in this area, I surmised, that the dreaded spooners festered.)

Months earlier, a mailing had arrived from the R&A, asking if there was any fellow R&A member I wanted to be seated near at dinner, and without hesitation I'd penned in the name Rees Jones. The golf architect and I had been good friends for many years, and I felt better the moment I saw him standing at the seat across from mine at the head of Table 1.

At the front of the room, just off my right elbow, was a raised dais for the redcoats, and at the far right side of that dais was the podium. Except that there *was* no podium—just a bulbous chrome-plated microphone that looked like something Rudy Vallee might have used. This was an extremely disquieting discovery. I'd be speaking nude— nothing to lean on when the knees went weak, nowhere to hide my text for desperation peeks when I blanked out, nowhere to duck if the spoons began to fly.

Extremely disquieting discovery number two came when I looked at the dinner program, an elegant ecru-colored folded card with the R&A emblem embossed on its cover. Inside, printed in dark blue script on the left-hand side, was the evening's bill of fare and accompanying spirits, and on the right-hand side was the agenda. The first item was "Toast to the Queen" and the last—roughly a dozen items later—was "Reply to the Toast to New Members, from George Peper." It would be two torturous hours—maybe three—before I got up there.

Three it was. Three hours of eating, drinking, listening to speeches, drinking, awarding prizes, and drinking. By the time the last medal was handed out, I'd consumed two glasses of red wine, one glass of white, and either two or three glasses of after-dinner port—in addition to the three double scotches. I was no longer feeling nervous. I was not, in fact, feeling anything. The red line had long been passed. Indeed, I'd all but forgotten about my oratorical duties when, from the dais, I heard someone say "George Peper." It was Michael Bonallack.

"I know we're all looking forward to hearing from Richard Cole-Hamilton and George Peper," he said, "but first let's take a very brief intermission."

As four hundred men funneled toward eight urinals, I sat staring blankly across the table at Rees.

"I think I may be too drunk to speak," I said.

"C'mon, let's get up and take a quick walk," he said.

"I'm not sure I can do that, either. I think my feet and my brain are going through a trial separation."

"Up you go," said Rees, steering me into the loo-ward traffic.

The proposer of the toast was Richard Cole-Hamilton. (Coincidentally, fifteen years later—on the very night I returned to the dinner—he would become the captain of the club.) Richard, the managing director of the Clydesdale Bank, had no particular credentials as a speaker, but he was barely twenty seconds into his remarks when I knew I had a tough act to follow. His material was only vaguely humorous to me—the typical sort of semi-bawdy stuff that the Brits seem to like—but the way he delivered it was hilarious. He was one of those guys who tells jokes and then laughs at them himself well before the punch lines, laughs so long, hard, and infectiously that he gets everyone in the audience laughing with him.

The only story I remember was his closer, about the Scotsman who had been invited by a wealthy matron to a formal ball to be held at her manor, where all the men were required to wear kilts.

"I'm afraid I won't be able to attend, your ladyship," he said.

"What a shame, Mr. MacTavish," she said. "May I ask why not?"

"Yes, I'm afraid it's the dress code. I refuse to wear a kilt."

"And why may I ask is that?"

"It's the flies, madame. I'm afraid of the flies."

"Mr. McTavish," she said indignantly, "I will have you know, there have never been and there will never be any flies at my balls!"

"Nor at mine, madame, nor at mine."

Cole-Hamilton laughed so hard at that one he nearly fell off the dais into Table 6. Then, sensing he'd hit a home run, he suddenly fell solemn and quickly, almost perfunctorily, raised his glass and said, "To the new members! Welcome to you all."

And so it was my turn.

Somehow, adrenaline had neutralized alcohol and I managed to deliver my speech without slurs, stumbles, or spoons. I know this for sure only because a tape recording was made and sent to me a month later.

33

The Wedge-Away

Oddly, I've always felt a kinship with Jack Nicklaus. We're both of Germanic descent, both Aquarians, and both have a habit of putting our feet in our mouths. (That last trait may be the reason we've both had hip replacements, by the very same Boston surgeon.) On top of that, when asked our two favorite places to play golf, the Bear and I have identical answers—St. Andrews and Pebble Beach.

Of course, there are some differences as well, beginning with Jack's eighteen major championships and my none. For most of my life I'd been able to live with that inequity, but now, suddenly I was living alongside one of those beloved courses—a course where he'd won two big ones. My game was as good as it had ever been, and yet I still hadn't won a tournament.

So I invented one—the Wedge-Away Championship. Obnoxiously exclusive in concept, it was restricted to people whose residences were within a wedge shot of the 18th hole of the Old Course. A quick census told me this was a good thing—there were only about a dozen such denizens and all of them were older than I. On paper, at least, this was an event I could win.

The idea took its final shape when I invited Gordon Murray and Andrew Lang-Stevenson for a drink. We appointed ourselves tri-chairmen of the First Annual Wedge-Away Championship, an 18-hole event to be played at full handicap. Gordon became the captain, Andrew the managing director, and I the president. Andrew generously donated the prize—an 1880-vintage hickory-shafted cleek—and I got it mounted and framed with room to display the names of two or three decades' worth of winners. On the trophy was a plaque that read: THE WEDGE-AWAY CHAMPIONSHIP—Where Everyone Finishes Close at 18.

The tournament was scheduled for the Saturday after the R&A Autumn Meeting. The format we chose—the Stableford points system—suited me just fine. I'd already won a Stableford tournament (though not on the Old Course), an annual event that Andrew and one of his orthopedic surgeon colleagues, John Ireland, had kindly invited me to join, although my victory was due as much to dumb luck as good play. It was played over three days, but each player counted only his two best of the three scores. There was also a quirky regulation intended to keep the competition tight until the end. After round one, the player in first place had his handicap reduced by four strokes, the player in second had his handicap reduced by three, the player in third by two, and the player in fourth by one. Conversely, the player who had posted the worst score of the day became the beneficiary of four additional handicap strokes on the morrow, the second-worst player received three more, the third-worst two more, and the fourth-worst one more. After the second round, the same cuts and raises were applied.

A 77 on the New Course in round one gave me 37 Stableford points and put me in second place among the twenty or so competitors, so my handicap went from 7 down to 4. The next day, on the Eden Course I so detest, I sprayed the ball all over the place and came in with an 86, good for 26 points, the worst in the field—so back up went the handicap, all the way to 8.

Then, on the final day at nearby Elie, I played one of the better rounds of my life, a 72 that was good for 42 points. After throwing out my Eden round, I had a total of 79 points, which turned out to be the winning score. The prize was a lovely silver salver on which my named was engraved, although my joy in victory was tempered by the fact that the guy I'd beaten was my good friend and neighbor—and the fellow who had invited me in the first place—Andrew. He and I had been paired together that final day at Elie, and he had played every bit as well as I had—a 78 off his handicap of 13 worth the same 42 points—but I'd begun the day a stroke ahead of him. It had come down to the last green, and had his six-footer found the cup, he would have won on a tie-break, having played the better final round.

In any case, my game was in fine shape, and knowing that, I felt some added pressure as the Wedge-Away Championship approached. We were able to muster only six of the twelve eligible competitors (hey, the Open Championship had a modest beginning, too) but a strong six it was—organizers Peper, Murray, and Lang-Stevenson plus three neighbors from up the street: Scotsman Bryce Hogarth and two Americans (members of the R&A as well as the San Francisco Golf Club), Maynard Garrison and Hank Kuechler, each of whom owned a flat on Pilmour Links, the eastward extension of Gibson Place.

Gordon, Bryce, and Andrew went out in the first group, about an hour in front of Hank, Maynard, and me. As we approached the eighth green, I saw them on the 11th tee, and their body language told me none of them was playing well. Gordon, when I hailed him and asked how the group was doing, gave me a thumbs down. In return I gave a shrug that suggested we were hot and cold. The truth was, Hank and I were both pretty hot while Maynard had struggled.

It would come down to me and Hank. I'd played the front 9 in two over par, he (off 14) had shot four over, so we were about even. We stayed that way for most of the back 9, too, as I was able to grind out pars, except for bogeys at 11 and 17, while Hank had made about an equal number of pars and bogeys. My score was 76, a net 69 good for 39 points. Hank shot 84, for a net 70 and 38 points.

I'd done it—won a tournament on the Old Course! Granted, the elation of victory was tainted by the fact that I had, uh, invented the tournament, restricted the field, and held it on my favorite course. But I felt guilty only until I realized this: In 1977 and 1984 Jack Nicklaus had won his own Memorial Tournament on his own Muirfield Village course in his own hometown of Columbus, Ohio.

Yeah, any way you look at it, the Bear and I are two of a kind.

34

The Partisans

n late September, St. Andrews underwent a dramatic trans-
formation as thousands of summer tourists were replaced
by thousands of university students. Suddenly, the same streets that
had been clogged with portly chaps from Pittsburgh and Abilene
sporting tartan "Old Course St. Andrews" tam-o'-shanters with white
pompoms now were alive with slim young men and women in blue
jeans and Ralph Lauren shirts. In the space of one metamorphic weekend, the days became quieter, the nights became louder, and the toon
became much less auld and grey.

The R&A saw a similar change as the several hundred members
who had converged for the Autumn Meeting returned to their homes
around the world and the cavernous stone clubhouse suddenly belonged to the few dozen guys who lived locally. Except on the rare days
when a golf competition was organized, you could fire off a shotgun in
the Big Room and not strike a soul (although you might rouse one or
two supernumerary members from leather-chaired slumber).

I'd joined an unofficial winter-season group—the Monday

Club—made up of local members who played Monday mornings and then repaired to the clubhouse for a couple of drinks, a bottle of wine (or two), and lunch, followed by coffee and perhaps a liqueur in the Big Room. All very civilized.

During the same period, however, I'd met a bunch of guys who were members of the two other men's clubs in town, the New Golf Club and the St. Andrews Golf Club. The New Club, at 3 Gibson Place, was less than twenty steps from our door. Despite its name, and motto—Semper Nova—it was over a century old, formed when the members of a dozen golf clubs in town—none of them with the bene- fit of a clubhouse—consolidated under one roof. The membership was and remains largely business and professional men.

It was in the New Club on a Sunday afternoon in 1908 that Old Tom Morris took his last steps. Still going strong at age eighty-six, he'd made his usual visit to the club for a few pints—perhaps a few too many—and en route to the bathroom he'd passed through the wrong door and tumbled down a flight of stairs.

Old Tom's original club, the St. Andrews Golf Club, was formed in 1843. Back then it was known as the St. Andrews Mechanics' Golf Club, mechanic in those days referring to a variety of skilled trades. Its eleven charter members were mostly tradesmen but also included a dancing master and a butler in the person of George Morris, Old Tom's brother. The first captain of the club was a blacksmith.

One hundred and sixty-one years later, in the same year the R&A was captained by His Royal Highness the Duke of York, the St. An- drews Golf Club captain was a rangy good-looking fellow named John Devlin, a local plumber. It remains the most democratic club in town, a place where craftsmen and shopkeepers gather to swap beers and barbs with cabbies and caddies. The first clubhouse was on Golf Place in the building now occupied by Auchterlonies golf shop. In 1933 it moved to its present location opposite the 18th green of the Old Course, just steps from the R&A, and 100 yards up the street from the New Club with which there was a not so subtle rivalry.

"We may not be as high-falutin' as the boys in the New," an SAGC man said to me one afternoon in the club bar, "but I bet we have more members who are millionaires."

"Aye," said another. "They may be professional men but we know what we're about—many of us have skills we're very proud of. We're the partisans!"

"Not partisans, you idiot," said one of his buddies. "Artisans—we're the artisans' club, aye."

One thing was certain—the best golfers in town belonged to the SAGC and always had. In the main lounge, a massive gold-lettered plaque attests to the fact that SAGC members have won two dozen British and U.S. Opens.

I probably should have joined the New Club—it was closer to me both geographically and demographically, but the gritty camaraderie of the St. Andrews Golf Club guys was irresistible. When Gordon Murray, a member of both clubs, offered to sponsor me for the SAGC, I accepted, and I was delighted to be accepted by them.

As it turned out, the St. Andrews Golf Club had plenty in common with both the New Club and the R&A, to the extent that they all lacked certain things I'd grown accustomed to in American clubs—things like annual assessments, valet parking, 30-handicappers, locker fees, range fees, trail fees, corporate attorneys, cigar nights, pool parties, bond traders, golf carts, teaching professionals, monthly minimums, Hawaiian luaus, investment bankers, and tennis. Perfect. It was golf, pure and simple—you hung your hat on a hook, slung your clubs over your shoulder, and played the game—played it with passion, reverence, deference, and speed.

As to the speed part, I'd always wondered why the Scots made their way around a course so much more quickly than Americans do. After a couple months at the SAGC, I knew the answer—they wanted to get to the bar. Indeed, on some days, the golf seemed merely foreplay to the drinking.

I had to admit, it was an inspiring place to get snockered. Most of the club's first floor was an elongated bar/lounge, fronted by a large bay window that looked out on the 18th green and the sea. It was here that everyone gathered after their games, assembling in club chairs around simple wooden tables or in the green leather sofas just a few feet from a full-service bar that offered several brands of beer and ale as well as—to my extreme delight—ten-year-old Macallan at one pound twenty (about $2) for a very generous dram. Not even the R&A had Macallan! The walls were clad with century-old photos of bearded, sport-jacketed past members wielding their hickories, and a large, illuminated display case housed a shrine to Old Tom that included, among other treasures, the gold pocket watch he wore.

Shortly after I joined, the lounge got a paint job, new carpeting, fancy power-operated drapes, and a couple of flat-screen TVs, in exchange for serving as the set of one of the Titleist NXT commercials that featured John Cleese and "Old Tom Morris," played by David Joy, a fourth-generation St. Andrean and one of the most talented individuals I'd ever met. Although best known for his portrayal of Old Tom, he was an accomplished writer, actor, illustrator, artist, engraver, golf historian, and after-dinner speaker. Perhaps more importantly, he'd applied his good mind and good heart to a number of local charities, including the St. Andrews Preservation Trust, the Byre Theatre Trust, and the Keepers of the Green, a group that provided powered wheelchairs to the needy. In 2002 the St. Andrews Golf Club had recognized David's contributions by making him an Honorary Life Member of the club.

David, along with Gordon Murray, was also a member of the Thursday Club. The concept was the same as the Monday Club at the R&A, a group of roughly twenty guys, most of them retired, who played golf on the Old Course each week from October through March.

But there were also major differences between this group and the fellows from the big clubhouse across the way. Whereas the members of the Monday Club played their matches either for no money or for a modest 25 pence on the front 9, 25 on the back, and 50 for the match, the SAGC boys had a couple of established games and the stakes, although not crazy, were appreciably higher. First, each four-ball played a two-pound Nassau and then there was an individual Stableford competition where each player anted £5 and the winner took all.

Took all, that is, until the drinking began. An unwritten rule was that the winner bought the first round of drinks—the first of many. On the couple of occasions I'd been invited to join the group (strictly as a guest—membership in the Thursday Club was carefully controlled), it seemed that not only the winner but each of the competitors bought at least one round. That was the other difference from the Monday Club, which usually adjourned at a reasonable early-afternoon hour. On Thursdays the golf began at eight and usually finished by noon—the drinking began at noon and often finished after eight.

Four rounds of drinks—one bought by each member of your group—was the minimum. If you didn't hang in for four rounds you were considered either a wimp or a cheap bugger. If you stayed for the fifth round it was a tacit signal you'd be in until round eight, or twelve.

Most of the Thursday regulars were the kind of characters you'd envision running into in a Scottish pub. One of the classics, Jake Fleming, loved his red wine almost as much as he loved his golf, and in recognition of same he had a standing arrangement for a taxi to transfer him from the club to his home on Thursday night. Most of the other guys, happily, were within stumbling distance, with the award for shortest walk going to Jack Willoughby, a burly, affable Texan who for eleven years had owned the Dunvegan Hotel, less than a hundred steps around the corner.

"Yeah, I look forward to every Thursday," Willoughby told me, "but I'm afraid I've never been able to read the St. Andrews Citizen [published Friday] without a hangover."

They were quite a collection, the partisans. In addition to David "Joy Boy," the Renaissance man, Gordon the fisherman, Jack the hotelier, and Jake who designed and sold custom-made kitchens, there were two accountants, a golf shop owner, two restaurateurs, a caddie, a policeman, two oil riggers, two salesmen, an interior decorator, a golf tour operator, an R&A porter, a horse trainer, and an owner of a chain of radio stations. The late-afternoon conversation, as you might imagine, ranged widely—everything from European economic policy to the comparative merits of Liz Hurley's left and right breasts.

One day we spent nearly an hour trying to guess how many swings Wee Raymond Gatherum had needed on the afternoon he'd taken a sand wedge and golf ball to the beach and played his way to the far end of the West Sands—where the St. Andrews Bay meets the Eden Estuary. I'm not sure what muse had called to the little man that day and I'm even less sure why his exploit became such a rich topic of conjecture, but the answer turned out to be 82—and Raymond was a solid 2-handicapper, so that's a good target.

The centerpiece of the Thursday Club year was the Christmas lunch held the second week of December, when in addition to the £5 entry fee, everyone anted another £20 for a five-course dinner and several barrels of wine. Four of us were invited guests for that gala—as usual we were ineligible for the Stableford prize (which on that day was also the club championship, the winner's name being engraved on a crystal decanter), and that afternoon we had to sit alone for an hour while the club members held their annual general meeting, but when they all returned they had some news for us.

"We've had a rather lengthy debate upstairs," said David Miller, the Thursday Club president, "and by a majority vote of three to two with eleven abstentions, the four of you have been elected to membership in the Thursday Club, which has hereby been capped until such time as one of us dies."

I was stunned, and extremely flattered. "I don't know what to say," I said to Miller.

"Don't say anything," he said. "Just buy us a drink."

The SAGC guys may have been lower on the social register than the R&A chaps, but for their weekly Stableford competitions they'd developed a more sensible system of handicapping than anything I'd seen on either side of the Atlantic. You started the season with your CONGU handicap, but if in any week you scored 36 or more Stableford points (in other words, played to your handicap or better), your handicap was reduced by one stroke for the rest of the season, with no possibility of going back up. If you won the weekly competition you were cut by two strokes and if you won it with 40 points or more you were cut by three.

In the course of the twenty-six-week season, just about everyone won at least once while also bettering his handicap a few times. As a result, by March all of the 15-handicappers were down to 10, all the 10s were down to 5, all the 5s to scratch or even plus figures. At the end of the season I was a 1 and Wee Raymond, who had started at a 2, was a +4. At that point, the system was operating at peak efficiency: No one had a chance—which meant that everyone did.

And so it was that a second day of my week became reserved for golf and not much else. I must admit I found it difficult to embrace the Thursday Club with the same thirst as Jake Fleming, but like Jack Willoughby I did look forward to it every week—not for the golf, not for the drinking but for the good companionship of these twenty men: Colin Balsillie, Tommy Douglas, Jake Fleming, Raymond Gatherum, Stewart "Care Bear" Gatherum, Bill Hicks, Bryce Hogarth, David Joy, Robert Laing, Bob Marshall, Andy McGlashan, John "Shaky" Mc-Gregor, Gordon Murray, Ian Murtaugh, Neil Ogston, Sr., Neil Ogston, Jr., John "Pro" Philp, Willie Tait, Roy "Sadaam" Verner, and Jack Willoughby.

35

Reunion

There remained just one major downside to our St. Andrews sojourn. An ocean separated us from our sons, Tim and Scott.

Libby felt it more acutely than I. On almost a daily basis she connected with one or the other of the boys, either by phone, instant messaging, or e-mail. I assumed my accustomed backup role, chiming in from the bedroom extension, doing the occasional IM guest spot, and reading whatever e-mails Libby saw fit to forward. But we both missed our boys.

Prior to our trip, I'd thought I'd found a brilliant way of staying in visual contact—Webcams—and I'd bought three of those eyeballs that attach to the computer. It all seemed so easy—install the software, clip on the camera, log onto e-mail, and beam into each other's laptops.

Well, we all installed, clipped, and logged on just fine, but nobody got beamed. The issue with Tim seemed to be an incompatibility between his Mac and our PC, whereas with Scott we were unable to hurdle the Princeton intranet's firewall. (At least that's what our sons told us—could be they just didn't want the long-distance parental snooping.) We actually came close to connecting with Tim—messages on Libby's laptop read "Tim Peper is logging on . . . Tim Peper is locking in . . . Tim Peper is clearing his throat, combing his hair, and preparing to speak . . ." Then there would be ten minutes of nothingness. Tim Peper had left the building.

So we Webcammed with the most telecommunicatively advanced of our friends, Mary Tiegreen. That turned out to be great for me because Mary also was my design collaborator on *The Secret of Golf,* the book I was writing—she was actually able to hold layouts up to her camera for me to see and comment on. She and Libby also had several jolly face-to-face chats and Millie became almost as mesmerized by the Webcam as by television, especially when Mary's two golden retrievers appeared in the frame.

Happily, neither son seemed to be in major need of parenting. Tim's acting career had progressed nicely. In the two years since he'd graduated from NYU he'd played the title role in an Off-Off-Broadway production of Kenneth Lonergan's *Lobby Hero,* had snagged a small role in the Disney/Touchstone movie *The Greatest Game Ever Played,* and had sung, danced, and generally strutted his stuff in an offbeat independent film called *Glow Ropes: The Rise and Fall of a Bar Mitzvah Emcee,* which had won the grand prize in a New York City film festival sponsored by HBO. He'd also landed a small but recurring role in *Conviction,* an NBC pilot from the creator of *Law & Order.* Of course, he'd had a few frustrations, too—narrow misses for roles in movies and TV pilots—but he'd managed to pay his bills through a series of commercials for the New York Lottery, Dr. Pepper, Cascade, Degree, and Ask Jeeves. In a profession where the likelihood of success is about the same as in pro golf, he'd gotten off to a great start.

Scott had adjusted well to college—pledged a fraternity, joined the ultimate Frisbee team, and developed an interest in a narrow area but one that was growing in importance with each day—the legal and ethical issues related to technological development. For instance, he told me there would soon be a box that could be hooked up to a U.K. television that would enable me to download all my favorite shows from the U.S.—and that would raise numerous questions for broadcasters, advertisers, and cable operators on both sides of the Atlantic. Few people were addressing such issues, and Scott had decided he wanted to be one of them.

We'd rented a modest apartment in Edgewater, New Jersey—about halfway between Tim in Brooklyn and Scott in Princeton—and we'd been able to make a couple of brief visits, but in fifteen months the four of us had not spent more than a few days together. That, however, was about to change. They were coming to Scotland for Christmas.

Libby and I had been priming for weeks. I'd asked around and learned that there was a farmer in Strathkinness who sold fresh-cut Christmas trees, and the first Sunday in December Libby, Millie, and I had driven out for a look. Sure enough, there on a hill beside an immense barn full of sheep and cows was an impromptu tree store. Surprisingly, the trees weren't from the farmer's own land; they'd been trucked in from Cornwall, England, dozens of firs, spruces, and pines. Since the ceilings in our place were twelve feet high, I picked out the largest tree I could find, a nine-footer, which the farmer bound with string and fitted with an ingenious base—a three-foot-wide, four-inch-thick slab from a tree trunk with a hole at its center in which the trunk of our tree was inserted.

Since the tree was roughly the same length as our Honda—and since neither the farmer nor I had any rope with which to lash it to the roof—we opened the hatchback and jammed it straight up the center of the car, its trunk pressed against the windshield, its tip dangling over the rear bumper. It was a bitterly cold ride home, but the interior of the car assumed a pine-fresh scent that would linger until April.

A brief panic occurred when we were unable to find the tree ornaments, but eventually they surfaced in the upper reaches of the guest bedroom closet. Libby tastefully festooned every mantel, chandelier, and newel post with *objets de Noël* and baked roughly a thousand cookies while I dredged Bing Crosby's *Christmas Classics* from the bottom of the CD stack. A full three weeks before the boys were due, we were in all-out festive mode.

So was the town. I'd always wanted to spend a Christmas in the U.K., and St. Andrews had begun to look like the fulfillment of my vision. Strings of simple white lights suspended across the cobblestone streets, storefront windows transformed into celebrations of the season, the scent of sugar and spice seemed everywhere. People bustled along the sidewalks and up and down the little alleys carrying packages and smiling and greeting one another even more cheerily than usual. It was all rather Dickensian, or at least Burnsian.

To be honest, neither of the boys was particularly enthralled with the notion of spending an entire week in St. Andrews. Oh, I know they wanted to spend Christmas with us as much as we did with them, and I knew they were curious about the home Libby and I had made for ourselves, but I also knew they were cringing at the prospect of seven straight winter days in the Auld Grey Toon. For people their age, Christmas week was just about the deadest week of the year, since the university was closed and almost all the students were gone. Any other time, there was plenty of nightlife (well, at least for a small Scottish town). Allegedly, there were more pubs per capita in St. Andrews than in any city in the U.K., and during the school year every one of them kept busy—but not over the holidays.

So we bought the boys off with a pre-Scotland jaunt to Amsterdam, Europe's most relaxed city, thanks to a lenient policy on recreational drugs. Scott had stopped off there after his visit to us in the spring, had loved it, and knew his older brother would, too. So they took a sort of long weekend there before meeting us.

Also joining us was a good friend from the U.S., Tori Scalzi and her daughter, Clare, a freshman at Vanderbilt. On Christmas Eve the six of us piled into the Honda like a bunch of circus clowns and drove into Edinburgh for sightseeing and last-minute shopping. Libby cooked a beautiful tenderloin dinner. There were games of charades and Monopoly, much eating and drinking and merriment, lots of attention for Millie, and a Christmas Day walk on the beach. That day the boys went out on the Old Course and played the first hole with a Frisbee, scoring a pair of 5s.

The next day—Boxing Day as it's known in the U.K.—we invited our neighbors in for an afternoon of caroling and cheer. I played the piano for about the third time since its arrival, Gordon and his brother-in-law, Ken (who made Gordon look like a shrinking violet), led the group in song, and twenty-two people consumed sixteen bottles of wine. The next day, I somehow roused myself for a round of golf with Eric and Margaret Reid's son, Athol, and two of his friends, each of whom was even more hungover than I was.

Was it like the Christmas we'd known back home? No. It never could be, especially for the boys, who had always celebrated in the same living room in front of the same fireplace. Our sons knew that, while we were doing our best to make things merry and bright, this house in St. Andrews would never, could never be their home, that when we'd sold our house in New York, we'd all lost something forever. But I think, at least I hope, they also knew that life is not perfect, that change is not bad, and that other fine Christmas homes—both ours and theirs—loomed in their future. In the meantime, we were together.

36

Winter Wonderland

During the holiday season the Scots embrace a series of odd traditions. Boxing Day is almost as big a deal as Christmas. (Boxing refers to a time when the tradesmen received a "Christmas box" from their patrons—money in appreciation for the work they'd carried out during the year.) All the banks, shops, and offices are closed as everyone generally continues the eating, drinking, and merriment of the day before. A few days later, they gear up for Hogmanay (a word for which no one has a cogent explanation). An ancient pagan festival that culminates in New Year's, Hogmanay in Scotland is much *bigger* than Christmas (possibly because, for four hundred years following the Reformation, the celebration of Christmas was actually banned in Scotland). In Edinburgh, where it has become a huge ticketed festival, the Hogmanay street parties begin on around the 28th and things don't settle down until January 2.

And then there is the whole business of First Footing. Scottish folklore holds that the first person to step across your threshold in the New Year is a harbinger of the luck you will have—good or bad—over the next twelve months. The desired visitor is a tall dark stranger bearing a cake, a coin, or a lump of coal for the fire. Blond men are said to be undesirable, possibly relating back to the Vikings, who were door-to-door pillager/rapists of the Scots for the better part of eight centuries.

We got a blond. He wasn't a stranger and he wasn't even particularly tall. At eight o'clock on the morning of January 1, 2005, Gordon Murray appeared at the door. He'd come to pick me up for golf.

Yes, golf on New Year's Day. A week earlier, in a colossally unguarded moment, I'd agreed to partake in another harebrained tradition, this one strictly St. Andrean, known as the New Year's Prizes, wherein roughly three hundred demented townsfolk try to determine who has the least debilitating hangover.

I had parted company with Gordon only five hours earlier, after a festive evening with our wives that had begun with a champagne dinner at The Barns, a delightful inn and steakhouse in Kingsbarns, owned by fellow Thursday Clubber Ian Murtaugh, and had concluded at a ceilidh (sort of a Scottish square dance) at the New Club. Concluded, at least, for Libby, me, and Shelagh. Gordon had closed the place.

"C'mon, get a move on, my man," he said cheerily. "I almost won this tournament a couple of years ago, and I think this could be the year." Gordon, more than anyone I'd ever encountered, had an ability to drink and carouse all night and then bolt out of bed the next morning as perky as if he'd had ten hours of sleep. Meanwhile, my head felt like the size of Jupiter, I could barely lift the spoon to stir my coffee, and my stomach was a cauldron about to boil over.

Yet oddly, I was looking forward to that round of golf.

A year earlier, I would never have considered it. In the winter after our arrival, I'd sat for hours at the bay window, staring incredulously at the procession of fools—heads down, hands in pockets, bundled like Eskimos, trudging doggedly into the gale. Here we were, on a remote and rugged extremity of the Scottish coast—at about the same latitude as Moscow. Rain pelted down one day in three, wind whistled almost constantly at 25 to 50 miles per hour, and daylight lasted barely eight hours (and that was daylight, not sunlight—if you wanted sunlight, figure on about two hours). Yet there was golf—unremitting, indomitable, exuberant golf. The daily ballot for the Old Course looked like midsummer—every tee time was taken. And this parade of the intrepid prevailed not only on the Old but on the New, the Jubilee, the Eden, the Strathtyrum, and the Balgove as well.

It was a very different world from the one I'd known. Back in New York the likelihood of my playing golf any day between November and April was about the same as my playing Othello at the Met or middle linebacker for the Giants.

I'd held out until February and then entered the R&A Winter Shotgun. What a mistake. To begin with, it was my first entry in a club competition—that had me more than a bit nervous. I knew no one in my assigned group, and that didn't help. And the competition was foursomes—alternate shot—the most pressurized format of all.

And then there was the weather. The appointed day happened to be the most viciously cold and windy of the year. Had I not been playing golf, I would never have left the house. The thermometer read 39 and the anemometer outside the R&A had the wind speed at 45 mph with gusts over 60.

In a shotgun, the competitors disperse across the course, each foursome starting on a different tee. Everyone begins simultaneously, with the firing of a shotgun (or in the U.S. an airhorn—or at the R&A a nineteenth-century cannon).

My group was slated to tee off at the 9th hole, just about the farthest point out on the Old Course. Had I not been a total neophyte, I would have known that it was okay to drive my car out onto the links, to an area behind the 8th tee where, for the purpose of shotgun events, cars could be parked. Instead, I trudged the two miles, straight into the biting wind.

On the way, I did some strategizing. The foursomes format meant I would tee off on either the odd-numbered holes or the even-numbered holes. Number 9 was an easy par-4, and as downwind as it was on that day I could reach the green with a long iron, but I really didn't want to have to hit the first shot of the day—especially a long iron. Besides, if I drove off 9, it meant I'd have to drive off 11, the second hardest hole on the course, 17, the hardest hole on the course, and 1, where I still hadn't gotten used to the pressure. So I'd decided I'd take the even-numbered holes.

I arrived fifteen minutes too early, having lost all feeling in my extremities. The conditions were so brutal I hunkered on the lee side of a bunker like a medieval sheep. My partner was Jamie Barber, a distinguished-looking fellow of perhaps seventy years. We shook hands, commiserated a bit about the weather, and then he said, "Well, George, you're the low handicapper, why don't you lead us off."

"Oh, no, that's all right, Jamie," I said. "You show me the way— I'm just a rookie."

"No, no, I insist," he said.

"Are you sure?" I said, voice cracking.

"Yes, absolutely," he said. "You see, if I were to tee off here it would mean I'd have to tee off on 11 . . . and 17 . . . and 1. I'd rather not put myself through that."

So I took out my 2-iron, assumed a numb-fingered grip, and wrenched the club convulsively upward, whereupon the wind grabbed it like a kite. My tee shot was a soaring slice that crossed two fairways and embedded in a gorse bush somewhere on the back 9. And that turned out to be one of my better efforts that day. Jamie and I ended up with 26 Stableford points. We would have had more, had we not 4-putted the 13th green from 4 feet. We didn't finish last, but we gave the guys in last place a good run. I didn't play golf again until the spring.

By the second winter, however, I'd hit a rhythm through the Monday and Thursday Club games, which had just kept going, week after week through the late fall. There was no Labor Day letdown, no packing in of the clubs—everyone just kept on swinging, and I kept on swinging with them, partly in fear of being labeled a dilettante, a pansy, or both. Before I knew it I'd become one of those steadfast, idiotic winter golfers.

In fairness, it's not quite as nutty as it looks. Rain, wind, and darkness notwithstanding, the winter conditions in St. Andrews are pretty darned golfable. On average it's a dozen degrees or so warmer than in the U.S. Northeast and the annual snowfall is only an inch or two, as opposed to a foot or several. Perhaps most important, the blessed sand-based fairways and greens stay in remarkably good nick. Since most of the daily play comes from locals—hardy locals at that—there's no mucking about. Four-ball rounds finish in three and a half hours or less. Indeed, on some days only the swift survive—slackers risk freezing in place, blowing out to sea, or running out of light. The conditions also breed a special camaraderie, similar, I suspect, to the bond shared by Siberian letter carriers.

I found that the Old Course played both easier and harder than in summer. Easier because many of the tees were moved up and the cold hard ground ran fast, with the result that even a player of moderate power could drive a par-4 or two. The pins tended to remain in the same low-traffic positions for days, sometimes weeks, and more than ninety of the course's vaunted bunkers had become Hallowed Ground Under Repair, in readiness for the upcoming Open Championship. Thus, when we hit into the Cottage or Strath or Principal's Nose or Hell, instead of wading sadly into the abyss, we simply plucked the ball out, no penalty.

At the same time, however, the bone-hard ground and brisk winds combined to stiffen the strategic assignments. Before every swing— whether a drive or a pitch—it was necessary to stop and say "Wait a moment now, just exactly what do I want to do here?"

The only major change in the course came at the 11th, the hole most exposed to the elements, where both the tee and green were given the winter off. On December 1, a temporary tee was carved out of the fescue, roughly 20 yards beyond the 10th green, and shots were aimed in the general direction of the 12th tee at a narrow, fiercely sloped temporary green. It played about 180 yards, invariably, into the teeth of the wind, and for three months a year it was the hardest hole in town.

But adjusting to the course was only part of the challenge of winter golf. There were numerous more subtle things to learn. Booking tee times, I discovered, was something of an art: With daylight scarce, the 1st tee was open only four hours, from eight until noon, but if you tried for the window between eight and ten, you took a risk. The Links Trust closed the tee on mornings when there was frost, reviewing the situation every half hour until it was clear. If you had an 8:50 A.M. tee time and they didn't open the course until nine, you were out of luck. Wily veterans knew to make a last-minute check of the weather report before submitting their ballot cards.

The practice center in St. Andrews is half a mile from the 1st tee of the Old Course, so almost no one makes a pre-round visit. Having been spoiled by the fine range at Sleepy Hollow, my club in the States, I was used to hitting fifty or so balls and an equal number of chips and putts before my weekend games, and I'd needed several weeks to adjust to the reality that my first strike of the day would be the tee shot at number 1. Winter golf brought a whole new problem—the need to warm up. What saw me through was an old Johnny Miller tip: When there's no range, take your driver and make twenty swings in a row without stopping—no more, no fewer—twenty swings. It's actually not easy to do—and you start to look and feel foolish after about the eighth swing—but I found it enabled me to get the first shot or two airborne without hurting myself.

Then there was the other aspect of warming up—haberdashery. I'd always assumed you couldn't play winter golf without five layers of clothing. Now I know you can't play winter golf *with* five layers of clothing. My sartorial epiphany came on the day I learned it's okay for guys to wear silk underwear. A set of paper-thin long johns, a pair of corduroys, two sweaters (one sleeveless, one turtleneck), a ski cap, winter golf gloves on both hands, and I was good to go—except on really rough days when I added a rain suit. (The myth that everyone carries a flask of hooch in the golf bag is just that. In the course of fifty or so winter rounds, only once or twice was I offered an adult beverage. Okay, maybe six times.)

But the ultimate challenge was the business of taking it to the mat. On November 1, a large wire trash can appears next to the 1st tee of the Old Course. It's filled with dozens of slabs of artificial turf, each the approximate size and conformation of a haddock. This is the signal that, in the interest of protecting the sacred turf, over the next five months all iron and wood shots from the fairway will be played off a mat.

My mat and I got off to a poor start. Attached to it was a loop of white string that I assumed was meant to be slipped over some appendage of my bag. So I slipped it over my umbrella handle. By the time I reached my tee shot the string had twisted itself into a braid that Heidi would have been proud of—two minutes later it was unraveled, but so was I.

Most of the wily veterans, I noticed, shoved the mats into pockets of their bags. At least two guys dragged them along the ground behind them, like haddocks on a leash, and one rather corpulent bloke shoved it down the back of his rain pants, an abrasive butt-warmer. I settled on a bag pocket.

When your golf ball sits on a mat, it's approximately one half-inch closer to your hands. Naturally, I failed to compensate, with the result that on my first few swings I made excellent contact with the mat but horrible contact with the ball, propelling both about the same distance. After four mighty swipes at the opening hole I was a yard short of the Swilken Burn, about to learn that the toughest of all mat shots is the soft wedge. When both ball and mat flopped summarily into the drink I nearly returned to the warm sanctity of my home.

By the 5th or 6th hole, I began aiming my shots for the rough so I wouldn't have to deal with the little green monster. My score that day, under excellent weather conditions, was 94. Round two was marginally more successfully only because I hit every shot of less than 80 yards with a putter.

It was nearly a month before I broke the code. But once I did, my mat and I became fast friends. By pointing it to the right of my target, I realized, I could induce the more inside-out swing path I'd been working on for over a year. By positioning the ball at the very back edge of the mat, I was able to hit a driver into the wind when needed (although an R&A edict later decreed this to be "bad form"). By flipping the mat on its back and hitting off the rubber bottom, I could get some check on my pitch shots. One day I actually slapped the mat down on the upper tier of the 17th green and instead of putting used a lofted wedge to flop the ball down to the pin on the lower level, where I sank a 4-footer for par. I then parred 18 for a round of 72—my fourth 72, but still no scores under par. Oh, how I would have loved my first red number to have come on a morning in the middle of December.

For two or three months, in addition to my Monday and Thursday games, I'd had a semi-regular Saturday game, with Gordon and two kindred golf spirits, our neighbor Bryce Hogarth and David Sandford. Each of them, like Gordon, was a couple of years older than I, and each of them, like me, was a 7-handicap. Bryce, a six-foot-two gentle bear of a man with dark eyebrows and a white burr haircut, had had a successful career as a salesman, and I could see why. He knew how to chat people up, draw them out, and let them talk about themselves, and he also had a near-photographic memory, for which I had a respect bordering on awe, my own memory rarely extending back more than a few seconds. Bryce was a student of golf history—particularly European competition—and could cite stats on every player and performance from Tiger Woods to the 1860 Open. Despite my own three decades of steeping in the game, when Bryce and I disagreed on a fact or figure, I deferred to him.

David had an elegant drawling sort of Scots accent. I loved the way he greeted me on the tee each Saturday with a "Guud mahwning, Jahwge." He was actually Commander David Sandford. His career in the Royal Navy had included command of one of the Queen's submarines as well as an exchange-program stint with the U.S. Navy in Norfolk, Virginia. Upon his retirement, David had followed the time-honored path of British military men with a bent for golf: He'd become a club secretary (general manager in American parlance). His club was one of Edinburgh's oldest and most distinguished—Bruntsfield (which David pronounced "B'duntsfield")—its fine parkland course offering views of the Firth of Forth. Bruntsfield served a sumptuous daily lunch. One of my most surprising rounds of golf had come when David had invited Gordon, Bryce, and me for a day's outing. After a fine but bloating meal of shrimp, pâté, roast beef, and trifle, I'd gone out and made six pars, six bogeys, and six birdies.

Gordon, Bryce, David, and I always played a one-pound Nassau. Gordon, being Gordon, took charge on the 1st tee and tossed our four balls into the air to determine who would become partners. Gordon, following U.K. convention, got five strokes—three fourths of the difference between his 14-handicap and our 7s. He was by far the worst ball striker in the group but by far the best putter, and no matter how the teams shook out, the match usually came down to the last hole or two.

Each week when the final putt was holed we faced a conundrum—where to go for drinks. Bryce, Gordon, and I were members of the St. Andrews Golf Club, David and I were members of the R&A, and Bryce, David, and Gordon were members of the New Club. More often than not, we ended up at the New, joining Eric Reid and three of his contemporaries who assembled there for lunch each Saturday. Along with them, we'd settle the world's problems for an hour or so and then disband.

Except on the Saturday before Christmas. That week, all four of us put on coats and ties and went in for a proper lunch at the R&A. A long liquid lunch—two beers to start, followed by two or three bottles of wine with the food and concluded by a series of brandies and liqueurs, the precise number of which I don't think even Bryce could accurately recall.

And so for five months a year, I embraced this game of winter golf—on Mondays, Thursdays, and Saturdays. We played in hail and sleet, played on days when the ball blew off the tee and the flagsticks blew out of cups, when 300-yard par-4s could be reached with 4-irons and 160-yard par-3s couldn't be reached at all. Our eyes watered, our noses ran, our ears burned, and our joints ached, but our passion never wavered. Indeed, to walk a brisk 18 holes in winter with three good friends, the wind lashing at your cheeks, the turf crunching beneath your feet, is to know a noble sort of joy.

The New Year's Day Prizes began ominously, when I carved my opening tee shot deep over the OB fence for a triple-bogey 7. I would take another 7 at the 14th hole. Walking to our tee shots on that hole I'd turned and said to Gordon, "You know, it's astounding to me that, in over a year of playing this course—what is it, fifty rounds—there are two things I've never done: I've never hit a ball into Hell Bunker and I've never made a 3 on the 18th hole."

Immediately, I hit a 4-wood into Hell Bunker.

"Well," said Gordon. "Maybe this means you'll birdie 18."

I was already several strokes over par, and at that point I didn't care. I cared even less after the 17th tee, where I hit a pushed pop-up that was so bad it didn't reach the hotel, barely fifty yards away, leading to an 8. Then at the home hole all hope of a birdie vanished when I left myself a putt of 80 feet.

And in it went. There was nothing to do but laugh. Despite taking 22 strokes on three holes, I'd managed an 83 on a day when the wind had blown hard. It turned out to be good for a tie for fourth place. Hardly a tall dark stranger with a piece of coal for the fire, but not a bad way to start the year.

37

Stalking Prince William

What were the chances that two of the world's most attractive and fascinating males would converge in the same little Scottish town? George Peper of America and Prince William of Wales, together in St. Andrews—sometimes truth is stranger than fiction.

I must give him credit for being the first to arrive. It was early in the year 2001 when Wills, as he is known to those of us on the inside, made the surprise decision to matriculate at St. Andrews (rather than Cambridge, his crown prince father's alma mater). Immediately, applications to the university soared by 50 percent, most of them from females.

Allegedly, two tabloid newspapers had bought houses in town and made payoff arrangements with bartenders to provide scoops. But when Prince Charles arrived with his son for Freshman Week it went almost unnoticed—it was the week of September 11. Only after I came to town, precisely two years later, did St. Andrews began to generate a full frenzy of press attention. The combined presence of the two of us was, I suppose, simply too enormous to ignore.

As an Anglophile, I'd always been something of a royals watcher, and I'd been shamelessly infatuated with William's mother, Diana. I can still remember exactly where I was and what I was doing when I learned the shocking news of her death. The only other public figure about whom I can make that statement is John F. Kennedy.

So I was hoping to get a glimpse of the lad. In fact, I was sort of expecting it. This was not a big town—just three main streets, circumscribed by the sea on one side and the golf courses on another, with the main route in and out passing right by our door. I figured a bump-into was inevitable, but in nearly a year and a half neither Libby nor I had had a royal sighting.

What made this all the more frustrating was that just about everyone we knew *had* seen him—on the street, in a pub or restaurant, even on the golf course. The final straw came on the morning that Margaret Reid reported she'd seen Prince William pushing a shopping cart in Tesco. I'd had it. If he was not going to make himself conveniently evident to me, I'd simply have to seek him out.

I was armed with a few facts. He had two residences, one in a guesthouse on the grounds of Strathtyrum, an estate less than a mile outside town. However, since my inquisitiveness didn't extend to posing as a gardener or stable boy, that was out of the question. Ah, but he also had a room in a house on Howard Place, three blocks from our home. We were neighbors!

"You can tell when he's in residence," a friend told me, "by the plainclothed cops standing around outside the door to the place." Thus, for the better part of a month Millie and I walked into town with a slight detour past Howard Place. This, I must say, was totally contrary to my sense of ethics—as I've stated earlier, I never walk anywhere if I can ride. Once or twice I did see a pair of gray-suited goons who eyed me suspiciously, making it awkward to stop and lurk for any respectable period of time. With my unremarkable clothing and horn-rimmed Harry Potter glasses, I probably looked just harmless enough to be a serial killer—or at least a deranged stalker—and the last thing I wanted was for my friends in the States to see a newspaper photo of me grimacing while being wrestled and strip-searched against the back bumper of an unmarked Rover.

Wills was an athlete, had actually made the all-England water polo team, and I'd known he had a ritual of early-morning workouts at the St. Andrews Bay spa. Inasmuch as I'd decided not to join there, however, I had only one option. One day at 7:00 A.M. I appeared at the front counter of the spa, posing as a potential member and asking for a tour of the place.

"Certainly, sir," said the muscular young man on duty, "this is a perfect time—there's not a soul here at the moment," before leading me on a meaningless fifteen-minute walk of the facilities.

A couple of friends had spotted Wills at Ma Bells and the West End, two town pubs favored by the students, but I'm just not much of a pub guy, especially when I'm conspicuously twice the age of every other patron, so I limited myself to lingering, fruitless peers through the windows of those establishments.

In mid-March, with William's graduation looming barely two months away, I finally got a break, and from a most unlikely source. The R&A, realizing the Prince had never visited the club in his four years at the university, had wondered whether he'd like a tour of the place, with lunch to follow—lunch with members of the R&A Club Committee—and he had accepted!

I'd circled the date on my calendar, I'd polished my shoes for the first time in six months, and I'd just about mastered the slight bow of the head that is recommended when greeting anyone known as "Your Highness" when the news came that Wills had reconsidered. Presumably, upon reflection he'd decided that four hours in the company of eight fawning golf gits in blue blazers did not make for a big afternoon.

So the young Prince never got to meet me. But a handful of other lucky students did. Again it was the R&A that served as matchmaker—literally. Each year the club invites interested members to volunteer for a series of matches against the golf teams of four local universities—Dundee, Edinburgh, St. Andrews, and Stirling. These are essentially calls to slaughter. The six-point matches in which six two-man teams play better-ball against six teams from the university are contested at scratch, and the R&A has very few scratch players, especially among those who live locally and can make themselves available to play. To fill out its team, the club must therefore reach well down the skill ranks, and for the Stirling match in 2005 they reached all the way down to me.

Perhaps because it was my first such match, I was paired with the team captain, Jim McArthur, a local chartered surveyor who was a member of the R&A Championship Committee (which runs the Open Championship, among others) and a 2-handicap golfer. With those qualifications he might have been expected to be a serious sort, but I knew Jim to be a delightful fellow with a puckish wit and an ability to make people feel at home, which was exactly what I needed.

The match was on the Old Course, preceded by lunch at noon in the clubhouse. We met in the library, where drinks were served. I was the last to appear (people in Scotland are extremely prompt about engagements, particularly where free alcohol is involved) and I noticed that everyone was holding adult beverages.

"A Bloody Mary, please," I said to the barman on duty.

"Good choice," said Jim, "we're going to need all the blood, sweat, and tears we can muster against these lads," and he introduced me to our two young opponents. They were clean-cut, well-mannered boys, this was their first visit to St. Andrews, and they were clearly thrilled to be in the R&A. One of them was a 2-handicap, the other a scratch. We chatted with them and their teammates for a while, and then Jim took me aside.

"On paper, you and I have only one chance against these boys, George," he said.

"And what's that?" I asked.

"Get them bloody pissed before they play," he said.

"Pissed. Do you mean the American pissed—angry—or the Scottish pissed—drunk?"

"Scottish. Now the good news is we're the last of the six groups off—that gives us plenty of time. Just leave it to me."

"You're the captain," I said, and took a very small sip of my drink.

Jim then called for everyone's attention.

"You lads from Stirling have a reputation as one of the most fearsome golf teams in Great Britain," he said, "and it was therefore incumbent on the R&A to assemble a squad of twelve strong and distinguished players to battle you. Unfortunately we weren't able to do that, so you'll have to play the twelve blokes who've shown up."

He then dispatched the first two matches to the dining room. The rest of us ordered another drink, and a half hour later Jim and I and our two opponents took a third drink to the lunch table. With several ounces of vodka now coursing through my veins, I was beginning to question my captain's strategy. After all, the drinking age in the U.K. was eighteen—these kids surely knew how to handle their liquor at least as well as I did.

At lunch Jim ordered a bottle of the club claret, which the four of us polished off somewhere between the appetizer and main course, at which point a second bottle arrived. Never had I consumed this much alcohol before a game of golf—and we weren't done. As we changed into our golf togs in the locker room, a silver tray arrived with four large cordial glasses filled with a clear liquid.

"Ah, the nectar of the fairways," said Jim. "Kummel, everyone?"

Kummel (pronounced alternatively "kummel" and "kimmel") is sort of the haggis of postprandial libations, its origin and ingredients a bit mysterious. Ninety percent of the world's consumption seems to take place in St. Andrews at the R&A and in the town of Gullane (pronounced alternatively "Gullin" and "Gillin") at the Honourable Company of Edinburgh Golfers (pronounced Muirfield). It tastes a bit like liquefied rubber bands.

Thus infused with eight drinks, we made our way festively to the tee where, for the first time in my life, I felt absolutely fearless. My drive split the fairway and traveled nearly 300 yards and my wedge approach nearly hit the flagstick before stopping 20 feet past the pin. The putt for birdie barely missed and one of the young lads had to sink a 5-footer to tie us. I parred the next hole and then birdied 3 after hitting a drive onto the front of the green. The old guys were 1 up! Two holes later both Jim and I birdied the par-5 5th to go 2 up.

My swing was free and easy, no shot seemed beyond my skill, and best of all I was putting like a kid. If I'd known that abundant quantities of liquor could be so salutary for one's game, I suspect I would have become an alcoholic at age fourteen.

We made the turn 2 up. Then we both hit the wall. The booze, combined with our age—an aggregate half century more than that of our adversaries—took its toll and we lost three holes in a row. At the 12th, having made double-bogeys on the two previous holes, I topped my tee shot ingloriously into the steep face of a bunker that was no more than 50 yards from the tee. Let me tell you, there are few golf experiences more demeaning than to wade into a bunker and hit backwards, reducing a 50-yard drive by 30 yards. At that point I'm not sure whether I needed a gallon of coffee, a pint of kummel, or a needle of morphine.

I never really recovered, but Jim played heroically, halving the lads on the next four holes, parring 17 as they both bogeyed, and then birdieing the 18th hole for a 1-up victory. Two of our other five teams managed to squeak through and miraculously, virtually without precedent, the R&A halved its match with the college boys, 3–3. The whole thing was way more fun than meeting Prince William.

38

Dazzled by a Puffin Crossing

One area of Scottish culture with which I'd made little attempt to familiarize myself was the world of team sports—or team sport as they refer to it in the U.K. Although I felt a bit guilty about this—and more than a bit left out when in the R&A or the St. Andrews Golf Club the topic of conversation turned to the latest big match and I had nothing to contribute—it was not inconsistent with my attitude toward sports in the U.S., where I'd never had more than a casual check-in-once-a-month interest in the New York Yankees and the New York Giants. Other than that, I was athletically clueless, asportual.

I suspect, however, that even a rabid American sports fan would have a challenge with the offerings on the British calendar. Cricket was totally bewildering, a gaggle of ice cream men playing stickball on steroids. Soccer, which the locals call football, was fun to watch but I couldn't get past the hooligan aspect, both on the field and in the stands. And then there was rugby, with two different versions in play—one with thirteen players, the other with fifteen. I figured if they couldn't sort it out, I didn't need to.

So when my friends began to prattle on about the Australian Chinaman's economy rate at Lords, or Scunthorpe's throttling of Man U, or the brilliant last-minute try by the Wigan Warriors, I took it as a signal either to shut up and gaze out the window or pay a lingering visit to the loo. And on the morning when Gordon Murray knocked on the door with the breathless news that he'd snagged a ticket for me to the Scotland-Ireland Six Nations match in Edinburgh on Saturday, well, I fear I may not have reacted appropriately.

"Uh . . . what sport is that?"

"Rugby, of course," said Gordon. "This is the biggest match of the year—a grudge match—and it comes to Scotland only once every two years. Ireland's better on paper, but they've lost a couple of key players to injuries recently, so it could be close. Besides, a bunch of the guys are going—we're going to make a day of it, drive into the city in the morning, have a few pints, go for a proper lunch, head out to the stadium for the game, and then do a bit of pub crawling afterward. There are thirty-two pubs on Rose Street and one year after the game we hit every one of them."

It all sounded a bit too manly for me, especially the pub-crawling part. There were twenty-four pubs in St. Andrews and in the course of eighteen months I'd hit only one of them, for a cheeseburger. But Gordon had done a typically brilliant sales job and seemed incredulous I was even mulling over his offer. Besides, I figured this was as good a time as any for me to thrust myself into the Scottish sporting scene.

"Okay, I'm in," I said with as much enthusiasm as I could muster.

By the morning of the game, I was ruing that decision. The evening before, Libby and I had been invited to a dinner party where I'd taken in alcohol as if I was preparing for a university match. I think it was the three after-dinner liqueurs that did me in. I'd awakened feeling significantly less than one hundred percent, hoping some fresh air would snap me out of it.

Half an hour later, I was in the back seat of Gordon's car with a little white-haired fellow named John. I'd never met John and it seemed Gordon barely knew him except as a fellow New Club member who needed a ride to the game. He was also a devout smoker, dragging hard on a succession of unfiltered Marlboros. Had John asked whether I minded his smoking, I would surely have let him know. I've always wanted to be asked that question and then have the courage to answer, "No, I don't mind if you smoke—do you mind if I fart? Then we can both enjoy our dirty habits." But being a nonconfrontational sort, I'd said nothing, just perspired profusely and belched surreptitiously into my corner of the car.

When I'd set foot in that car I'd entered a sort of personalized torture chamber. I can think of only two things in the world that are guaranteed to make me sick to my stomach—sitting in the back seat of a vehicle for any length of time and sitting in close proximity to someone smoking a cigarette. Now I was doing both, and on a stomach that had been marginal to begin with.

It was too cold to open a window, especially at the rate we were traveling. We'd gotten a somewhat late start so Gordon had taken the back roads and was doing his best imitation of James Bond in an Aston Martin, rocketing down the straightaways, working the gears furiously, and whipping through the S curves with more gusto than finesse. Barely fifteen minutes into our journey, I knew I had a major problem.

"Uh, Gordon," I said weakly, "I don't think I'm gonna make it."

I'd been silent since we'd set out—now suddenly the attention of all three of my fellow travelers was focused on me. John had even removed his cigarette.

"What do you mean?" said Gordon, slowing briefly to warp 7.

"I'm feeling a little ill, and I don't think my stomach is going to be able to handle things today," I said. "I think maybe you should just drop me in the next town and I'll take a cab home."

A brief discussion ensued during which they offered me the front passenger seat, offered to stop and let me take a few breaths of secondary-smoke-free air, and generally tried to convince me to hang in there, the most effective inducement being Gordon's reckoning that he wouldn't be able to unload my ticket and I'd therefore be out 80 quid.

I suppose I could have toughed it out another twenty miles to Edinburgh without consequences for the interior of Gordon's car, and once there I might have rallied for the rest of the day. Essentially, at that moment, my body was speaking to me firmly and what it said was "Take me pub crawling tonight and you're a dead man tomorrow."

And so, after another brief discussion, it was decided that I would be deposited in the town of Markinch from whence I would get a train to Leuchars followed by a cab back to St. Andrews.

The name Markinch is derived from two Gaelic words, Marc (meaning horse) and Innes (meaning meadow). Although now a singularly unremarkable town, Markinch was once the capital of Fife—back in Pictish times—presumably before any other town, village, or hamlet had been discovered. The population reached a peak of 6,800 in 1901 when several small industries were in full flower, but during the twentieth century, when just about every other town multiplied threefold, nearly 5,000 Markinchians bolted. The most illustrious citizen, it seemed, had been one Norman Wilkie, who in 1982 had achieved a degree of fame by shooting history's fattest wild rabbit, the bulging bunny weighing in at 8.25 pounds, fully five pounds heavier than your average feral cottontail.

So there I was, nauseous in Horsemeadow. The single main street offered a hairdresser, a minimart, and, blessedly, a pub that happened to be open at ten in the morning. I only hope that pub is still in business today after everything I left in its men's toilet.

Architecturally, the most arresting building in town was the Tudor Italianate train station, built when rail travel came to Fife in 1847. Inside, the kindly lady at the ticket window had good news for me—the next train to Leuchars was in half an hour. I wandered to the minimart, bought a bottle of Diet Pepsi and a roll of Tums, returned to the station, and settled myself gingerly on a bench on the northbound platform.

It was a busy morning in Markinch—in the course of my brief wait, over a hundred people appeared, most of them large, tattooed males wearing kilts, Team Scotland rugby shirts, and work boots. Clearly, they were headed to the Big Game I'd just aborted.

I managed to make my half-hour trip safely home, where Libby served me a soothing bowl of lentil soup. Then I went straight to bed. By the time I awoke the game was over, Scotland had been trounced, and Gordon and his band of merry men were, I suspected, into pub number eleven or twelve.

I felt much better until I looked at the day's mail and saw that a letter had arrived from our car insurance company. Essentially it told me I needed to get a U.K. driver's license. The company had insured me with my American license for a year but the honeymoon was over.

I hadn't renounced my U.S. residency, just obtained a writer's visa, which allowed me to do work for American companies while living in the U.K. I was thus sort of a man without a country, a situation that had worked beautifully from a motoring standpoint. Granted, the speed cameras had nabbed me twice—and I'd had to pay hefty fines— but inasmuch as I didn't have a British license, there was no way for the vehicle Nazis (either British or American) to slap me with penalty points. After each citation I'd received a peevish letter from the Fife Constabulary saying, effectively, "We're really mad at you, Mr. Yankee wise guy, and one of these days we're going get you, but for the moment you have us over a barrel." The nicest aspect had been that I didn't have to worry about losing my license as a result of a failed Breathalyzer test, overwhelmingly the number one fear among adult male Scots. But now suddenly things had changed. For a moment, I had a terrifying vision of having to go everywhere on foot, or worse yet, ride in the back seats of other people's cars, seated next to guys like Nicotine John. There was never a question, even if we were going to leave in six months—I would take the damned test.

Then I looked at what was involved. It was not one test but three of them—a Theory Test (analogous to what we in the U.S. call the written test), a Hazard Perception Test (in which you view videos of traffic situations and identify potential problems as they develop; the faster you spot them, the higher grade you get), and finally a Road Test, said to be among the most stringent in the world. I'd always seen the U.K. drivers as uncommonly knowledgeable and courteous—it was no wonder.

The Theory Test turned out to be first and foremost a cottage industry. The exam fee was £20, and if you wanted any chance of passing it you needed to buy a book entitled *The Official Theory Test for Car Drivers,* which was another £20. And why not—it was 430 pages.

Much of it was the same as in America, but certain aspects were quirkily daunting. To begin with there was an entire Highway Code, comprised not only of rules for car drivers but rules for motorcyclists, rules for bicyclists, and rules for pedestrians (although the pedalers and walkers didn't have to take tests). There was also a section entitled "Rules About Animals"—stuff like "Don't honk at sheep" and "Never trust a horse to signal before turning." As an American motorist, the only animals I'd dealt with were road hogs.

I'm not sure how many signs, traffic lights, pavement markings, and assorted electronic signals we have in the U.S., a nation with more than eight million miles of roadway, but I imagine it doesn't come close to the 234 signs that were depicted in my Theory Test book. They came in a variety of delightful shapes, colors, sizes, and symbols, including one with a Sisyphean fellow pushing a boulder with a stick and another—this one a surefire attention-getter—showing a car hurtling off the edge of a cliff.

In Great Britain, I learned, it's important to know when you're "dazzling" other motorists (and not with the halter top worn by your friend in the passenger seat). Dazzling in this case refers to the injudicious use of one's high beams. And speaking of lights, you are expected to know that bomb demolition vans have flashing blue lights, doctors' cars have flashing green lights, and powered wheelchairs have flashing amber lights (in the event you are otherwise unable to distinguish those vehicles).

Then there is the whole matter of pelican crossings, puffin crossings, and toucan crossings (yes, those are their actual names), the traffic-light-controlled areas intended to aid the transit of pedestrians. Pelican crossings, I learned, were those where the red light changed to flashing amber before going to green. I never learned how to distinguish a puffin from a toucan.

The Theory Test was thirty-five questions, and one needed to answer thirty questions correctly to pass. The test was administered at dozens of centers around the country, and the nearest to us was in Dundee. "Allow plenty of time to reach the test center," said the information booklet, "as you don't want to feel rushed. Also, if you arrive late, you may not be able to take the test."

Suitably intimidated, and being a morning person anyway, I booked the earliest possible slot, 8:30, and set out at 7:30 on what is a twenty-minute trip. The test center was "conveniently located in the city center, just a few short blocks from the Tay Bridge."

Now, nothing in the city of Dundee is conveniently located, least of all the city center, which is in fact impenetrable during the day, when the main streets are restricted to pedestrians. My guess is that, a few years back, the city planners became so exasperated with the inner city's byzantine infrastructure that they just threw in the towel and closed everything down.

The few arteries that are open are one-way streets leading to places with evil-sounding names—Arbroath, Crieff, Glamis. And if, after a series of wild-guess turns, you are fortunate enough to randomly approximate your destination, you are still screwed, as there is absolutely nowhere to park.

I crossed the Tay Bridge into metropolitan Dundee at precisely 7:45 and spent the next forty-five minutes navigating the few short blocks. The usual maze was exacerbated on this day by a string of road excavation projects that looked like Dundee's version of the Boston Big Dig. In typical British fashion, fawning signs explained and apologized for the disruption, but I didn't have time to read them—I was too busy terrifying fellow motorists and barreling through puffin crossings. On three occasions, being the sole car in a pedestrian-only area, I asked passersby for directions. Each of the first two times, I was within two hundred yards of the test center, yet neither person had any idea how to get me there. My third friend turned out to be a drunk who, having heard my plea, just laughed convulsively and stumbled away.

Finally, at 8:28 I screeched into the parking lot next to the test center. Half an hour later I'd passed the test with a score of 34 out of 35 and completed the Hazard Perception part with a score of 70, which sounded weak to me but according to the test administrator was "outstanding."

A couple of weeks later I took the Road Test, which turned out to be similar to a colonoscopy—the worst part was the anticipation. Indeed, the examiner seemed to pay almost no attention to my driving skills. I think I know why. The information sheet I'd handed him had shown that I'd taken the Theory Test in Dundee. When he saw that, I figure he knew I could drive anywhere.

39

Two Trips Home

On most mornings, the bleak, treeless landscape outside our window offered no clue as to the time of year. In May, the gorse bushes lining the Old Course fairways burst forth with bright yellow blossoms, but those same flowers might return in midwinter after a sufficiently warm spell. There were no such things as spring showers, summer heat waves, fall foliage, or winter blizzards. Except for the wide variance in daylight—a full twelve hours more in summer than winter—the four seasons in St. Andrews were indistinguishable.

That bothered me at only one time of year, when winter wore on without a trace of spring. Late one February afternoon, sitting in the St. Andrews Golf Club with Gordon and Wee Raymond Gatherum, I began to hold forth on the glories of the Masters.

"It's golf's rite of spring," I said. "There's just no place like April in Augusta. I wish you guys could see it."

"Aye," said Wee Raymond, "I'd love to go to the Masters. I've always wanted to play some golf in America, too. Thirty years ago, when

I was the drummer in a band, we toured all over the U.S., but I never even brought my clubs—what a missed opportunity."

"Well then, why don't we just go," said Gordon, "the three of us and our neighbor Andrew. We'll play some golf and then go to the Masters."

"And just how do you propose to get tickets to the Masters?" I said. "You realize I can't help you. I'm a has-been. I don't have the clout I used to have at Augusta, and even the clout I used to have was minimal."

"Tickets will be no problem," said Gordon, a bit too confidently. I knew he had more connections than AT&T, but the Masters is the toughest ticket in sports. I was forced to continue my line of questioning.

"How in hell do you have a line on Masters tickets?"

"I was recently offered four tickets by a friend," said Gordon, coyly enjoying the moment.

"And who was that?"

"Sir Michael," he said, raising his chin with a self-important smile.

"No way. Michael Bonallack offered you tickets to the Masters?"

"That's right, about three months ago. And I told him that if Stephen made the field I'd take him up on it."

Stephen was Stephen Gallacher, a young Scottish professional (nephew of Bernard Gallacher, the former Ryder Cup captain) who was a member of the St. Andrews Golf Club and—more significantly—a member of the international brotherhood of Friends of Gordon. After a sparkling amateur career he'd struggled as a professional before winning, appropriately, the Dunhill Cup on the Old Course in October, a victory we'd all celebrated that evening at The Barns, the highlight coming with the singing of "Happy Birthday Gordon and Stephen," the two of them having just turned sixty and thirty within a day of each other.

"So did Stephen get an invitation?" I asked.

"No," said Gordon, "but I'll give Michael a call tomorrow—the tickets might still be available."

They weren't, but David Fay came to the rescue, and the trip was on. Thanks to the generous hospitality of *Links* magazine owner Jack Purcell, we were set up to stay and play at Reynolds Plantation in Greensboro, Georgia, for two days followed by three days at the Harbour Town Yacht Club in Hilton Head Island, South Carolina. Meanwhile Gordon, through British Airways FOG Bill Williams, managed to get everyone upgraded to first class from London to Atlanta, found a house in Augusta for the week for $3,000, (about a third the going rate), called in some markers with members of the Augusta Country Club for three rounds of golf, and somehow set up a final night at the Château Élan resort near Atlanta and a final round at the exclusive East Lake Golf Club.

We were an odd foursome, Gordon, Raymond, Andrew, and I—a fisherman, a horse trainer, a knee surgeon, and a golf writer; two Scots, an Englishman, and a Yank—but we got along just as famously on the road as we had in St. Andrews, albeit exhibiting our respective idiosyncrasies.

Gordon the ambassador addressed everyone from cart boys to hotel magnates as "my man" and wasted no timing letting them know we were all citizens of the cradle of golf. "Yeah, three of us live on the 18th hole of the Old Course" was a phrase Andrew, Raymond, and I heard often. In ten days Gordon would make dozens of new contacts and secure sufficient invitations to set us up for a fully hosted return trip the following year, the only caveat being that we play host to each of the new FOGs if and when they came to St. Andrews.

Wee Raymond had a perpetual smile on his face and reveled in the sheer grandeur of everything. On the flight over, when he reclined his first-class seat, his heels couldn't reach the footrest. In his suite at Château Élan, the overstuffed king-sized bed was so high off the ground he had to take a running leap to get into it, and he pronounced the endless, elegant morning buffet at the Four Seasons Hotel at Reynolds Plantation "without question the biggest and best breakfast I've ever had." His only difficulty was with the gallerying at Augusta, where he could have benefited from a small stepladder.

As always, however, Raymond played the best golf of all of us. If there were a world ranking for amateur golfers under five foot four he would probably be among the top 100. He was my length off the tee but a far better shotmaker, those drummer's wrists and hands serving him with an endless variety of shots from 80 yards in. (He tried to teach me his bread-and-butter shot on the Old Course—a low sand wedge that took two bounces and stopped dead. After a couple of hours of practice, I reached the point where I could hit it about once in five attempts, the other four being sclaffs, fats, and shanks.) But Raymond had some good genes going for him—his grandmother was Old Tom Morris's sister.

Andrew my upstairs neighbor was his ethereal self, never quite zeroed in on what was going on. Before our first round, the four of us assembled in carts in the staging at the first tee. Raymond and I hopped into one cart, Gordon got into the driver's seat of the other, and Andrew plopped down in the passenger seat of a third cart, where he sat staring blissfully down the fairway until the three of us approached and pointed out that the fellow sitting next to him was not Gordon.

It was wet that day so the carts were restricted to paths. On one back-9 hole Raymond and I pulled up in back of Andrew and Gordon's cart and waited for them to return from playing their shots. Gordon arrived first and as he reached his bag said, "Ohmygod, I'm missing two clubs. You guys don't have my 4- and 5-irons, do you?"

We didn't. After a few confused seconds, we all looked out at the fairway where Andrew had just played his approach shot and was heading our way.

"Andrew," shouted Gordon, "are those two clubs in your hand yours or mine?"

Briefly befuddled by the question, Andrew stopped, looked down at the clubs, looked back at Gordon, and, with no change of expression, said, "Yours."

We played five fine courses—the Nicklaus and Fazio designs at Reynolds Plantation followed by Haig Point, Secession, and Berkeley Hall in the Hilton Head area. Having fought through a stern winter's golf at St. Andrews, I'd figured my game was in better shape than it had been in any spring of my life. The reality was exactly the opposite.

Faced, for the first time in eighteen months, with the tree-lined courses of my homeland, I was unable to cope. The free, fearless swing I'd enjoyed on the expansive Old Course had disappeared somewhere over the Atlantic, replaced by a fearing, steering, veering lurch. Virtually every second shot was played from some sort of trouble.

I'd spent over a year developing a punch shot that could hold its head in the wind, but now the only use for it was to play recoveries from the trees. On the rare occasions when I found fairways, I had trouble finding greens—the same low ball, when it managed to clear fronting bunkers, bounded into peril beyond.

That might not have been enough to sink me, but my Scottish programming had also left me bereft of a short game. On the Old Course, the only shot you really needed was a bump-and-run. Cuts, lobs, and flops were once-a-month assignments. Now, when faced with anything more complicated than a straightforward chip, I locked into panic mode, issuing a rich variety of skulls and chunks.

And then there were the greens. Gradually, I'd transformed my languid, American arm-and-shoulder stroke into a vigorous rap, the best way to traverse the enormous and slow greens of the Old Course. Now, suddenly, I needed the soft stroke back, and I couldn't summon it. In fact I couldn't summon much of anything. I was in putter's purgatory.

So that week I played some of the most remarkably awful golf of my life, culminating in a round at Secession where I parted company with eight balls and made only two pars. The truth was incontrovertible—I'd lost the ability to play American golf. As we drove to Augusta, I felt almost glad that a prior commitment had forced me to curtail my stay and I would not be joining my three pals for the last few rounds. I wanted to get back and be sure that the only game I'd lost was American.

The day after my return to St. Andrews, I took Millie out for a dawn round on the New Course. It was a cool, breezy morning— about 50 degrees, about 25 mph of wind—ideal conditions. Suddenly I was comfortable again. At the 18th hole, using Wee Raymond's two-hop wedge shot, I chipped in for a 75. Two weeks later, in similar conditions in the R&A Spring Medal, I started 7-6 but managed an 80 that, after four windy days, turned out to be among the top 15 of more than 400 scores. All was not lost.

Still, I was sad that I'd lost touch with the American game. One month later, however, I got another chance. When *The Secret of Golf* was published, Libby and I returned to the States for a launch party at the driving range at Chelsea Piers in New York City, after which I headed out on a four-week, twenty-two-city tour, making visits to bookstores and appearances on morning TV news shows. Week one took me through the South (Miami, Orlando, Tampa, Atlanta, Birmingham, Washington, and up to Philadelphia), weeks two and three the middle of the country (Minneapolis, Chicago, Milwaukee, Columbus, Houston, Dallas, Denver, St. Louis, and Toronto), week four the West (Portland, San Francisco, Los Angeles, San Diego, Tucson, and Phoenix). On the weekends, since there were no breakfast news shows, I flew home to our apartment in New Jersey and sneaked in a couple of rounds at Sleepy Hollow.

My home course had changed for the better in the season I'd been away—dozens of irrelevant trees had been removed and the views of the Hudson River were more spectacular than ever. It remained one of my four or five favorite places in the world to play golf. But not the kind of golf I was playing. There were no excuses this time. Sleepy Hollow's classic C. B. Macdonald design was almost as wide open and welcoming as the Old Course and I was fully familiar with its requirements. I just couldn't seem to get comfortable the way I used to. I'd always been able to step to every tee with a plan, knowing how and where I wanted to hit my drive, how I wanted to tack toward the hole, how to read putts and coax them across the sloping greens. Now I didn't feel that comfort and confidence—not at Sleepy Hollow. Now I felt it at the Old Course.

The book tour had also left me with a strange feeling. Each day was the same—a publisher's escort picked me up at my hotel, ferried me from TV studios to bookstores to radio stations to a lunch interview to more bookstores and to the airport for my flight to the next city, where it all began again. I was a perpetual tourist, never staying anywhere more than a few hours, looking at everyone and everything from the outside. I suppose that was to be expected. More disturbing were the weekends. Living in a small one-bedroom apartment several miles from where our home had been, I felt starkly removed and alone. Constantly, the same five words came to mind. "I don't live here anymore." This big, gorgeous, dynamic country—still, despite its myriad problems and challenges, the finest nation in the world, not to mention the place where my two sons lived—no longer was my home. There was something very unsettling about that.

40

Herbicide

My month in the States had taught me that, when you live away from your home for any extended period of time, you simply lose touch. Each day during the book tour I'd seen new things, things that hadn't existed when I'd left—new magazines, new television shows, new dog foods and laundry detergents—not to mention a slew of elected officials I'd never heard of, let alone voted for.

I'd also missed out on a lot of news. Not big news like wars and scandals and hurricanes—the London *Times* and *Telegraph* and the BBC had kept me on top of those things. No, I mean the lesser stories, both local and national, ranging from a change in state tax rates to a change in garbage pickup days. And obituaries—deaths of the sort of people who live on the edge of one's consciousness, people who are important in America but not worldwide.

I'd learned, for instance, that both Captain Kangaroo and Mister Rogers had died. That led me to wonder whether Soupy Sales and Pinky Lee were still around. General William Westmoreland had saluted his last. Could Alexander Haig still be among the ranks? Sandra Dee was gone—what about Frankie Avalon? I simply hadn't kept abreast of the Grim Reaper's progress.

The only area where I'd stayed on top of things was golf, thanks in large part to the Golf Channel U.K. and *Golfweek Digital.* With impeccable timing the Golf Channel had launched its British version just weeks after our arrival, and *Golf Central,* the half-hour news program that is broadcast at dinnertime in the U.S., reran to the U.K. audience continuously from seven to nine each morning. Meanwhile, *Golfweek* had come out with a digital version beamed as a mega-attachment to one's e-mail—an exact replica of the magazine, right down to pages that turned when I pushed the Page Down key. It arrived each Tuesday morning—a day earlier than I used to get the paper version in the States—complete with color photos and in-depth reports of the previous week's play. I was literally wired into the world of golf.

I didn't expect the rest of St. Andrews to be as well informed as I was, but I must admit I was astounded one evening while sipping a whisky in the Big Room of the R&A to see that one of the lockers had a brass plate on it with the name H. W. Wind.

H. W. Wind was Herbert Warren Wind, the most elegant chronicler of golf America ever produced. Born in 1916, he studied at Yale and Cambridge, and after a stint in World War II went to work for *The New Yorker* magazine, where his graceful essays on golf and other subjects won him a large and loyal readership. For the better part of four decades, golfers looked forward to his reports from the major championships. Wind was a friend of Bobby Jones, co-wrote books with Ben Hogan and Jack Nicklaus, and although sports in general and golf in particular were his specialties, he could have written knowledgeably and articulately on politics, theater, or music.

Golf never had a more careful researcher. I can remember sitting next to him in the press room of the Country Club at Brookline, early in the week of the 1988 U.S. Open. Herb, in his trademark jacket and tie despite the summer heat, was interviewing Rees Jones, who had done a major renovation of the course. They chatted for nearly two hours and Herb's questions probed into everything from the name and hometown of Rees's chief bulldozer operator to the granularity of the sand in the Brookline bunkers.

I suspect the Masters was Herb's favorite. On a couple of occasions I was able to tag along as he walked the course, absorbing his insights. It was he who coined the term "Amen Corner" for Augusta's holes 11 through 13 (a reference to an old jazz song, "Shoutin' at the Amen Corner"), and his words in tribute to Bobby Jones are as moving and eloquent as golf prose gets. In 1948, eighteen years after Jones had won golf's Grand Slam, he was diagnosed with a crippling disease called syringomyelia, which he fought bravely until his death in 1971. Wrote Wind: "As a young man, he was able to stand up to just about the best that life can offer, which is not easy, and later he stood up with equal grace to just about the worst."

Herbert Warren Wind was one of my heroes. After his retirement from *The New Yorker,* I'd contacted a golf collector friend, the late Joe Murdoch, who had kindly photocopied and sent me every one of Herb's essays, and they remain a treasured part of my library. In 1987, when I was elected to membership in the R&A, nothing gave me greater pride than to know that I was the first American golf writer to become a member since Herb, thirty years earlier.

All of which added to my horror that evening in the Big Room when I saw the locker with his name on it. You see, lockers in the Big Room—there are about fifty of them—are reserved for the longest-standing members of the club. Generally, you have to have been a member for forty-five to fifty years before you get one. Herb certainly qualified—that was not the problem I had. The problem was that Herbert Warren Wind, sadly, had passed away.

The moment I saw the plaque, I jumped from my chair and went to the hall porter's desk.

"Ford," I said, "I just saw there's a locker with Herbert Warren Wind's name on it."

"That's right, sir," he said.

"Well, I'm afraid Herb Wind is dead," I said.

"Oh my," he said. "We knew he'd been ill and confined to a home for the last few years, but never got the news. I'm sorry to hear that. We'll take the plaque down right away."

I began to return to my whisky, then turned around.

"Uh, Ford," I said, "just a quick question. What do you do with those plaques when the members pass on?"

"Well, sometimes the wives or descendants ask for them and we send them along, but Mr. Wind didn't have any family . . ."

He'd noticed the opportunism in my eyes. "Would you like to have the plaque, sir?"

"Yes, I certainly would. Herb Wind was both a friend and an inspiration to me."

"Fine, then. When we remove it, we'll put it in your pigeonhole—you can pick it up tomorrow."

The next day the H. W. Wind plaque sat prominently on a bookshelf in my library, just in front of his classic *The Story of American Golf.*

A week or so later, my USGA friend David Fay came in for a series of meetings with R&A officials. As usual he stayed at our house, and one day we met in the Big Room for a drink before lunch.

"Do you know how the lockers in this room work?" I said. "They go to the longest-standing members—when one of these guys dies, the next guy on the list moves in. Almost none of the lockers are used but it's a point of honor—or at least longevity—to get your name on one of them."

"Yeah, I know," said Fay. "Bill Campbell [former USGA president and R&A captain] has the post position over there next to the fireplace."

"Right. Well, can you believe it, I'm sitting here a couple of weeks ago and whose name do I see on one of the lockers but Herb Wind's. They didn't know he was dead!"

At that point Fay fixed me with an incredulous stare and said, "Herb Wind isn't dead!"

It was as if he'd spoken Swahili, so incomprehensible was the message.

"What? Of course he's dead," I said. "I'm sure I saw a report, just a few weeks ago."

"Where?"

"Well, I can't tell you specifically, but . . ."

"There's no way," said Fay. "If Herb were dead, I'd know about it. He's a recipient of our Bob Jones Award—the USGA would have issued a formal statement of some kind."

"Ohmygod."

I ran out the door and all the way home, where I powered up my computer and in the Google search box typed "Herbert Warren Wind dead died obituary." It returned the message I'd dreaded: *"Your search did not match any documents."* I'd prematurely shelved my hero, committed precipitant Herbicide.

Back to the R&A I ran, straight to the porter's desk.

"Ford," I panted, "I can't believe I did this, but when I told you Herbert Warren Wind had died, well, I was, uh, wrong. Here's his plaque. Can you put it back right away?"

"Well, no sir, I'm afraid we can't," he said. "The next member on the list has already been informed and his name is on the locker."

"No!"

"I'm afraid so. But I wouldn't worry. I'll hold on to the plaque and we'll see that Mr. Wind gets reinstated at the next opportunity."

I was absolutely sick. It wasn't as if Herb would ever learn of what I'd done to him—he'd been severely infirm, both mentally and physically, for years. And I was only minutely concerned that someone like Bill Campbell would one day walk the periphery of the Big Room and ask "Where's Herb?" Mostly, it was the dreadful feeling of having stripped a fine man of the recognition he deserved, not to mention stripping him of his life.

"Don't you tell a soul about this," I implored a guffaw-stifling Fay, knowing he would tell everyone. Incredibly, less than two weeks later, on the morning of June 1, I was going through my e-mail when I saw a message from *Golf Digest* editor and fellow R&A member Jerry Tarde with the subject listed as "Not That You Had a Rooting Interest, But . . ." There was in fact no message from Jerry, just an attachment from the obit page of the previous day's *New York Times* entitled: "Herbert Warren Wind, Golf Essayist, 89."

That afternoon the plaque was back on my bookshelf.

41

Summer Son

St. Andrews, as you might imagine, has inspired no shortage of memorable golf shots, both magnificent and mortifying. Since the day in September of 1858 when Allan Robertson made 3 at the home hole to record the first sub-80 score on the Old Course, golfers great and small have been making their marks.

Most of the well-known shots have occurred in the championships, from Bobby Jones's 130-yard hole-out from the Cottage Bunker in the 1930 British Amateur to Jack Nicklaus's drive of the 18th green forty years later in the Open. Likewise the disasters such as Tommy Nakajima's calamitous 9 after a battle with the Road Hole Bunker in the 1978 Open, Doug Sanders's missed putt at the 18th in 1970, and Ian Baker-Finch's drive out-of-bounds left at the first hole in 1995.

Among the local players, all have at least one stroke of genius to share with anyone who will listen. Tip Anderson, the legendary Old Course caddie who took Tony Lema to victory on the Old Course in 1964 and Arnold Palmer to both of his Open wins, was a pretty fair player himself, and right up until his death, a few months after we arrived, he held court in the Dunvegan Hotel pub, where he reveled in describing how in a St. Andrews Boys Championship back in the 1940s he'd once hit his second shot on the par-5 14th hole into the infamous Hell Bunker and from there holed a 7-iron for eagle.

Gordon Murray, at the least provocation, would relive the putt he'd once made from the right side of the 7th green into the hole on the left side of the par-3 11th, a distance of 200 feet up a 20-foot slope with at least 30 feet of break. (Those were the most recent numbers I'd heard—they seemed to increase with each telling.) And when the talk turned to legendarily long tee shots, Wee Raymond Gatherum had a stopper: "I once drove the 1st hole."

"Did you really bounce it across the Swilken Burn?" I asked him.

"No, it was a good long shot, but there used to be a wooden bridge on the right side, much closer to the center of the fairway than the one there now, and my ball hit it, caromed left off the guardrail, and rolled onto the green. In the group in front of us was a friend of mine, a big strong bloke who always hated being outdriven by the likes of me, and when they all saw the ball roll onto the group he looked back at the tee and said, "I know who hit it, it's that wee bugger Gatherum!"

There were even some unofficial fraternities in the town—those who had played the Loop (holes 8 through 11) in four straight 3s, those who had driven at least five par-4s—generally, holes 3 (352 yards), 9 (307), 10 (318), 12 (316), and 18 (354)—and on the dark side, those who had completed the Ignominious Quadrilateral, hitting tee shots OB left and right on the 1st and 18th holes.

I'd come within one swing of each of those clubs—a couple of times I'd made three 3s and a 4 through the Loop, I'd driven all the drivable holes except 18, and I'd visited all the OBs except left on 18, which seemed to require the nightmare confluence of a strong following wind, a fast-running fairway, and a stupendously pull-hooked shot.

I suspect I'd excluded myself from those last two clubs for the same reason—I tended to swing carefully (for me) on 18, often protecting a score. The fast lane to the green was up the right side, tight to the OB fence, and on most days I didn't have the guts to take that route, aiming instead at the right edge of the R&A clubhouse. On a few occasions I'd driven pin high left, and on a few others I'd managed to roll into the Valley of Sin, within a yard or so of the front edge of the green, but I'd never joined the elite corps who have walked proudly from tee to green with no swing between.

At least seven or eight par-4s on the Old Course, and perhaps two or three more, were drivable. On a sufficiently blustery day, the 6th (374 yards) was within reach and so was the 7th (359), if the drive were as accurate as it was long. I'd heard tales of people driving both the 2nd (411) and 4th (419) holes and I could well believe it, as both of those holes were dead flat with plenty of room to roll onto their right fronts.

On the inward 9, number 15 (401) could be bounced and rolled upon with a following breeze, and in one Thursday Club outing I'd seen Neil Ogston, Jr., reach the 16th (351). There were only two par-4s I'd never heard of anyone driving—holes 13 (398) and 17 (455).

Then, incredibly, one day I saw someone drive 13. The wind was blowing, but not ridiculously so, perhaps 25 miles per hour from the northwest, which put it directly at our backs for the inward 9. It was a busy June day and my long-hitting guest, just over from the States, was not familiar with the Old Course, so I'd been careful to delay our group's tee shots until the group in front of us—four R&A guys— were safely out of range.

At the short par-4 12th, we didn't hit until they were all on the green, and we should have waited longer than that. Two of us put it on the front apron and then our big hitter flew his drive clear over the green, landing in the rough beyond.

Thus, on 13, I was extra-cautious. It's one of the stronger holes on the course, a very slight dogleg left with a series of deep bunkers called the Coffins down the left side. At about the 275-yard mark the fairway stops abruptly at the face of a ten-foot-high ridge that is covered with rough and dotted with a couple of bunkers. The ridge extends perhaps forty yards and then dips down to a final patch of fairway that slopes slightly upward for another fifty yards or so. At the end of that stretch, just in front of the green on the left, is a small depression with more rough and the Lion's Mouth Bunker, while on the right, at greenside, is the Hole O'Cross Bunker for which the 13th hole is named. The entrance to the green is barely fifteen yards wide.

The R&A guys had made their way to that entry area and were playing their third shots when my friend came to the tee. Now, given his length, the wise strategy was to hit a 2- or 3-iron to the base of the ridge, then a short iron approach. But he was one of those players with more talent than sense, he'd been going at every hole with a driver, and this time was no different. The moment club struck ball I knew it was his best strike of the day—smack on the sweet spot, majestically high, and on the ideal line. It would certainly find the ridge, possibly even bounce down to the finishing stretch of fairway.

Since my graduated bifocals and I don't get along very well on the golf course, I play without glasses and can't see beyond 6-iron distance. My guest was similarly sight-impaired, so it was one of our partners who first reacted to the shot. "My God," he said. "I think it's on the green. John Rankin is standing near the front fringe and something just rolled passed him."

Sure enough, he had carried the ridge—a flight of over 330 yards, and bounded forward another 50 or so, skirting both bunkers. There it was on the front edge of the green, a drive of 375 yards. Immediately, I apologized to my bombarded friends.

"That's quite all right," said Rankin, a seventy-year-old, 7-handicap retired attorney who had been playing the Old Course several days a week for decades. "In fact, I feel as if I've witnessed a bit of history. Just who is that young fellow with you, George, a professional from the States?"

"No, John," I said proudly, "that's my son."

Scott, after some indecisiveness about what to do with his summer, had opted to join Libby and me in St. Andrews, and we couldn't have been happier. That round on the Old Course was the first of several he and I would play together—on the Old, the New, the Jubilee,

Kingsbarns, Elie, and elsewhere—rounds that, I suspected, would constitute our last spate of father-son golf for quite some time. The summers ahead would likely involve him in more serious things— jobs, internships, maybe academic pursuits—but not golf.

But he had not come to St. Andrews simply to hang out. He'd had a solemn mission—to get his 3-handicap game honed sufficiently to try out for the Princeton golf team in the fall. Thus, roughly half of his waking hours were spent either playing or practicing. The nearby Drumoig Golf Centre, onetime headquarters for the Scottish PGA, had a terrific practice facility and I'd arranged for Scott to get the same deal as Scottish university students—an all-inclusive fee of £5 per day gave him access to a magnificent covered range, an area of real turf to hit off, a large short game and bunker area, and three practice holes. Some days he spent five or six hours there, hitting hundreds of full shots, chips, and putts.

To earn his keep, he caddied, thanks to Gordon, who introduced him to the caddiemaster at Kingsbarns. He didn't go out more than once or twice a week, but the pay was good—$90–$100 for a single loop of 18 holes. In the evenings he hung out with a couple of other Americans who were caddieing at Kingsbarns and with one of the girls in the shop, Louise Sandford, a St. Andrews University student who also happened to be the daughter of my Saturday golf buddy, David.

Scott had always had a fine, flowing, natural swing, and his slim, limber frame enabled him to get his hands very high at the top of the backswing (à la Davis Love), giving him a huge arc and enormous power. Since the age of sixteen he'd been outdriving me and now, when we both caught our drives on the screws, he was a full 50 yards longer than I. Apart from Tour players, I'd seen only two or three people who could hit a ball farther.

But over the previous eighteen months he hadn't played much golf. That was due in part to the fact that we'd deserted him, left him without easy access to a course in the States. He'd spent the previous summer working a job that averaged over fifty hours a week and at college he'd played only a handful of times.

Thus, he hadn't expected much when he arrived in Scotland and perhaps for that reason his first few rounds were good ones, including a 73 on the New Course, something I'd never managed. But curiously, after that his game went inexorably downhill. It seemed that, the harder he worked, the worse he got. Being a cerebral type, he spent almost as much time thinking about his swing and game as practicing, and when one theory didn't bear results he moved quickly to another. At one point, he contracted the worst of all golf afflictions, the shanks. It was painful to watch him thunder a 300-yard drive into the heart of the fairway, only to shank his next shot into a gorse bush. When the shanks finally receded, he couldn't sink a putt (one day on the Old Course he shot 77 with 34 shots from tee to green and 43 putts). And when his putting returned he couldn't find a fairway with his driver.

The golf gods tortured Scott relentlessly until his last week or so with us, when everything began to fall into place. "I think I finally understand my swing," he said. "I think even if I putt poorly now I can get it around in 75." He was right—the last round I played with him was a 73 on the Old Course that could have been a few strokes lower if a couple of birdie putts had dropped instead of lipping out. When he headed home for some last-minute practice in the U.S., he was cautiously optimistic. He had not gotten his game to the level he thought he would, given the time and effort he'd put into it, but he was close.

In the end, however, it would be moot. In September the Princeton golf coach told Scott and the half dozen or so other hopefuls that the seven-man squad was set—a couple of scratch-handicap freshman recruits had filled the gaps left by graduating seniors. The walk-ons were allowed the formality of a three-day tryout but in order to make the squad they'd been required to play 54 holes on the university course in 6 over par—something most of the team members themselves would have had trouble doing. It rained on the first day. Scott never told me what he shot, only that it was high enough that he didn't need to bother to return for days two and three.

Thirty-five years earlier, I'd tried to make the same team and also had fallen short. For Scott, it was the first time in his life he'd tried really hard to do something and not pulled it off, and I think that hit him hard. Golf does that. On the other hand, he'd known all along it was a long shot, and I think he got over it quickly.

Besides, he'd returned to the States having mastered another skill—he'd learned how to drive a stick shift. As the designated driver-educator, I'd decided that the ideal training ground would be the lightly trafficked road that begins with Grannie Clark's Wynd, crosses the Old Course, and runs another two miles, between the Jubilee Course and the beach. That was a bad decision—yes, it's lightly trafficked but that doesn't mean it isn't busy. On a summer day that little road can serve up a smorgasbord of surprises for the motorist—kids chasing runaway soccer balls, dogs chasing hares, kites dive-bombing across the dunes, not to mention the odd strafing golf ball.

But none of those was Scott's biggest problem. Scott's biggest problem was his instructor. I just couldn't get him to master the let-out-the-clutch-as-you-give-it-the-gas concept. After two or three sessions he was still popping clutches, I was still being hurled into the dashboard, and every unsuspecting man, woman, child, and hound on that little road was carnage-in-waiting. The nadir came on the afternoon when we nearly hurtled our neighbors Sydney and Deirdre Cohen into a ditch. They'd been out for a quiet stroll until Scott down-jolted into a mini-roundabout from which he'd made a rather serpentine recovery.

Finally, Libby took him out for a lesson. In less than ten minutes she had him driving perfectly.

"Dad, you didn't tell me I could let the clutch out gradually," he said. "I thought I had to time everything in a split second."

"Oh . . . uh . . . that's right," I said. As one of the world's most notorious clutch riders, I should have been able to articulate the concept.

Scott was with us only six weeks, one of which he spent with some college buddies in London, and for Libby and me his stay ended all too quickly. The three of us watched *Simpsons, South Park,* and *Seinfeld* reruns together and bonded in disgust over our myopic president and his fiasco in Iraq. Since Libby loved to feed him his favorite foods, I got a welcome break from the chicken-fish-vegetable regimen and helped Scott consume tons of tortellini with red sauce. Scott cleaned the digital detritus from my computer a couple of times, sat through a couple of R&A lunches with me, and, on several warm evenings—usually around nine o'clock—we sneaked onto the St. Andrews Links Trust practice area and took on each other in viciously competitive pitching and chipping matches that lasted until dark. I savored those twilight contests with my son, knowing that in the third week of August he'd be heading back to school, and I'd be losing my favorite golf partner.

42

50,000 People in Our Backyard

For the better part of a year the town had been sprucing up—a handsome new sea embankment (financed by the R&A's 250th anniversary fund) had been built along the road parallel-ing the 1st hole, new retail shops had sprung up, a new St. Andrews town sign had been installed on the main road, an immense floral dis-play had been planted at the east entrance to the town, and everywhere the conversation had turned increasingly to one subject—the advent of the 134th Open Championship.

With a month to go, topic number one had become the mistreat-ment of Jack Nicklaus. In April Keith McCartney, a former chairman of the St. Andrews town council, had put forth a proposal to make Jack an honorary citizen of the town. However, not all the council mem-bers had agreed, and the proposal had been voted down, causing an outcry among the local residents and politicians who said the council had let the town, the sport, and the nation down. The pressure had caused them to reconsider and a second meeting was held, but once again they'd rejected the proposal, whereupon one of their members,

Murdo Macdonald, had handed in his resignation and stormed out of the meeting.

By that time, the story had become prime fodder for the press, both in the U.K. and abroad. A written apology had been extended to Nicklaus, who had responded graciously. In reality, I think Jack is secure enough that it didn't matter to him one bit—but in St. Andrews it had become a cause célèbre.

Meanwhile, Wee Raymond and I had been arguing for weeks over how viciously Tiger and company would rip apart the Old Course. As easy as it had played for us locals all winter and spring—albeit from the middle tees—I was convinced that the pros, in the absence of a big wind, would add several pages to the record books.

"It's running like concrete, but the greens are still accepting shots," I said. "I bet we'll see several sub-65s, and I wouldn't be at all surprised to see a 59. Certainly someone will shoot 62—and that, by the way, would be the lowest score ever in a major championship."

"Come off it, George," said Raymond. "Those boys won't play the course the way you and I do, they'll hit lots of irons off the tees, and you watch, there won't be a lot of short birdie putts, not on these greens."

"Sorry, Raymond, someone will have a go at it," I said. "Look at that no-name kid who shot 62 here in the qualifying for the Amateur last year. The Old Course can be had, and if there's no wind, it *will* be had. Besides, why in hell would a pro play an iron off the tee at a hole like number 9? Most of those guys can easily carry those two bunkers at the 275-yard mark and then they'll bounce right onto the green with an eagle putt. Hell, we do it every week from the front tees."

"Yeah, but we're not as smart as they are. Why don't you ask your friend Tiger about number 9," said Raymond. "In 2000 he hit a 7-iron off that tee four days in a row and made two birdies and two pars."

"Fine, but I'll bet you £5 he doesn't do that this time. The Tour's biggest hitters are 15 yards longer than they were five years ago, and I've heard talk that the R&A won't even be using the new tee they created at the 9th. Tiger knows damn well that Ernie and Phil and Vijay and the rest will be ripping drivers—maybe even 3-woods—onto the green, and he won't give them that kind of advantage, no matter how much confidence he has in his wedge. Not when he hits it longer than any of them."

"Rubbish," said Raymond. "In 2000 Tiger had his game plan— stay out of the bunkers. He followed it and he won by eight shots. He won't change a thing this time. And, by the way, unless he regains some more of the accuracy he had in 2000, neither he nor anyone else will be shooting any 59s—maybe something in the low 60s, but no 59s. I've been playing the Old Course for forty years, and I can tell you this—she won't be giving up those kinds of scores, no matter how long and strong those boys are."

"Well," I said, "we'll find out soon enough."

We'd toyed with renting our place for Open Week. A real estate agent had assured us that, given our location, the top players would be interested and a corporation might want it as a hospitality center. They advised us to ask $35,000 for the week. That kind of money was tempting, even if it meant the Pepers would have to camp out in a university dorm room for the week. In the end, however, we had to ask ourselves, why had we been living here for these two years if not to enjoy the week of the Open Championship?

Besides, this was before Scott returned to the States, and both he and I had jobs to do. I'd volunteered to help out as a marshal and Scott had gotten an intern position with Turner Network Television, or more accurately, I'd gotten it for him through an old friend, Chris Carmody, who was the producer of TNT's golf coverage. Turner had the U.S. broadcast rights to the Thursday and Friday as well as the early-round coverage on Saturday and Sunday before handing it over to ABC.

Carmo, as I'd always known him, had stopped by to see us a year or so earlier when he'd been in town for meetings with the R&A championship staff. When he'd mentioned that TNT would be need- ing a couple of kids as temps during Open Week, I'd been quick to suggest Scott, and Carmo had been kind enough to reserve a slot for him.

There was an amusing irony in that. Roughly thirty years earlier Carmo had tried to help me get a job in sports television. We were both bachelors at the time, living in apartments on New York's Upper East Side. I was working for a book publisher, and he'd landed a great job in the production department of ABC Sports. During the summer, we played coed softball Monday nights with a bunch of guys and girls in similar circumstances, recent college graduates living in the city and working their first jobs. After the games we adjourned to places like Allen's, Melon's, Churchill's, Pedro's, The Mad Hatter, and The Raveled Sleeve—Upper East Side saloons that catered to yuppies like us.

One night over beers at Allen's Carmo said to me, "You like sports and you're a journalism guy, George. You might be interested to know there's a production assistant's job opening up at ABC Sports."

"Well, yeah," I said, "I'd love to be like you, 'spanning the globe for the constant variety of sports—the thrill of victory, the agony of defeat.' " At the time, ABC, under executive producer Roone Arledge, was the leading network in sports coverage, and the opportunity to work side by side with the likes of Jim McKay, Chris Schenkel, Frank Gifford et al had put stars in my eyes. Two guys of roughly my age named Bryant Gumbel and Jim Lampley had just been hired by ABC and were already making their marks as on-air reporters on the sidelines of NFL games.

Carmo gave me the number to call and the next morning I set up an appointment. Two days later, when I entered the ABC waiting room, I saw a dozen guys who looked just like me—clean-cut types in navy blazers, oxford button-downs, and rep ties, most of them strongly projecting one of two personae—spoiled preppy or dull-witted jock. One by one they disappeared into the inner sanctum and returned twenty minutes or so later looking less than elated. I was feeling encouraged by default.

The interviews were running behind schedule and I'd been there almost an hour when Carmo appeared. "You'll be interviewed by two guys," he said, "a couple of young producers named Geoff Mason and Terry O'Neil. They're asking everyone the same question and everyone's getting it wrong."

"Okay, what's that?" I said.

"What was the most important international sporting event of 1974?"

"Hell, I have no idea," I said. "All I know is golf."

"Okay," said Carmo, "the answer they're looking for is the World Cup. ABC has rights to the World Cup, so they want people who believe in it."

"Got it," I said.

Moments later I was called in. The interview was barely underway when, sure enough, Mason said, "George, what in your view was the most important international sporting event of 1974?"

I feigned cogitation for a moment and then said, "Well, as much as I enjoyed Gary Player's win in the British Open at Hoylake, I'd have to say it was the World Cup."

Mason and O'Neil exchanged glances. "Good answer," said Mason. Then he uttered the two words I least wanted to hear: "Who won?"

I think I said "Cincinnati." End of interview.

Scott's job sounded glamorous but turned out to be four days sitting inside TNT's production trailer, watching the broadcast and making note of the exact moment and second that every significant shot and putt was made, for later use by the replay and highlights producers. However, they paid him £500 for the four days, gave him a snappy TNT windbreaker and hat, and he seemed to enjoy the experience.

My job brought no cash remuneration, but like my son I got a hat and a windbreaker, mine emblazoned with "134th Open Championship" along with my own personal "Quiet Please" paddle. Over two hundred townies—most of them members of the three men's golf clubs—had volunteered to help out, and on the Saturday before the championship we were assembled to receive instructions from our marshal-in-chief.

Much of the meeting focused on security. Just two days earlier several terrorist bombings in London had killed fifty-two people. There was a fear that, with the Open attracting forty to fifty thousand people a day, not to mention millions of TV viewers around the world, St. Andrews might be the next target.

"This week, we need you not only to help control the gallery but to keep your eyes open for people who look as if they don't belong," our commander told us. "If you see someone who seems more interested in watching you than in watching the golf, report him or her to the nearest police or security officer. Likewise if someone leaves a briefcase or piece of luggage under the grandstand, report it immediately. Do not be a hero—do not confront the individual yourself."

Then, to lighten things up a bit, he said. "This applies equally to streakers—and I can assure you, there will be at least one streaker, a fellow who is actually paid to do his thing at events such as this. He wears a simple black jumpsuit with a Velcro closure that can be opened in a flash, excuse the pun. Even if you think you've identified him, stay away from him."

As he spoke I smiled, recalling the Wednesday of the 2000 Open at St. Andrews when a fellow had dashed naked across the Swilken Bridge. The next morning, one of the tabloids ran a front-page photo of him, taken from behind with the 18th green and R&A clubhouse in the background. The accompanying headline was classic: "The Most Famous Hole in Golf." It made me wonder now whether the streaker's patron was from Fleet Street.

Our commander next delineated the duties of the various marshals—tee marshals, fairway marshals, spectator crossing marshals, green marshals, grandstand marshals, roving marshals, and traveling marshals—and closed by impressing on one and all the importance of keeping a low profile.

"I know you're all familiar with the BBC's commentator Peter Alliss," he said. "Well, you know how during golf telecasts the camera sometimes departs from the action on the course and pans to people in the gallery or to strange events that have arisen outside the ropes, at which point Peter invariably offers a wittily scathing observation? Your primary mission this week is to be sure you do not become fodder for Peter Alliss."

Before leaving we were given our windbreakers, hats, and badges. The R&A loves badges. I'd been to more than a hundred major championships before this one but never had I been so comprehensively credentialed. Attached to the zipper pull of my new windbreaker, like a week's worth of ski-lift tickets, were badges saying Marshall, Working Press, Locker Room, R&A Member, and R&A Marquee. In addition, since I was moonlighting as a glorified bouncer at the door of the R&A clubhouse and at its Forgan House annex, I was required to wear a little plastic nameplate saying "R&A Club Committee." It all made me feel very official, and officious.

By Sunday I started seeing famous faces. While walking Millie I bumped into ABC/ESPN anchor Mike Tirico and one of his sidekicks, Nick Faldo, both of whom seemed genuinely excited to be in St. Andrews. Later I saw a fellow I'd partnered with in the AT&T Pebble Beach Pro-Am fifteen years earlier, Bart Bryant. Back then he was a winless journeyman, but in the past year he'd won twice, including Jack Nicklaus's Memorial Tournament. Jack had invited him to play a practice round on Monday and he was looking forward to that. We reminisced a bit about the laughs we'd shared at Pebble, courtesy of the other amateur in our group that week, Bill Murray.

"He's like an institution out there now," said Bart.

"Yeah," I said, "I think it's a perfect fit. He loves playing every year and they love having him. He does a lot of behind-the-scenes stuff for the charities, too. Those who say he's not good for the game need to take themselves—and the game—a little less seriously."

"Amen to that," said Bryant.

We talked a bit about Bart's overnight success at age forty-two, then he asked me a question.

"You must know the Old Course pretty well," he said. "When the pin's way left on 17, I'm figuring I should hit my approach long and left, toward the 18th tee instead of taking on that pot bunker."

"Absolutely," I said. "We don't see the pin there very often, and you may not see it there this week, but if you do, that's the play—it's dead flat over there, an easy up and down for you."

Bart would have a strong showing, especially for a British Open rookie—a tie for 23rd that included, to my relief, four straight pars at 17.

Other celebrities that Millie and I came upon that day included Mike Cowan, better known as Fluff, currently caddieing for Jim Furyk and before that Tiger. I knew him from his pre-Tiger days with Peter Jacobsen. We saw Phil Mickelson's two coaches, Dave Pelz and Rick Smith. They'd had a tougher than usual assignment this week, helping Phil navigate the humps and bumps of the Old Course. Rick was reveling in the St. Andrews atmosphere ("There's just nothing like it, anywhere in the world"), while a fatigued Dave was looking forward to the start of the tournament ("Once the bell rings, no more walking—I'll be watching all my golf on television").

The R&A had added 165 yards to the Old Course, with the result that this Open would be played on not one course but four. The new tee for the 2nd hole sat on the Himalayas putting green, the new 9th tee was on the 8th hole of the New Course, and the new 13th tee was on the 3rd hole of the Eden. The intent of all this was to protect the sanctity of par from assault by the prodigiously long-hitting pros, essentially, to Tiger-proof the course. In the eyes of many, however, they'd simply played into Tiger's hands while making things difficult for shorter hitters—they'd Funk-proofed.

There was no question that Fred Funk needed a secret weapon coming into this Open and a week prior to the championship someone whispered a name in his ear, a name that, according to the whisperer, could make all the difference for him. Who was that? Who else—Gordon Murray.

"Yeah, a pal of mine from Aberdeen knows Freddie and he rang him up and told him I could help him find his way around the Old

Course, so Freddie's asked me to walk the three days of practice rounds with him," said Gordon. "Do you know him?"

"Only as a fan," I said, "but my guess is that you and he will get on well."

Sure enough, on Monday afternoon, there was Gordon striding regally up the center of the 18th fairway side by side with Fred Funk. I'm not sure what sort of wisdom he imparted, but it wasn't enough to overcome the Funk-proofing. Fred opened with a 77, followed with a 71, and missed the cut by three strokes.

Monday was as warm a day as I'd ever seen in St. Andrews—temperatures in the high 80s—and Tuesday started the same way. My marshal duties began that morning at six. I'd been fortunate to get a plum job—guarding the walkway that separated the bay window of the R&A from the first tee. Only players and their caddies were allowed on my turf.

In the course of my four-hour stint I was able to get an up-close look at about two thirds of the field. Even better, I was able to stand in the shadow of the clubhouse, out of the searing sun. (A year and three quarters in St. Andrews had reduced my tolerance for warm weather.)

Looking at the list of 156 competitors, I felt very old. Most of the field was about twenty years younger than I. Two of the young English players had in fact struck up relationships with daughters of my Saturday-game friends, Ian Poulter with David Sandford's Louise and Graeme MacDowell with Bryce Hogarth's Katie. If only Paula Creamer could find my Scott!

Nameless faces and faceless names passed by all morning, politely nodding at the all-but-superfluous marshal. The only ones who stopped to say hello were my three more or less contemporaries—Greg Norman, Tom Watson, and Jack Nicklaus. Jack, despite his snub by the town council, was the big story of the week. Four years earlier the R&A had announced that it would return to St. Andrews in 2005 rather than 2006 as had been expected, in the hope that Jack, turning sixty-five that year, would play. (The R&A eligibility requirements prohibit competition by players over the age of sixty-five.) Flattered by the gesture, Nicklaus had agreed to play and had announced that this, his 164th appearance in a major championship, would be his last.

He'd established quite a record in the Open—three wins and an agonizingly impressive seven second-place finishes in thirty-seven appearances. The last two of his victories had come at St. Andrews, and I'd been fortunate enough to witness the second of them in 1978.

It was my first overseas assignment for *Golf Magazine* and sort of an immediate second honeymoon for Libby and me—we'd been married just two months earlier. It was during that week that we both fell in love with the town of St. Andrews.

I don't think I will ever experience a moment in golf to rival the close of that championship. Along with a few other press guys I'd taken up a position on the stone steps to the left of the 18th green, and during the last fifteen minutes or so of play we were joined by Ben Crenshaw and Tom Kite, who had tied for second with Ray Floyd and New Zealand's surprise contender Simon Owen.

"Boy, this is just amazing," said Kite, surveying the scene that surrounded us—the sea, the R&A, the town, the tens of thousands of golf fans. "There is just nothing like this place." Crenshaw nodded reverently. The two Texans, friends and rivals since their grade-school days, briefly compared notes on their rounds, on how the course had played that day, and how they would be coming back to the Open for as long as they could qualify. I just listened, pinching myself occasionally. It had been a Forrest Gump sort of week.

Then their words became inaudible, drowned by a wave of cheers and applause from down the fairway. Striding purposefully toward the green was Nicklaus, his shaggy blond locks blowing and glowing in the Scottish sunshine. With each of his paces, the ovation grew louder and deeper, a swelling roar of affection and acclamation. They stood six deep in the road alongside the fairway, they stood in the grandstands, they stood on stone walls and balconies and rooftops, leaned from hotel windows, club windows, and shop windows—men, women, and children of every age, shape, and size, cheering with a golf passion perhaps only the Scots can know.

When at one point Jack raised his putter in gratitude and the crowd responded, tears began to form in my eyes. Blinking them back, I glanced furtively at Crenshaw, hoping he hadn't noticed, and saw that he was in the same state. We all were. Thirty thousand people had assembled on that final hole, and each of us had just witnessed something special: the game's greatest player winning the game's oldest championship on the game's most legendary course.

I'd gotten to know Jack shortly after that 1978 Open, later had co-written a couple of articles with him, and collaborated on three TV projects with him. Libby and I had stayed at the Nicklauses' home in North Palm Beach, and in 1988 at a black-tie gala at the Waldorf in New York—the culmination of *Golf Magazine*'s celebration of the centennial of golf in America—I'd had the honor of presenting Jack a life-sized statue of himself as the Player of the Century. It may not have been the height of his career in golf, but it was certainly the height of mine.

All that history rattled through my head as Jack's 9:50 practice round tee time approached. In the area between the 1st tee and 18th green, a hundred or so members of the media had assembled. One of the Open's patron sponsors—the Royal Bank of Scotland—had issued a £5 note commemorating Jack's association with the Open Championship (and, not coincidentally, his association with RBS). It showed a rendering of Jack from 1978, hugging the claret jug. The ceremonial first note would be presented to Jack at precisely 9:30. (By that afternoon there would be a minor stampede for such notes at the St. Andrews RBS branch, which quickly limited customers to four notes each, and by Wednesday morning a few such notes, autographed by Jack, had made their way to eBay, where they were being offered for between £50 and £100.)

At 9:10 Jack and his son Steve turned the corner around the R&A clubhouse and made their way down my strip of turf. We shook hands and spoke briefly. I'd written to him and Barbara a month earlier, inviting them to drop by our place if they could find time during the week. He acknowledged receiving the invitation, said he'd try, but we both knew there was little chance. This would be my last contact with any of the Nicklauses, although a month after the Open a typically thoughtful note arrived from Barbara.

Once Jack was off the tee, things died down, and at ten o'clock I was happy to knock off for the day. After doing a few errands I took a nap and when I awoke, fall had arrived. A haar (Scottish for a summer sea fog) had drifted in, lowering the temperature by nearly 30 degrees. Now, I thought, all we need is a bit of wind and things could get interesting. Sadly, that never happened.

That evening was the annual dinner of the Association of Golf Writers, held in a large tent to the right of the 1st fairway. A few speeches were made and captain Bernhard Langer accepted an award on behalf of his victorious European Ryder Cup team. At the same time, up in the R&A clubhouse, the Past Champions Dinner had been held. The two functions concluded at about the same time and as I made my way across Grannie Clark's Wynd to my home I literally crossed paths with Tiger Woods. He had been the first one to exit the dinner, and while the other champions lingered, signing autographs, he beelined it straight down the 18th fairway to his room at the Old Course Hotel.

Having won the Masters with his made-for-Nike chip-in at the 16th hole, along with two other victories in the first half of the season and a second place behind Michael Campbell in the U.S. Open, Tiger was back on top of his game and a prohibitive favorite at 5–2 odds. (Typical of the British bookies, they'd also provided odds on Tiger again avoiding the bunkers for four straight days—12–1.) Looking for a more robust payout, I'd put my pounds on Phil Mickelson (14–1), Sergio Garcia (25–1), David Toms (30–1), Adam Scott (40–1), and Angel Cabrera (50–1), betting each of them both to win and to finish among the top five. They would prove to be a complete waste of money.

On Wednesday, with a day off from my marshaling duties, I made my regular early-morning visit to the spa at the Old Course Hotel. (Originally the hotel had told us locals we'd be banned for the week, to allow the resident competitors and other bigs to pump iron in privacy, but under a storm of pressure they'd relented.) So there I was at 7:00 A.M. plugging along on a treadmill while beside me Vijay Singh put an upper-body machine through its paces. When he left I checked the settings—on the same piece of apparatus where I occasionally grunted out 6 or 8 reps at 30 pounds of resistance, Vijay had been doing 30 reps at 80 pounds—just one of the myriad reasons his handicap was 13 strokes lower than mine.

Later that day I returned to the hotel for a cocktail reception. Passing by the fishbowl workout room I glanced in, hoping to spot another star. Only one person was there—and using my regular treadmill. When I realized who it was, I almost ran back to the house for my sweats. Yes, it was Woods—Elin Woods—perspiring magnificently in a skintight body suit.

By Thursday morning the heat was back and there was barely a breath of wind. As I headed up to the 1st tee for another six-to-ten shift, I was more convinced than ever that the pros would tear the course apart. In one of the practice rounds, Australia's Scott Hend had driven six par-4s—six of them! There was not another championship course in the world where that could happen.

The R&A had wisely put a trio of jackrabbits in the first starting time—Mark Calcavecchia, Rory Sabbatini, and Simon Dyson. Off the tee at 6:30, they finished three hours and forty-five minutes later, proving that not all pros are glacially slow. Of course, the second group— Sandy Lyle, Joe Durant, and Marcus Fraser—finished half an hour behind them and by midday the average pace was close to five hours.

My catbird seat gave me the opportunity to do some mother-in-law research on course management. The tee at number 1 had been pushed back almost to my sidewalk and the hole played straight into what wind there was, but not one player of the sixty or so I saw hit a driver. Most of them went with long irons or hybrid woods—everything from a 4-iron to a 3-wood, as far as I could tell. Surprisingly, Sandy Lyle, a former Open champion and a Scot, hit the highest ball of the morning, a lofted wood that soared like a steroidal 7-iron. The lowest came from Tiger, one of his stingers that never got much above eye level. When Tiger's group left the 1st tee, ninety percent of the people in the grandstand left with them.

The worst tee shot of the morning belonged to Colin Montgomerie, who pull-hooked a 4-wood into the Swilken Burn. When I saw that, I thought, There he goes again. Despite being Europe's best player for most of the last decade and a half, Monty had never finished better than eighth in an Open Championship, and during the previous year or so, apart from a hot week at the Ryder Cup, he'd played some of the worst golf of his career. He'd begun the season in 83rd place on the world rankings. But how wrong I was. Monty would play bravely for four days and finish in second place, sparking a return to form that, by year's end, would restore him among the world's top 10 players.

Toward the end of my shift a young player approached. He was a bit lost, had climbed under the ropes, and was about to walk in back of the tee while a group was teeing off. When I extended my arm to restrain him, he mistook it as a handshake and said, "Hello, sir. I'm Sean O'Hair."

The twenty-three-year-old PGA Tour rookie had qualified for the Open just four days earlier with a breakthrough victory in the John Deere Classic. At the time he didn't have a passport, but the White House had intervened and he'd made it for his tee time. We chatted while the group on the tee played their shots—he was an outgoing, unaffected, and polite young man, remarkably so given the tragic history he'd had with an overbearing father. In those two minutes I became his fan, and on Sunday I was delighted to see him tie for 15th.

My only real stress came not from people but sounds—two of them. The first occurred just as Game 9—Stewart Cink, Thomas Levet, and Peter Lonard—stepped to the tee. It was a loud piercing bark from the southwest, and I recognized it immediately as the voice of Millie.

Libby had left her in the little gated area just outside our back door, and something must have set her off. For an animal with lungs the size of teabags she had astonishing projection, especially downwind. Her strident yaps were as annoying from 200 yards away as they were from two feet, and for a long thirty seconds or so, Millie Peper was the voice of the 134th Open. When she went quiet, I prayed that Libby had shut her inside the house—Tiger's group was due on the tee in twenty minutes and the last thing I needed was for my mutt to let out a yelp just as the Striped One took the club back for his opening tee shot. Happily, we did not hear from Millie again, at least not on my watch.

The other sonar event occurred just before ten o'clock, when a strange man emerged from the starter's hut next to the 1st tee with a panicked expression on his face. Since I was the human being closest to him, I became the recipient of his news:

"An alarm is about to go off," he said.

"What?" I said, wondering what kind of alarm he meant. Air raid? Smoke detector? Snooze?

"I'm with the BBC," he said. "We have access to the hut to store equipment, but no one told me it had an electronic burglar alarm. I had a key to open the door, but I don't have the security code to—"

And then it began, a series of electronic honks, blared in one-second intervals at threshold-of-pain volume. Suddenly, everyone in the area—all the players and caddies on the tee, all the rules and scoring officials, all the R&A members in the clubhouse, all the concessionaires and media members, and all ten thousand or so people in the grandstands turned and stared—stared at the starter's hut, at the strange ashen-faced man, and at me. Blessedly, Peter Alliss was on a comfort break.

In no time half a dozen police officers arrived, quickly becoming as helpless and hapless as we were. Next came a phalanx of R&A championship staffers, walkie-talkies to their ears. It seemed the only ones with the combination were the Links Trust staff, they were all half a mile down the road, and none of them would agree to give the security code over the phone (lest it get in the wrong hands and the starter's box become the target of serial burglaries—imagine all the purloined pencils and pin sheets).

So the beeping continued. Game 19 timed their swings to the blaring beeps, as did Game 20. It was nearly fifteen minutes before affable, mustachioed J. J. Johnston, one of the Links Trust rangers, came to the rescue. When the alarm stopped, he got an ovation louder than the one that had greeted Tiger.

On that day Tiger would shoot 66 and take a lead he would never relinquish. The rest of the week would be less a tournament than a coronation, as a Woods victory never seemed in doubt. Indeed, the most dramatic moment between Thursday and Sunday took place at approximately 6:00 P.M. on Friday when Jack Nicklaus made his final march up the 18th hole.

A photographer from Getty Images had asked whether he could capture the event from our bay window, in exchange for which we would receive a framed print of the best shot. That seemed like a good deal to me, so there we were—the photographer hanging out window one, Libby standing at window two, and I sitting on the sill of window three, Millie in my lap and my feet dangling down the side of the building to watch, along with fifty thousand or so others, as the Golden Bear walked the last 354 steps of his major championship career.

I smiled to see him wearing a red sleeveless sweater. Months earlier, at a meeting of the R&A Club Committee, we'd discussed several options for the club's 2005 Christmas card and had decided it should be a photo of Jack waving farewell from the Swilken Bridge. A letter had been sent to Jack, asking for his approval, which he had granted. Now I wondered whether that festive red had been selected with the card in mind.

Sixty-five-year-old Jack had played well for two days, scores of 75-72 for a 147 total. Although he'd missed the cut by 2, he'd bettered the performances of several dozen players, including defending champion Todd Hamilton, Ian Woosnam, Nick Price, Jim Furyk, Davis Love, and Stewart Cink. When his birdie putt hit the hole at 18 and the crowd erupted, it was almost as dramatic a moment as in 1978.

Tiger's lead went from 2 strokes on Thursday to 4 on Friday and back to 2 on Saturday, when seven world-class players drew within striking distance. José María Olazabal was his closest pursuer, Colin Montgomerie and Retief Goosen were 3 back, Sergio Garcia and Brad Faxon 4 behind, and Michael Campbell and Vijay Singh 5. There was hope for an exciting finish, but I still had the feeling it would be a bunch of Fords chasing a Ferrari.

I was back at my marshal's post on Sunday morning when R&A chief executive Peter Dawson strolled by with a surprising statistic. "The fairways today," he said, "are running faster than the greens." They'd just put a Stimpmeter on the 9th fairway where the ball had rolled 11.5 feet—the green was rolling 10.5.

Monty would drive that 9th green and birdie the hole to draw within 2 strokes of Tiger—but behind him Tiger would do the same thing, crushing his fourth driver in four days and making his third birdie (a fact that, at the next Thursday Club outing, I would be quick to point out to Wee Raymond). Thereafter it was all Tiger—when he birdied the 12th after Monty bogeyed 11 and 13 the lead was 4, and it would grow to a 5-stroke victory on a final score of 274, 14 under par.

That was 5 strokes higher than he'd shot in 2000, and his pursuer's scores also were a bit higher than five years earlier. Wee Raymond had been right in terms of our larger argument. The Old Course had held up beautifully—and not because of its increased yardage. The calm conditions and rock-hard fairways had more than neutralized the added length. But it was that same hard ground—and 18 greens that had become increasingly firm—combined with numerous difficult pin placements that had enabled the old lady to defend herself.

During my chat with Peter Dawson, I'd pointed over at the flagstick on the 18th green, positioned just a couple of feet beyond the crest that climbs out of the Valley of Sin.

"Isn't that pin a bit more severe than in past championships?" I asked.

He'd looked at it for a moment, then, with a sly smile, said, "Yes, I believe it is."

When greens are hard, not even the pros can hit wedge shots that take two bounces and stop, and when you combine that with pins set at the crests of ridges on downwind holes, as they often were during the week of the Open, birdies tend to come mostly as a result of long putts.

And so the best ball strikers had risen to the top. The first ten included Woods, Olazabal, Fred Couples, Garcia, Langer, Geoff Ogilvy, Singh, Goosen, and Campbell, ample proof that the rewards went to those who were best able to choose the right shot and then hit the right shot right.

In a stiff wind, the Old Course is arguably the game's best combined test of brains and brawn—no tricking up required. Or as Henry Longhurst said after a similarly mild-weather Open at St. Andrews in 1958, "If we could experiment with holding the Open in September it would be a splendid thing. If we could hold it on the Old Course forever it would be still more splendid."

Once the presentation was over, people flooded across the course, and many of them stayed for several hours. The wait for photos at the Swilken Bridge was close to half an hour. (I was wishing I'd had the foresight to create a life-sized cardboard blowup of Tiger holding the claret jug—I could have made a fortune charging people for the opportunity to pose with it.)

During the slow exodus of the crowds, friends and neighbors wandered through our back gate for drinks and postmortem conversation. And as darkness fell a solitary figure crouched on the 18th green, stroking putt after putt to that elusive cup—Scott Peper.

The next morning, like clockwork, the chamber-of-commerce weather was gone, replaced by rain and chilly temperatures. We were getting back to normal now. That afternoon I learned that there had been some overnight excitement at Hamilton Hall, the large red building directly behind the 18th green. Owned by the university and used as a dorm throughout the school year, it had been pressed into service as housing for officials, press, and R&A members during Open Week. At about 3:00 A.M. someone had set off a fire alarm, flushing the hundreds of occupants onto the street in their pajamas and night-gowns. They were granted temporary asylum in the Big Room of the R&A but not without a brief confrontation with the night porter.

"There's a fire next door and we need to come in," said one of the R&A members.

"Yes, I understand that, sir," said the porter, "but the Open Championship is over now and that means ladies are not allowed in the clubhouse."

Yes, things had returned to normal.

43

Home

As the 2005 R&A Autumn Meeting approached I was feeling less than happy with my golf game. The putting touch that had taken me to the quarterfinals of the Jubilee Vase a year earlier was nowhere to be found, and my iron play was in a sort of mid-Atlantic limbo—I hadn't gained much confidence in the low drawing shot I'd decided was necessary for links golf and at the same time I'd lost the ability to play any other kind of shot. Even the enormous greens of the Old Course had become elusive targets.

I entered all the competitions—the Calcutta Cup, the Jubilee Vase, the Autumn Medal, the Town Match, and played without distinction in all of them. I did, however, make it to the final match of the Jubilee Vase, as a result of a phone call I received from the chairman of the R&A Club Committee, Julian James.

"George," he said, "as you know we will be losing two committee members this year and adding two new ones, with the result that various subcommittee assignments need to be made. If you're agreeable, I'd like you to be chairman of the Golf Sub-Committee next year."

It was a bit surreal, a bit hard to get my head around, the notion of George Peper chairing the committee that oversaw all competitions among members of the Royal & Ancient Golf Club of St. Andrews—something I would never have dreamed possible two years earlier. And equally surreal, when I walked the 18 holes of the Jubilee as the Club Committee's ceremonial steward of the match—the date was September 17, 2005—it had been two years to the day since we'd arrived in St. Andrews.

Maybe because of my Teutonic background, I'd always believed in the tidy portent—the *alles in ordnung*—of anniversaries. Three years earlier, I'd chosen a similar moment to leave *Golf Magazine*—after exactly twenty-five years, exactly three hundred monthly issues as editor-in-chief. Nice round numbers had a way of compelling me to action. Now another deadline had arrived—it was time for us to head back to America. But this time the move wouldn't be easy.

In college I'd written my senior thesis on "The Novel of Dépaysement." A French word, *dépaysement* describes an uprooting in which the central character leaves or is taken from his native surroundings and transported to a new and foreign place, a place that changes him in important ways.

I'd expected to experience that sort of thing from our St. Andrews adventure, but now, two years later, I didn't feel changed, and certainly didn't feel uprooted. In fact, it was almost as if I'd found roots, as if in the cradle of golf I'd found something seminal about myself.

There was, I knew, some geographical relevance. One hundred years earlier, my father had grown up near a small town on the North Sea. I'd never been to Husum, Germany, but I could remember his descriptions of it—a fishing village of a few thousand people, set on a windy, treeless coastal plain, once the site of a medieval castle. The parallels to St. Andrews were eerie, not the least of which was the town's nickname, bestowed by its most illustrious citizen, the poet Theodor Storm:

All my heart belongs to you,
You grey town by the sea;
The magic of my youth, evermore
Will rest and smile on you, on you,
You grey town by the sea.

For me, it seemed, St. Andrews held an attraction that involved something more than golf.

For Libby, however, there was no such pull. During our two years she had not taken up golf—after the lessons arranged by Angela Bonallack and a few practice sessions with Shelagh Murray, she'd packed the clubs away. But she had begun to do what she'd come here to do—paint—and on the days when she sat herself in front of her easel she could entertain herself creating a landscape almost as completely as I could walking one with my golf clubs.

Libby had been proposed for St. Rule, one of the women's clubs (both golfers and nongolfers), comprised largely of wives of R&A members (and also for the ultra-exclusive Ladies' Putting Club!). We had in fact gone a long way toward accomplishing the first goal we'd set for ourselves—to make friends and generally fit into the social fabric of the town. Many St. Andreans had welcomed us into their homes, and as each month had passed we'd become more comfortable.

We'd reciprocated by holding a couple of cocktail parties. Following one of them we were cleaning up when Libby said, "As Alison White was leaving tonight she said the nicest thing. I'd told her how grateful you and I have been for the welcome everyone has given us outsiders, and she said, 'Outsiders! You're nothing of the sort. You're one of us now.' "

Of course, we would never be insiders—St. Andrews is not a town where one becomes easily accepted as a local—not for a hundred years or so anyway—but we were encouraged nonetheless by the friends we'd made. Fundamentally, what gives any place its character is the people, and in St. Andrews Libby and I had been fortunate to meet some of the most generous, joyful, and genuine people we'd ever known.

"St. Andrews will never mean to me what it means to you," Libby told me, "but I can't think of anywhere I'd rather live. It's all about the quality of life here."

She was right. In two years we'd encountered no traffic jams, no road rage, no honking of horns, and no shaking of fists. We'd had few phone solicitations and no street solicitations, no arguments with salesclerks, no disputes with neighbors. St. Andrews was a bastion of safety, cleanliness, and crimelessness, a place where a trip to the post office or library could bring cheery conversations with half a dozen fellow citizens. At the same time, it was arguably the most cosmopolitan small town in the United Kingdom, the combination of the university, the rich history, the splendid beach, and the golf attracting a never-ending stream of residents and visitors from around the world. No other town in Scotland had such year-round vitality.

By contrast, our few trips back to the United States had convinced us that our nation had changed. Maybe it was 9/11, maybe it was just the digital age, but it seemed that everything moved at a frantic pace— everyone seemed in a hurry, compelled to accomplish things as if they feared another national tragedy might occur at dawn.

Advertising and marketing were everywhere, and the ads seemed even bigger and louder than we'd remembered. We'd become used to roads without billboards, towns without neon, TV without commercials. In the U.S. the sizzle had all but replaced the steak.

Moreover, under the Bush administration the country had become sadly polarized. People were either with the government and its policies or against it, and everyone seemed angry about one thing or another—the mess in Iraq, escalating gas prices, global warming, corruption in Congress, competition in Asia. America was still the greatest nation in the world, it just wasn't the buoyant, positive country we'd left. It was still my home, but it was becoming less and less the place where my heart was. During the Ryder Cup, I found myself rooting hard for Europe, and when London beat out New York for the 2012 Olympics I was as happy as a Piccadilly cabdriver.

On the other hand, our two sons lived in America, and that was enough to pull us home. We also knew that if and when grandchildren came into the picture the need to be near our boys would be even greater. Being boys, they could not be expected to make frequent vis-its—or visits at all—to the United Kingdom, not if they had wives whose families were based in America. And we would need to be based there, too.

But if we were going back, there were things I needed to do. First I would have to resign from the R&A Club Committee, barely one year into my four-year term. I'd have to renegotiate my just renewed con-tract with *Links* magazine inasmuch as the title of my column was "Letter from St. Andrews." I'd have to resign from the boards of two local charities and drop my resident memberships in three local clubs. All those things would be awkward, but at the same time, they were all doable. St. Andrews didn't need me.

But I needed St. Andrews. Two years in that town had brought me an addict's need to breathe its air, to walk its cobblestone streets. I'd come to look forward to its subtly changing seasons—to the impossi-ble green lushness of the hillsides in spring, to the warm sea breezes of summer, the return of the students in the fall, and the cozy fires of winter.

Then, of course, there was the golf. Bobby Jones once said, "If I were to set down to play on one golf course for the remainder of my life, I should choose the Old Course at St. Andrews." Well, I *had* set down, and for myriad reasons it would not be easy to get back up. I had, after all, some unfinished business—that third goal of mine. On four occasions over the past two years I'd shot even par on the Old Course—I'd managed a 33 on the front 9 and 34 on the back—but I'd never put two strong 9s together. I still had not bettered par on the Old Course.

Just before Christmas I was asked to represent the R&A and make a speech at the annual dinner of the Fife Golf Association, a group representing several dozen clubs in the area. What I delivered was generally lighthearted but these last few words came straight from the heart:

"Someday I hope to bring my grandchildren here to Scotland—not to show them what golf is but to show them what golf isn't—that it isn't $200 million resorts and $200,000 membership fees, that it isn't six-hour rounds and three-day member-guests, that it isn't motorized buggies, Cuban cigars, and cashmere headcovers. It's a game you play simply and honorably, without delay or complaint—where you respect your companions, respect the rules, and respect the ground you walk on. Where on the 18th green you remove your cap and shake hands, maybe just a little humbler and a little wiser than when you began."

As I was leaving that evening, a little gentleman approached me. White-haired and bespectacled, and at least eighty years old he was, but his posture was erect, his gait was sprightly, and the color in his cheeks told me he was still an active golfer. He did not introduce himself, just shook my hand, held on to it, and looked me straight in the eye for a few seconds, without speaking. Then he said something that touched me in a way that few words ever have.

"Welcome home, laddie. Welcome home."

Not long thereafter I came across this passage in *The Moon and Sixpence,* a novel by Somerset Maugham based on the life of Paul Gauguin:

"I have an idea that some men are born out of their due place. Accident has cast them amid strangers in their birthplace, and the leafy lanes they have known from childhood or the populous streets in which they have played, remain but a place of passage. They may spend their whole lives aliens among their kindred and remain aloof among the only scenes they have ever known. Perhaps it is this sense of strangeness that sends men far and wide in the search for something more permanent, to which they may attach themselves. Perhaps some deep-rooted atavism urges the wanderer back to lands which his ancestors left in the dim beginnings of history. Sometimes a man hits upon a place to which he mysteriously feels that he belongs. Here is the home he sought, and he will settle amid scenes that he has never seen before, among men he has never known, as though they were familiar to him from his birth. Here at last he finds rest."

And so, one fall evening, as the golden Scottish sunshine worked its magic and a cool breeze drifted in from the North Sea, Libby and I made the decision that had been coming for months. Using an all-too-large portion of our nest egg, we bought a two-bedroom apartment in New York City.

For our sons.

We will not sell our home in St. Andrews—we cannot leave this blessed town.

Acknowledgments

Few notes were taken and no traditional research was done for this book. Most of the words just sort of spewed forth after long periods of staring out the window. Unavoidably, however, some facts and figures were needed, and for the accuracy of same I'm indebted to four good St. Andrews men—two Peters and two Davids—Peter Lewis, Director of the British Golf Museum, Peter Mason, External Relations Manager of the St. Andrews Links Trust, and local historian/authors David Joy and David Malcolm.

Parts of this text have appeared, in slightly different form, in my column for *Links* magazine, and my thanks go to Jack and Nancy Purcell for their forbearance. Several of the photos inside were taken by friend and neighbor Iain Lowe, a professional photographer who took time out from a couple of books of his own to help with mine. The idea for this book never occurred to me, but it jumped immediately to the mind of my agent, Scott Waxman, when I told him I was absconding to Scotland. I owe him thanks not only for his support but for hooking me up with Simon & Schuster, where Bob Bender deserves the editorial medal of honor for his encouragement, guidance, and pa-tience with this occasionally insecure, rudderless, and foot-dragging author.

To our old friends, golf friends, and work friends from America and everywhere else, and to all the following who dropped by, teed it up, took us to dinner, and visited 9A Gibson Place, whether for five minutes or five days, thanks for making our first year anything but lonely: John and Suzy Barton, Mike Beckerich, Bill, Ginger, and Meg Bender, Furman and Linda Bisher, Mark, Laura, Natalie, and Scott Bluhm, Chris Carmody, Li Chao, Richard Cochran, Jeff and Alison Crowther, Brian and Tina Doyle-Murray, John Ellis, David Fay, Ed and Barbara Gowan, Jim and Harriet Finegan, Tom Flanagan, Steve Foehl, Ken Gilpin, Ed and Suzanne Grant, Dove Jones, David and Gillian Kirkwood, Dean and Suzanne Knuth, Herb Kohler, Tom Mackin, Greg Midland and David Midland, Mark Mulvoy, Don and Nancy Panoz, Hubert Pedroli and Mary Tiegreen, Paul Perkins, Rich and Nancy Preston, Jack and Nancy Purcell, Tom and Carmel Ram-sey, Ron Read, Ron and Kathy Riemer, Fred Ridley, Jim Robinson and Emily Robinson, Thos and Robin Rohr, Bill and Ellen Sedgwick, Semo and Fran Sennas, Grant Spaeth, Paul and Cindy Spengler, Larry Stewart, Jerry Tarde, Sally and Andy Unger, Connie Voldstadt, Fred Vuich, Ernie Wang, Natalie Wang, David Wasserman, Larry Water-house, Richard Wax, Peter Workman, Chuck and Nancy Yash, and David Yu.

Finally, my thanks go to Libby, for suggesting our St. Andrews so-journ in the first place, and for much, much more.

Index